TEACHINGS FROM THE TAP

Life Lessons from Our Year in Beer

MERIDETH CANHAM-NELSON

ISBN-10: 0985321407
ISBN-13: 9780985321406

Beer Trekker Press
PO Box 646 • Carmel Valley, CA 93924

This book is dedicated to Chris

My husband, travel companion, best friend and love of my life
Without you none of this would have been possible

CONTENTS

ACKNOWLEDGMENTS

Thanks go out to my mom for realizing that I wasn't ignoring her these past few years, just following my dream. Her unwavering support throughout my whole life has been a priceless gift.

Renee Brincks gets big hugs for her overwhelming encouragement, especially in the beginning, when I had no idea what I was doing. Everyone deserves a personal cheerleader in her life. Go team! Many thanks to David Ratcliff, a good friend and the little brother I never had, for his willingness to read early versions of the manuscript more than once. I owe you a beer (or two). Cheers also to Maia Merrill Gosselin, editor extraordinaire, for her invaluable support in getting things just right.

A toast goes out to all of our friends who believed in us following our hearts. Your well wishes kept our spirits up and helped us to see this whole endeavor through. And to the friends who shared in the Year in Beer adventures, cheers! You helped make it an experience of a lifetime.

Lastly, Porter and Stout would like to give dog kisses to Lilly for keeping them warm at night and to Baba and Gigi for spoiling them while we were gallivanting around.

INTRODUCTION

EVOLUTION OF A BEER GEEK

What can I say? I'm a beer geek. Much of my life I've tried to avoid being labeled a geek of any kind, but somehow it happened anyway. And I'm okay with it.

Merriam-Webster defines a geek as "a person often of an intellectual bent who is disliked." Doesn't sound very nice, does it? But similar to other words used to offend, the term "geek" has been co-opted by the insulted as a way to define the depth of one's enthusiasm for a particular activity or hobby. The craft beer community is one such group that now uses the term "beer geek" as a badge of honor. I, for one, proudly embrace the label.

Definitions vary, but all engender the concept of being an absolute fanatic of all things beer. Many define themselves based on the number of beers they've reviewed or by the size of their glass, bottle cap, or beer mat collections.

My husband Chris and I could easily justify our status with similar standards. We have hundreds of glasses and well over 1,000 beer mats. Our wardrobe is dominated by beer-related clothing. We even named our two dachshunds Porter and Stout. Beer is an integral part of our daily living. From our contributions to social media beer forums to planning beer events in our community, beer is our life, inside the home and out. But we're different from the average beer geek: we're beer travelers. We travel the world seeking the next great beer experience by going to breweries, pubs, and beer festivals.

For the last 20 years, we've maintained a list of the breweries we've visited. The number of breweries we can visit almost solely determines our vacation destinations. Over the last few years we've added an average of 60 breweries a year to The List. To date, we have been to over 700 breweries.

Pinpointing how I got to this level of beer fanaticism is difficult to trace. Despite my best efforts, I just can't seem to define an exact moment when I turned into a beer geek. The classic illustration of man's evolution from ape to an upright bi-ped comes to mind and it all makes sense. Mine was an evolutionary process that took nearly half a lifetime to achieve.

Like many beer geeks in my generation, my beer drinking role models mostly quenched their thirst with mass-produced American lagers. My father, for example, was a Coors man. The only change he ever made in his beer drinking habit was from Coors Original to Coors Light. It's fair to say that this upbringing did not predestine me for an interest in craft beer.

Fast forward to the late 1980s. Chris and I were attending U.C. Berkeley. At this same time, a growing trend brewed in the San Francisco Bay Area: craft beer. We were completely unaware of how being in the same place at the same time as this burgeoning interest might change our lives.

Today, younger craft beer drinkers take for granted the presence of multi-tap pubs and beer cafés. However, such places weren't always so plentiful. When Raleigh's Bar & Grill opened near campus in 1988, it was unique and intriguing. They offered newfangled beers with unfamiliar names. Some are still served at pubs today, but others, such as Iron Horse Alt from Devil Mountain Brewing, are long forgotten. A vast departure from our standards at the time, the beer list at Raleigh's opened our eyes to a whole other world.

In the years to come, our interest in craft beer would grow. Sierra Nevada Pale Ale–complete with yeast at the bottom of every bottle–replaced Henry Weinhard's Private Reserve and Lucky Lager in our refrigerator. Due to our lowered tolerance for non-craft beer, we often chose water over sub-par selections at parties. Beer posters squeezed out the Robert Doisneau prints on our apartment walls and our wardrobe expanded to include a multitude of beer t-shirts, sweatshirts, and hats.

In 1991 a new multi-tap, Barclay's Restaurant & Pub, opened in our Oakland neighborhood. We became original customers and a year later I started to work there while attending graduate school. The job was a challenge; keeping a rotating selection of 28 beers straight in my mind was no simple matter. The difference between Guinness and Rogue Golden was easy, but what style of beer was Anchor Steam? What made it different from Anderson Valley's Boont Amber? One day, something Chris told me moved me beyond the simple concern of which beer was which. He had watched as a Barclay's co-worker of mine approached a table.

"What's the Santa Rosa IPA?" the customer asked.

"It's an Indian Pale Ale. It's from India," the waitress said.

"Then why does it say Santa Rosa?" the confused customer replied.

The waitress, flustered about the seeming interrogation, insisted that the beer was from India and walked away.

In the context of today's craft beer popularity, that story seems unlikely. Now most people are familiar with IPA as a style of beer, even if they're not familiar with what IPA stands for or where it originated. But in the early 90s, we were all students learning about this emerging beverage called "micro-brewed" beer.

That story fueled my determination to gain as much information as I could about the beers served at Barclay's. I yearned for the knowledge to answer customer questions with intelligence, make educated beer recommendations, and offer people a positive beer experience.

At the time, it was generally assumed that women didn't know anything about craft beer. I experienced the male bias not so much on the job, but as a customer. Bartenders frequently ignored me and spoke directly to Chris, even when I asked the question. They just couldn't grasp that I was a real beer drinker, too. It became clear that my beer education was not going to come at the hands of bartenders. Chris suggested we go straight to the source: the breweries.

Those early brewery visits made an invaluable contribution to my evolution as a beer geek. Sampling tasty beers and learning about the brewing process was as fun as it was informative. My confidence on the job strengthened. I better remembered the beers and mentions of visits to the breweries lent me credibility with customers. They trusted me as someone who had a real interest in craft beer.

When we started keeping track of our brewery visits, we developed rules for inclusion on The List. The rules, which have changed little over the last 20 years, are simple.

1. The beer must be brewed on the premises.
2. The beer must be consumed on site.
3. Chain breweries count only once, even if multiple locations are visited.

By 1993, our list of breweries was already lengthy. Soon I realized that we had traveled to more breweries than anyone we knew. We'd morphed into beer travelers before we even had a label for it.

In the beginning, our beer travels were primarily day trips and weekend getaways around the greater Bay Area. As our college days receded and our funds and aspirations grew, we began to venture out of state, and in 1998 we headed to our first international destination: Ireland.

It only took one trip out of the country for us to understand that beer is best experienced within its own context. To drink a pint of Guinness in Barclay's was one thing. To drink Guinness in a village pub with a turf burning stove and traditional Irish music, was quite another. Listening to locals, with their thick Irish brogues, chat amongst themselves helped us do more than simply drink the beer: we experienced it.

This new style of travel expanded our appreciation for the art of beer drinking, but also altered our worldview. On trips, we started to let go of our self-conscious, shy natures and began actively seeking to connect with the locals. We met people in other countries who enjoyed beer as much as we did and gained an understanding of the role beer has played in other parts of the world. This knowledge made the world seem smaller, friendlier. The travel bug took hold and has yet to let go.

In 2005, Chris created the website *thebeergeek.com*, focusing it on himself as the Beer Geek. I assisted with content and was mentioned as a traveling and tasting companion, but Chris was the center of attention. *Thebeergeek.com* became the vehicle for us to share tales of our adventures, post pictures, and offer travel guides.

In November 2006 Chris's brother-in-law informed him about the Four Points by Sheraton's search for a Chief Beer Officer. The position involved acting as a brand ambassador for the hotel's Best Beers program. Although Chris thought it a long shot, he applied.

Several months later, a large box arrived. Chris received a Best Beers pint glass, two bottles of beer, and a letter stating that out of 7,800 entries from 31 countries, he was one of 15 candidates for the job. Continued consideration of Chris's application required a video submission due within a week. Over two days, Chris scripted, filmed, edited, and mailed off a five-minute video made with a borrowed camera describing why he would make a great Chief Beer Officer.

Chris was one of the final four candidates and even flew to New York for an interview. While in the end he didn't get the job, Chris started to realize that people enjoyed hearing tales of our beer travels. Interviewers told Chris that they especially liked that he shared his love of beer with me. That didn't seem unusual to us, though. We did everything together.

The experience inspired us to transform our love of beer travel from a hobby into something more serious. In its first major change, the website shifted from Chris as the Beer Geek to us as a beer traveling couple. We added my "beerography," edited the content to reflect us both, and I contributed blog posts.

One night at home we were watching *Passport to Europe* on TV and Chris exclaimed, "Why can't **we** have a travel show?" Occasionally, over beers, we fantasized about a show of our own. We sculpted the concept, worked out a theme, and brainstormed episode ideas. What we created was *The Year in*

Beer, a twelve-episode series featuring a different beer destination each month.

Our idea combined the practical information of public television travel personality Rick Steves with the cutting-edge attitude of Anthony Bourdain's show *No Reservations*. Our program would give people an alternative view of travel, where good beer ranked up there with museums, castles and cathedrals on a tourist's to-do list. We wanted to promote the discovery and exploration of other cultures specifically through beer and show that any traveler, not only the hardcore beer lover, could enjoy the experience.

For example, every visitor to Munich, even the non-beer drinker, goes to the Hofbräuhaus. It's on par with watching the noontime glockenspiel joust in the Marienplatz. But what few people realize is that across the courtyard is the Hotel Am Platzl, a place to enjoy excellent German food with the famous Ayinger beer. It's less crowded and not as loud, but every bit as authentic as the world-renown beer hall across the way. To us, stepping off the beaten tourist path is an essential part of beer travel and we wanted to share that philosophy with others.

We had no idea how to pitch a television show. Although even if we did, we also recognized that the chances of *The Year in Beer* becoming a reality were slim. Instead, we used the idea to add a video component–called *beergeek.TV*–to the website. Adding videos seemed the logical next step to chronicling our travel adventures. The framework we had developed for *The Year in Beer* became the basis for *One Pint at a Time* on *beergeek.TV*. In June 2007, we traveled to Munich with our new video camera. "Munich: The Greatest Beer City" was our inaugural episode.

A chance meeting during a trip to Olympic National Park in Washington State one month later renewed our thoughts about *The Year in Beer.* While driving, we picked up a couple that, unable to negotiate their RV down a narrow road, were hitchhiking to the trailhead. We started talking and learned that they traveled throughout the United States in search of waterfalls. We told them about *The Year in Beer* and they suggested we write a book, as they had done about their waterfall adventures. The wheels turned in our heads. Could *The Year in Beer* be reinvented as a book?

Once home, we declared 2008 to be the "Year in Beer" and started discussing, researching, and planning. Chris had a rough idea of the endeavor's cost, but we had no business plan to finance it. We jumped right in and hoped our limited savings and credit cards would be enough. In fact, if a business plan had been created, *The Year in Beer* would have never taken place. It was our passion–our hearts and souls–that provided the backing for the Year in Beer. Chris worked from home, so time off was not an issue for him. Also, at the time, I had a large bank of vacation and comp time, as well as an understanding and flexible supervisor. As far as we could see, there was nothing stopping us from undertaking this major endeavor.

So why on earth would we want to take on a yearlong beer adventure without solid financial backing? Well, we're obsessed with beer, love to travel, thought it'd be fun, and wanted to take our beer hobby one step further. Some might add that we're just plain crazy.

The final schedule included trips to ten major beer events and two prime craft beer destinations. Three side trips presented themselves early in the year as well. In 12 months, we visited over 90 new breweries and attended some of the biggest beer gatherings in the world: the Oregon Brewers Festival, Great British Beer Festival, Great American Beer Festival, and Oktoberfest.

Some adventures seriously tested our resolve, while others were remarkably stress free. We met interesting people, made new friends, and re-connected with old ones. The endeavor presented us with unforeseen opportunities and allowed us to discover unrealized parts of ourselves. In an amazing and unexpected way, our Year in Beer taught us valuable life lessons. The road leading to this granddaddy of all beer adventures took many years to build and one year to complete, but we did it. And best of all, we did it together.

JANUARY

FOLLOW YOUR HEART

Some things seem like a good idea at the time. Like one more Guinness at Gus O'Connor's in Doolin, County Clare, Ireland, or a third liter of beer at Oktoberfest. Or leaving the house at 3 o'clock in the morning to travel to Alaska in January.

After talking about it for close to a year and planning our calendar for months, the Year in Beer had finally arrived. We decided to kick the year off with the Great Alaska Beer and Barley

Wine Festival in Anchorage, Alaska–a festival Chris knew little about when he suggested that it be included in the schedule. Admittedly, he first looked toward a warm winter location, such as Hawaii, but with a limited choice of beer events going on in the month of January, he narrowed it down to Alaska.

Over time, the idea of traveling to Alaska in the middle of winter grew on me. Many of our friends thought the Year in Beer was crazy. A few friends took it seriously, but most just humored us. I came to embrace our Alaska trip as a way to show just how determined we were to live out our dream. At the very least, Chris and I expected to experience the year of a lifetime.

Our 6:30 A.M. flight to Anchorage flew out of San Jose, an hour and a half drive from our house. Chris always seeks my final approval for flight itineraries, so there's no one else to blame for my failure to fully consider the implications of approving such an itinerary. A fair number of sacrifices were anticipated (and accepted) as part of the quest for our dream and without serious consideration of the facts, the early departure was chalked up as sacrifice number one.

About a week before our trip, reality hit. First, we needed to arrive at the airport an hour and a half before the flight. For a 6:30 A.M. flight, that meant getting there at 5:00 A.M. That's early, I thought, but not too bad. Then Chris informed me that to be on the safe side, he planned on two hours travel time to the airport. I again calculated the time. Huh. To get there at 5:00 A.M., we need to leave the house at 3:00 A.M. Then, in my final calculation, I determined that leaving on time required waking up at 2:00 A.M. It was an unappealing prospect to say the least, but there was no way around it.

"A dream sure is a lot more fun than reality," I told Chris.

The morning we left, I slid into the passenger seat half asleep. As Chris pulled onto our street, I looked out the window into the dark. It was so quiet. Nothing stirred this early in the morning. A quarter mile down the road, though, a chance encounter jarred us awake: a mountain lion, unaware of our presence, strolled across the road. His long tail gently bounced as he walked. His large thick paws punctuated his graceful saunter with power and strength. The car slowed and we watched the cat until he disappeared into the brush along the side of the road. Mountain lions are common in our area, but rarely seen. Blurry eyed when we left the house, the sighting left us awestruck and alert. Chris thought the rare sighting was a good omen.

Virgin territory for us, episodes of *Northern Exposure* and the picture of the Eskimo on the tail of Alaska Airlines planes shaped my mental image of Alaska. Did moose really wander the streets? Possibly. Did people actually use dog sleds to get around? Without a doubt. But whatever crazy stereotype was conjured about our first destination of the year, it quickly disappeared when I caught my initial glimpse of Alaska's stunning landscape.

Shortly before 11:00 A.M., the plane started its descent into Anchorage. Staring out the window, the brightness of the low cloud cover caused me to see spots. I shielded my eyes and turned away from the light to regain my vision, but the anticipation and excitement of landing somewhere new was too great. I looked out the window again and saw the ice-filled Cook Inlet. Sitting in the aisle seat, Chris was unable to see out the window. After several attempts to get a good look, he gave up. I, on the other hand, had a perfect view of the snow-capped mountains and the runways lined with mounds of dirty ice.

At that moment, an unexpected sense of belonging ran through me. The strength of Alaska's draw pulled at my heart with the power of a real spiritual experience. More likely, however, it was simply my body's physical reaction to the gravitational pull of the change in elevation. With a jolt, the wheels hit the ground, jerking me to my senses.

The thrill of possibly having my first metaphysical awakening stayed with me as I stepped out of the jet way into the terminal. My expectations of Alaska were now higher than ever as we walked through the airport to collect our baggage.

Glass cases with taxidermied wildlife decorated baggage claim. Forever frozen in a ferocious snarl, a brown bear loomed over me on his hind legs. This once powerful animal that would have no qualms about ripping my head off in the wild could now only stand there motionless. I wondered what life events led him to this point, including the process of preserving him.

A man with a weathered face and crumpled, stained clothing approached me. His bushy gray beard move up and down as he spoke.

"Great, aren't they?" He nodded in the direction of the stuffed creatures.

"Uh, yeah," I replied.

"Be sure to look through there in the other case." He pointed as he offered his suggestion.

I peered around the brown bear whose life I'd contemplated just moments before. A wolf. Before I could ask the man the importance of my seeing the wolf, he walked away. It wasn't clear if he was trying to enlighten me to the deeper meaning of wolves, sharing his own spiritual connection with them, or simply offering me friendly hospitality. Whatever his intentions, his appearance made me think I had just been introduced to the more colorful side of the Alaskan population. Pondering the encounter, I joined Chris at the baggage carousel.

Dragging our bags behind us, we walked out to the taxi stand and were soon seated in the back of a cab. Taxi rides frequently offer adventure and our trip into Anchorage was no different. Years of travel have convinced me of the existence of an international cab driver's code of conduct manual. It doesn't matter where in the world or what the weather conditions are, all cabbies drive like they were a half hour late to their own wedding.

Despite the snow on the ground and muddy slush covering the road, our cabbie drove as fast and aggressive as any other cab driver. He pressed his foot on the pedal and the engine revved deeply as it strained to change gears. We surged forward, passing the car next to us.

Chris and I glanced at each other somewhat uneasily. Professing my undying (or possibly, dying) love and telling Chris any remaining secrets before our most certain untimely demise seemed an appropriate consideration in that moment. In the end, I decided we were perfectly safe. Since the cabbie was a local, he probably knew how to drive in such conditions.

Once at the hotel, confusion ensued regarding the readiness of our room. We waited in the expansive lobby while the front desk staff sorted it out. A taxidermied polar bear guarded the entrance to the hotel bar. This one looked more menacing than the playful polar bears at the zoo or the cuddly cartoon versions pedaling cola on the TV. In the midst of pondering the Alaskan obsession with stuffed wildlife, I looked back to see Chris chatting with an unfamiliar couple.

Matt and Michelle Venzke recognized Chris from our website, *thebeergeek.com*, and introduced themselves. Matt and Chris had been communicating through the internet for over a year, ever since Matt contacted him to say that he and his wife also traveled for beer. When we found out that our beer lives were converging in Alaska for the festival, we planned to meet. Coincidentally, we'd booked rooms in the same hotel.

Matt remarked that it was weird meeting people that he had seen on the internet. For the first time, I realized that more people than just our friends and family viewed our site. While far from being celebrities, the lack of anonymity we created for ourselves with our website became clear.

Thirty minutes later the hotel clerk informed us that our room still required cleaning. We left our bags with the front desk and, in the balmy 20°F weather, walked the four blocks to Glacier Brewhouse. I expected extremely cold weather in Alaska and the fact that the temperature bottomed out at 12°F below zero the previous week did nothing to change that. In preparation, I even purchased a long, heavy coat for the trip, a thrilling event since residents of the California coast have little need for heavy outerwear.

Now with this warmer weather, such a coat wasn't completely necessary, but I still wore it proudly, along with my gloves and hat. The good weather also eliminated the prospect of stories about the bitter cold penetrating to my core, which was admittedly a little disappointing. The improved weather brought me relief, though, because I hadn't really been looking forward to my California body going into complete shock.

Just over an hour after landing, we placed ourselves in our favorite position: at a brewpub bar enjoying a taster set of handcrafted beers. Nothing like a good beer and another brewery added to The List to get a trip started. Our yearlong adventure was officially on its way.

Chris characterizes Glacier Brewhouse as "rustic swank." The large restaurant feels as cozy as a winter cabin with its high-beamed ceilings and large open fireplace. The shiny granite bar and black-clad waitstaff, on the other hand, add a touch of class. Even with the haggard look of someone who'd been up since 2:00 A.M., I felt welcome and comfortable.

Before the trip, Chris developed a personal survival strategy for drinking beer in Alaska. The backbone of his plan included focusing on beers from Alaska and avoiding barley wines and other high alcohol brews. (This somewhat puzzled me, as the festival was called the Great Alaska Beer and *Barley Wine* Festival.) An English-style strong ale with a sweet malt flavor, barley wines were traditionally reserved for special occasions. Today, many breweries offer a barley wine all year long. In a place as cold as Alaska, they're a winter mainstay.

Living in Alaska requires a strong survival instinct. Our friend Jim told me that Alaska is "the place where the cowards don't show and the weak die." As such, the state's beer culture reveals how inhabitants have adapted to survive the frosty winter months. Breweries in Alaska brew seasonal beers with enough taste and alcohol to keep the blood flowing on freezing days, including barley wines, smoked porters, Belgian-style beers, and double India Pale Ales.

This hearty beer culture contrasted sharply with Chris's well-intentioned drinking strategy. He took one look at the Glacier Brewhouse beer menu and knew he'd been beat.

"A double IPA on cask?" he sighed. "You people are killin' me."

The bartender laughed as Chris ordered his beer. He simply could not pass up a double IPA on cask. What is the saying?

Something about best laid plans… Or is it the one dealing with good intentions and the road to hell? Chris turned to me.

"I don't know how I'm going to get through this weekend," he said.

Over beers, I told Chris about the experience I'd had as we landed. "Yeah, it probably was just the elevation drop," he said. "I'm such a dork. Do you know what I was thinking?" I shook my head no. "I wondered if the plane had skis to land."

Chris and I laughed. "You are a dork," I said.

When Chris planned our January Year in Beer trip, he corresponded with Alaska beer writer Jim Roberts, who goes by the pen name "Dr. Fermento." He hoped for a local's perspective on what a first time visitor needed to see and do while in Anchorage. Chris expected to exchange a few emails and gather some information. He didn't anticipate the level of hospitality that Jim offered. Eager to show us the local beer scene, Jim suggested we meet during our visit. He made us feel welcome before we even stepped foot in Alaska.

Jim, a native of the San Francisco Bay Area, moved to Alaska in 1979 and his love for his adopted state clearly showed the first time we met him. When we thanked him for the offer of hospitality, Jim replied, "I love my state and I love to show it off."

He invited us to a special event that evening at the Snow Goose Restaurant, home to Sleeping Lady Brewing. Unsure of the exact nature of the event, Chris thought it had something to do with the unveiling of a new beer. As it turned out, Jim had a very personal connection with the memorial brew tapped that night.

We finished our beers at Glacier Brewhouse and found our way to the third-floor pub of Snow Goose Restaurant. I was nervous, wondering how we'd fit in at this private function. I worried about my ability to muster the outgoing personality needed to meet new people.

The warm wood features of the pub projected a homey, relaxed feel. We sat at a table near the bar and ordered a taster set. I needed a boost, so I also ordered a cola, what Chris and I refer to as my "buck-up beverage."

As people gathered, greeting each other with warm hugs and hellos, reticence set in; everyone knew somebody else. Without the confidence to jump right in, blending into the wall behind me seemed a better option.

Chris spotted Jim and went to introduce himself. Forcing my shyness aside, I gave myself a pep talk before joining them. "I am girl beer geek. Hear me roar." Being a representative of *thebeergeek.com* required the confidence of a natural extravert, something I was not.

Jim's friendliness and his interest in talking with us made it easy to converse with him. He wanted to learn more about us as people, as well as how we contributed to the craft beer community. We explained the Year in Beer, an endeavor to which Jim responded enthusiastically. He went out of his way to make us feel welcome and introduced us to his friends, including Don and Tracey Lewellyn, a homebrewing couple. We told them about our life as beer travelers and they reciprocated with homebrewing stories. Before we knew it, the ceremony began and the socializing subsided. I had successfully jumped my first social hurdle.

Jim addressed the group first. On January 20, 2007, his son-in-law, Jeff, was killed in Iraq by a roadside bomb. Jim, who received the call from his daughter while on his way to the Great Alaska Beer and Barley Wine Festival, drove home to be at his daughter's side.

"At the house it was your typical somber affair," Jim said. "The military was out front with the company chaplain, the commander, and all the dignitaries."

The pub was silent. Jim hadn't said anything to us about his deeply personal connection to the event and it stunned us. The man who had been so gregarious just a few minutes earlier was now somber and reflective.

"It was the start of a very traumatic part of my life, my daughter's life, my family's life," he continued.

Jim then said that his daughter, in the midst of it all, suggested that he go on to the festival because Jeff would have wanted it that way. And so Jim did.

One year later, Anchorage homebrewer Lisa Urban proposed that Jeff, a beer lover, be honored with a memorial brew. Lisa's husband and fellow homebrewer Dennis teamed with Snow Goose Restaurant and Sleeping Lady Brewing Company to create Spartan Warrior Imperial Stout. This special brew recognized Jeff and the other soldiers from the local 4th Brigade Combat Team, 25th Infantry Division at Ft. Richardson who did not return from their mission.

As Jim and a few others spoke about Jeff, the keg of beer was tapped. Glasses of the dark brew made their way around the room. Chris got one for us to share since the style was a bit heavy for me to drink a glass of my own. Together with soldiers, locals, and Jeff's widow, Chris and I joined in honoring Jeff and his fellow soldiers with a silent toast. I found the bold, rich flavor of the imperial stout a fitting tribute to the strength and bravery of fallen soldiers.

Jim went on to announce the creation of the Spartan Warrior Memorial Fund to construct a monument on base. A man with a bucket weaved through the crowd collecting donations.

Chris added our contribution. The emotional, thought-provoking speeches from family and friends moved me, but they struck an especially deep chord with Chris.[1]

As the beer flowed and the group became increasingly animated, the gathering morphed into a celebration. It testified to the spirit of survival, perseverance and kinship that defines Alaska. We considered ourselves privileged to be part of the event that night.

Around 8:30 P.M., the crowd in the pub thinned as people made their way to the downstairs banquet room for the monthly meeting of the Great Northern Brewers Club, the local homebrew organization. Jim invited us to join them. He predicted a larger than usual crowd, not only because the festival attracted homebrewers from all over the state to Anchorage, but also because of the guest speaker's popularity.

Club members mingled as they shared their homebrew. Doing our best not to be wallflowers, we talked more with Don and Tracey Lewellyn. After a job transfer relocated the couple to Anchorage, they quickly grew fond of Alaska's sense of community and chose to make it their permanent home, a story I was hearing over and over in one form or another. Tracey suggested we try the homemade caribou summer sausage and moose salami. "The true way to experience Alaska," she told me.

She guaranteed the moose salami would be the best we'd ever had, explaining that the commercial product is often mixed with other types of meat. In contrast, the homemade variety is 100% moose. In general, Chris and I avoid red meat, and wild meats taste too gamey for us. But offered something

---

1 Later that night when Chris checked his cash, he made a surprising discovery. Extremely moved at the memorial, Chris didn't realize that he had donated all the money in his wallet.

as special as homemade salami, we could hardly refuse. Tracey was right; we'd never had any moose salami better than that one. Of course, it was the *only* moose salami we'd ever had.

The lighthearted mood of the homebrew club's pre-meeting social gave us a chance to interact with Jim in a more playful setting. Jim, with his tall, lanky physique, reminds me of John Cleese. He is smart, articulate and quite funny. Jim's favorite comedic topic is his prominent nose, something that is dwarfed only by his broad smile. With the amount of self-deprecating musings Jim offers about his most conspicuous feature, his smile is frequent.

While we ate salami and drank exceptional homebrews, a man with a 5 o'clock shadow, rubber chicken necklace and down parka tied around his waist commented on Chris's shirt. "Flogging Molly. They're a great band," he said. Chris agreed as the guy passed by and disappeared into the crowd.

The house lights flickered to signal the start of the presentation and people crowded to fill seats at the front, eager to get as close to the speaker as possible.

First came the club president's welcoming address followed by club business and a raffle. Finally the evening's speaker was glowingly introduced and who should walk up on stage but the Flogging Molly fan who looked like he'd just returned from a weeklong camping trip. It was none other than Sam Calagione from Dogfish Head Brewing. We laugh now that we failed to recognize him that night. A maverick trendsetter in the brewing community, Sam is a handsome guy who photographs well. Every major article, documentary, or television story on beer includes a comment from Sam. He is everywhere, including a Discovery Channel show.

Sam's passion for the craft beer industry is indisputable. Chris calls him a fire-breather for his fervent objection to macro-brewed beer. His speech that evening was an animated, no-holds-barred fight, as he took jabs at the big beer conglomerates. He also entertained us with stories of "extreme brewing," like the time he used lavender in a brew. Reading the amount in ounces, he measured the lavender in pounds. Sam recalled that a comment card at the brewery likened the taste to "toe kissing Laura Ashley."

Sam's stories were like good jokes building up to the perfect punch lines. "One of the first beers we distributed," he related, "was a Chicory Stout made with organic Mexican coffee, licorice root, and St. John's Wort." He paused. "It was the world's only anti-depressant, depressant."

He described making ale with vanilla bean and maple syrup from his father's farm, boasting that it was one of the first craft beers aged in an oak barrel.

"It had a price tag of $13 a six-pack so it was a hard sell," he said. "It tasted like trees, but it got me fucked up!"

The pace and content of the talk energized the crowd and the room bubbled with enthusiasm for craft beer. People mobbed Sam at the end, handing him bottles of homebrew and requesting his opinion. Sam–a seasoned socialite in the beer world and a genuinely affable person–graciously received each person and their beer. We simply shook his hand, said, "thank you," and called it a night.

Filled with the satisfaction of a successful first day, we walked the short distance back to the hotel room in the cold night air. Chris put his arm around me, "This has been a great evening. Good job, hon," he said.

"You, too," I smiled.

We had put ourselves out there and in response, people embraced us and helped us to feel part of things. The amazing feeling affirmed our decision to embark upon the Year in Beer.

Friday morning, the January Alaskan sun didn't rise until 9:52 A.M. I stayed in bed with the covers pulled up to my neck, figuring I might as well wait until lunchtime to get up. Chris used the time wisely and blogged about our first day in Anchorage. Then he called our new friend Jim.

To my surprise, Jim, who had the day off, generously offered to pick us up at our hotel and take us on a beer tour of Anchorage.

First, we lunched at Moose's Tooth, a pizzeria that brews beer. Unfortunately, the brewery was located separately from the restaurant, so we couldn't count it on The List. We ordered a sampler set at the bar while we waited for a table.

"Which beers would you like to try?" the bartender asked.

"All of them," Chris answered indignantly.

The bartender had the last laugh, though. One after another, she placed small glasses in front of us: Klondike Golden, Northern Light Amber, Prince William's Porter, and Pipeline Stout, to name just a few. With eighteen samples in total, we had amassed a pitcher's worth of beer. The problem with a big sampler set is that after the eighth or ninth beer, it's hard to tell the difference between one beer and the next, let alone remember what the previous ones tasted like. In our beer-centric world, waste is considered a no-no. Only on the rare occasion do we leave beer in the glass. This sampler set challenged us, but with the determination of true beer geeks, we finished them all.

Once we were seated at a table waiting for our gourmet pizza, I asked Jim how he came to live in Alaska.

"I came up here and loved it," he said. "Something drew me here and I decided never to leave."

"Wow, that's really weird because when we landed I had a sensation that the land was pulling me in," I said. Chris rolled his eyes.

"Yep, that's exactly what Alaska does," Jim agreed.

I shook my head in affirmation. Alaska has an untamed spirit, one that guides people not to think logically, but rather to follow their hearts. Just as Chris and I had done with the Year in Beer.

Lunch with Jim marked my first real sit-down with an experienced and successful member of the beer media. With a plan to chronicle our Year in Beer experiences in a book, I was eager to pick Jim's brain while I had the chance.

He offered me advice on writing, as well discussed his philosophy of beer and expounded on the microbrew industry. He also gave us a crash course in Alaskan culture.

"Alaskans are friendly people who really pull together to help each other out. There is a real sense of community here," he said.

As we got up to leave, the woman at the next table stopped us. She'd overheard our conversation and realized it was our first visit to Alaska. As if Jim's behavior was a direct reflection of her, she complimented him on his hospitality, then offered some facts about the state and told us a bit about herself before bidding us a good stay. Jim was right: Alaskans are both proud and friendly.

We drove to Midnight Sun Brewing Company[2], a brewery that did count on The List. Over the years, I'd seen Midnight Sun's ads in beer publications and our beer friends had

---

2 Midnight Sun has since moved to an expanded location. They now have a full service tasting room on the second floor of the brewery.

frequently mentioned them as an extraordinary brewery. The name was so familiar that I had to remind myself that we'd never been there. In fact, we'd never even tasted their beer. With limited distribution, the opportunity to drink it had never presented itself in our California neck of the woods.

Jim turned left across a busy street and into a small parking lot. A small sign on the door of the warehouse building to the right indicated we were there. Once inside, the concrete floors of the brewery offered about as much warmth as the pavement outside. The metal table that served as the bar and the corrugated siding on the wall added to the frigid feel. We joined several other people in the tasting area, including Shaun O'Sullivan from 21st Amendment Brewing Company in San Francisco. An unexpected encounter, Shaun was in Anchorage for the festival.

We'd last seen Shaun five months previous at a brewmaster's dinner at the Cathedral Hill Hotel in San Francisco. At the time, our friend Bruce Paton—aka "The Beer Chef" —was the Executive Chef at the hotel. Bruce held dinners where he created amazing menus to accompany the fine beers of a highlighted brewery. That particular night, Bruce paired 21st Amendment beers with five courses of exceptional food.

At the beginning of each course, Shaun stood and described the beer, which Chris videotaped. Prior to the third course, without warning, Shaun looked straight at him, pointed and exclaimed, "That guy is really freakin' me out!" Chris chuckled with embarrassment and promptly put the camera away.

At Midnight Sun, we introduced ourselves and Chris reminded Shaun of that night. He immediately remembered and it became our inside joke throughout the trip. Together, we sampled Midnight Sun's robust beers, which exemplify the character of Alaska. Jim explained, "We embody that [spirit] in our beer. When it's dark in the winter, you need a more sustaining, hearty, warming beer."

In addition to the standard lineup, we imbibed three beers from the Seven Deadly Sins series: Lust, an oak-aged Belgian-style dark strong ale; Envy, an imperial pilsner; and Gluttony, a triple IPA. These brews tasted as wantonly sinful as their namesakes. Not one-gulp beers, they were meant to be savored.

The bold taste of the beers was admittedly a little big for me and I took my time with the small samples as I wandered about. Sneaking a peek around the corner into the brewery, it wasn't much different from any other we'd visited. What *was* different, however, was that we were in Alaska, drinking beer with Dr. Fermento and Shaun O'Sullivan. This was turning out to be a special trip indeed.

I re-joined the others back in the tasting room and surveyed the beers in the cooler. Bottles of an oak barrel-aged chocolate pumpkin porter were lined up in the bottom left-hand corner. It was too good a combination to pass up, so I grabbed a bottle and set it near the register. Several other beers were added and the bottles clinked together as we squeezed more and more onto the metal counter.

Forty-five minutes later, it was time to leave, as Jim was due back to begin judging barley wines for the festival. We packed our beer purchase into Chris's backpack and prepared to leave. The warming effect of Midnight Sun's beer acted like anti-freeze and the chilly air could barely be felt as we dashed back across the parking lot to Jim's truck.

At 5 o'clock, we met Matt and Michelle in the hotel lobby and together walked the few blocks to the evening's main event: the opening session of the Great Alaska Beer and Barley Wine Festival.

Started in August 1994 as the Great Alaska Microbrewery Invitation, a few thousand attendees demonstrated that an appreciation of good beer and good food was alive and well in the state. The following year, the festival was moved to the William A. Egan Civic and Convention Center and renamed the Great Alaska Beer Festival. (Barley wines were added in 2000) The festival founder, Steve Shepherd, eventually combined efforts with Billy Opinksy, the owner of Humpy's Great Alaskan Alehouse, who had been organizing his own craft beer festival for several years.

Today, 4,000 beer lovers attend the annual Alaska Beer and Barley Wine Festival over three sessions. The event not only showcases great Alaskan beer, but also benefits the American Diabetes Association. Proceeds are donated to a fund supporting a summer camp for children with diabetes. Matt, Michelle, Chris and I were about to attend for the first time.

On the walk to the festival, Matt lost his self-consciousness as he realized we were dorky beer geeks, just like him. It was refreshing to meet Matt and Michelle because we rarely encounter other couples that drink beer together. And when we do, I often find myself pressed into the role of teacher. Michelle, an experienced craft beer drinker, required no schooling. I especially liked that Matt and Michelle traveled for beer. We exchanged stories and compared notes on the places we'd visited. With plenty of material for discussion, polite small talk was unnecessary.

Matt and Michelle stood in line outside while Chris and I entered the convention center to check in at the volunteer table. Although our shift wasn't until the next day, our volunteer status granted us free admission to all three sessions. We planned to attend two: the five-hour long Friday session and the three-hour connoisseur's session on Saturday.

With our wristbands on and our commemorative tasting glasses and drink tokens in hand before they opened the doors, we waited as Matt and Michelle made their way through the ticket collection and ID check. A dozen white haired men in lederhosen and red handkerchiefs were assembled off to the side. The deep rhythmic blasts from their Oompah band's tuba added to the festive mood brewing in the lobby. Spirits were high, as attendees were as happy about getting in from the cold as they were anxious to drink beer.

Explorer's Hall, the convention room where the festival took place, was smaller than expected (19,000 square feet) and surprisingly intimate. The carpeted floor, as opposed to the usual cement, and the relatively low ceiling made it cozy.

No floor plan was included with the program, so finding beers took a bit of exploration. When we saw a brewery we liked listed in the program, we roamed the aisles in search of it. Fortunately, the perfectly sized festival was small enough for random searches, yet still big enough to offer an interesting selection of beer. Colorful brewery banners of all shapes and sizes hung behind the rows of tables arranged into aisles. The Alaska breweries were conveniently clustered at the far wall to the left of the entrance. This is where we spent most of our time.

Buzz in the beer community said good things about Fort George Brewing in Astoria, Oregon so finding them became a priority. Chris Nemlowill, the owner and brewer, served one beer at the festival, a barley wine, which was enthusiastically received by both Chris and Matt. The opportunity for me to try some of Fort George's lighter style beers would have to wait until our visit to Astoria in July.

In addition to the Alaskan beers, Chris tried every IPA he could find, including Dogfish Head's 90 Minute. After the previous night's talk at the homebrew club meeting, I developed a beer crush on Dogfish Head's owner/brewmaster Sam Calagione. Sam served his own beer and the small size of the festival minimized the number of groupies around his table. This was my best chance to chat with him. Getting in line, however, was the extent of my plan and when it was my turn, I discovered that I had nothing to say. Handing Sam my tasting glass, I said, "I'll have the 90 Minute, please."

As we walked away, I asked Chris if he had footage of Sam. He assured me that he did. Chris and I attend festivals to drink beer, of course, but videotaping for *beergeek.TV* is always in the back of our minds. We capture some colorful memories, although admittedly, this sometimes includes ones best left forgotten.

That night marked our introduction to "the chicken." Every year, Phil Farrell, a homebrewer and Grand Master Beer Judge from Georgia, attends beer festivals all over the country with his rubber chicken. Festival attendees flock to Phil to get their picture taken with the famous fowl, and the lucky ones receive a necklace adorned with miniature rubber chickens. Sam Calagione's unusual accessorizing the night before now made a lot more sense.

We had no idea who Phil was, but others sure did. People surrounded him wanting to have their moment with the chicken. It took 20 minutes for me to muster the courage to introduce myself. A momentary break in the crowd allowed me the time to tell Phil about the Year in Beer. He told me about his travels with the chicken.

The original rubber chicken was the mascot of Phil's homebrew club, the Chicken City Ale Raisers. Unfortunately, in 2005 rambunctious children at the club's annual family get together ripped the original chicken apart. When chicken #2 arrived, Phil asked Charlie Papazian, homebrew author, founder of the American Homebrewers Association, the Great American Beer Festival and the Association of Brewers, and the current president of the Brewers Association, to christen it with good homebrewing mojo. Charlie poured beer into the chicken and took a drink from it. To document the momentous occasion Phil snapped a picture. Initially, as Phil brought the chicken to subsequent beer events, people balked at posing with it until he pulled out the picture and chided, "Charlie did it." The rest was history. Now people seek out Phil and the chicken at beer events.

Phil pulled out a thick stack of photographs. The chicken's well-documented history showed it drinking beer with industry notables, with its beak stuck in some woman's cleavage, and even diving down some guy's pants. Going for the conservative approach, I intended to kiss the chicken on the beak. Instead, however, the picture looked like the chicken was picking food out of my teeth. A blue-beaded necklace with a half-dozen small rubber chickens hanging off it and my picture added to the stack proved my encounter with the chicken.

While Phil and I talked, I inadvertently tucked the chicken under my armpit. Soon a crowd had gathered around us, waiting for their turn. Phil politely asked for the chicken back before moving on to someone else.

"Whoops. Sorry about that," I said.

Good thing he caught me! I definitely didn't want the reputation of attempting to steal Phil's infamous chicken, even if it was completely unintentional.

On Saturday afternoon, Matt, Michelle, Chris and I did the festival all over again. This time, we attended the "connoisseur's session." In general, a connoisseur's session is where a smaller number of higher priced tickets are sold and breweries often serve special releases or beers that are limited in supply. We received complimentary admission due to our volunteer status.

We sampled Alaskan Brewing Company's 1996 Alaskan Smoked Porter and the 2005 Darth Delirium from Moose's Tooth, both rare beers that we knew we'd probably never have another opportunity to try. While small sips of the bold brews were sufficient for me, the rest of the samples went to Chris, who savored every drop.

The sound of bagpipes echoed through the hall and we all turned to find the source. Dressed in red tartan kilts, the members of a drum and pipe band paraded through the hall, marching in and around the beer drinkers. Deep drum booms and the trailing shrill of bagpipes filled the air. I grabbed the video camera from Chris and ran ahead of the band, positioning myself to get some footage. The energy level dropped as the band filed back out into the foyer.

The Great Alaska Beer and Barley Wine Festival kicked off not only our Year in Beer, but also our volunteer service. When we started planning for the Year in Beer, Chris suggested donating our time at the festivals. It would help cut down on our costs, since complimentary admission was typically offered in exchange. We envisioned pouring beer, but because in Alaska volunteers must attend an alcohol server's class and distance prevented us from doing so, we got the inglorious job of "bread cutter." Our assignment surprised Shaun O'Sullivan who said, "You're, like, really big beer people and you're cutting bread?"

Being called 'really big beer people' had never happened before and it came as quite a shock, actually. The conversation quickly shifted to another topic, but the comment stuck in my head. Was it possible that the Year in Beer was going to bring us genuine recognition?

Several hours later, near the end of the connoisseur's session, Chris and I reported to the kitchen for volunteer duty. Convinced that "bread cutter" was a euphemism for a more unfavorable task like vomit clean up, the start of our volunteer shift caused a slight degree of anxiety and uncertainty. The discovery that the task of "bread cutter" literally meant cutting bread came as a great comfort.

Against a wall in the kitchen several bakers' racks overflowed with baskets of bread cubes, enough to feed all the pigeons in New York City for a week. So with plenty of bread already cut, our supervisor directed us to fill water pitchers and straighten up tables during the hour-long break in between sessions.

The connoisseur's session ended and attendees were ushered out the door. The noise in the hall simmered down. Without festival goers, the room was quieter, but still very active as brewers and brewery representatives straightened their displays and replenished the pens, stickers, and bottle opener tchotchkes. Chris and I started at one end of the room and swiftly worked our way down to the other, making sure that brewers were supplied with fresh bar towels and water.

We fulfilled our volunteer responsibilities in 45 minutes. It's true what they say, that one gets considerable satisfaction from volunteering. Free admission to a festival with hundreds of noteworthy craft beers was very satisfying indeed.

As we exited the hall in the late afternoon, a line of people waiting for the next session stretched around the block. Bodies bundled up in long coats, scarves, and woolen hats shuffled from one foot to the other with hands shoved deep into their pockets. Some groups huddled together for warmth. All down the line, puffs of breath floated just above heads. The festival wasn't due to open for another half hour.

I shivered my way down the few blocks to the warmth of Humpy's Great Alaskan Alehouse to wrap up our night. Opened in 1994, Humpy's was the first champion of Alaskan beer. Its impressive tap selection has made it a favorite with both locals and tourists ever since.

Coming in from the cold felt good and Humpy's was clearly the place to be. All the seats at the bar were occupied. Throughout the restaurant, groups of people laughed over pitchers of beer and plates of fish and chips, burgers, and steaks. We found Matt and Michelle at a corner table and joined them. While Chris heeded the recommendation of many others in ordering Humpy's famous halibut tacos, I enjoyed a fresh, local crab roll sandwich. Over beers, our table of first time Great Alaska Beer and Barley Wine Festival attendees discussed our impressions of the event.

The small crowd—4,000 people over three sessions—created an unexpected intimacy that encouraged leisurely discussion and interaction with brewers. Over five-dozen breweries from throughout the country and beyond were represented, yet the festival maintained a neighborly character. It seemed to reflect Alaska itself, as residents from the far corners of the state came together to form one close-knit community. The festival had all the amenities of a big event, but with a smaller crowd. Chris and I couldn't have enjoyed ourselves more. Matt and Michelle agreed.

Sunday morning, we accepted yet another kind invitation from Jim Roberts. He invited us to a post-festival breakfast for brewers at Café Amsterdam. While most beer industry people had already left the state, we remained an extra day in order to celebrate Chris's birthday. Café Amsterdam became the first of many great beer cafés we would visit during our Year in Beer.

Matt and Michelle joined us for the breakfast. Outside the café, nervousness filled my body. The generous offer sponsored by Café Amsterdam extended thanks to the brewers who made the festival a success, not beer geeks who attended. Chris told me to relax and reminded me that Dr. Fermento had personally invited us. If Matt and Michelle were nervous, they didn't show it.

The brick décor and faux stone archways in Café Amsterdam's interior reflected warmth and sunshine–completely opposite the weather outside. Climbing vines and an outdoor dining set added to the courtyard ambiance. A large sign behind the bar proclaimed, "Welcome barley wine lovers."

After polite pleasantries, it didn't take long for owners Ken and Shauna Pajak to wholeheartedly embrace us. A jolly couple with big hearts, they remind me of Mr. and Mrs. Claus. Ken summed up his perspective on life in Alaska with both humor and pride.

"People come in here and ask if they can use their American money," he reported.

"That can't possibly be true," I responded. It was hard to believe that people could be so misinformed. "I'm terrible at geography and even I know that Alaska is part of the U.S."

Ken assured me it was true and said, "It happens more often than you'd think."

Chris explained the Year in Beer concept to Ken, who reacted with great enthusiasm.

"That's fantastic! I'd love to do that! It's a little harder for us, though, because this place ties us down."

Ken told us nostalgic tales of his own beer travels and expressed words of good-natured envy. His reaction showed us that the Year in Beer invoked the same passion in the hearts of other people as it did for us. Throughout the rest of the Year in Beer, Ken followed our travels as we documented them on our website. His supportive emails of encouragement and light-hearted jealousy helped keep us in touch.

The visit to Café Amsterdam started Chris's birthday off right. With the gift of a heavenly beer selection, he enjoyed several pint-sized presents that morning. In the comfort and hospitality of new friends, all my insecurities disappeared. We met interesting new people and filled up on bacon, eggs and beer.

Matt and Michelle had planned a family gathering with her brother Jason that afternoon so they dropped us off at the hotel and we said our good-byes. Seeing them again in the future was a given since we had thoroughly enjoyed each other's company. Little did we know that the day would come much sooner than expected.

Our trip to Alaska ended where it started: Glacier Brewhouse. Not only did Alaska blow the top off Chris's well-intentioned beer drinking strategy, it burst the insulated beer bubble in which we lived at the time. The kind-hearted nature of the Alaskan beer community reached out to our deeply embedded extraverted side. The way in which they encouraged us to become part of the community brought something out in us we didn't know we had.

For several days, we'd been introducing ourselves, telling people about the Year in Beer, and engaging in general merriment. This new, more outgoing role tired us out. Reverting to our usual ways, the two of us quietly played Scrabble at the bar while drinking choice craft beer. An NFL playoff game in Green Bay, Wisconsin, where it was 35°F below with the wind chill, played on the television. Bar patrons around us chuckled as they compared that stiff temperature with the relatively warm drizzle that now fell in Anchorage. Who would have figured that any place could be colder than Alaska in January?

Monday morning, we boarded a plane to head home. I plopped into my seat with a sense of relief and the realization that we had really done it. This was the Year in Beer. My body hummed with excitement at the thought of the people we'd met and the beer notables with whom we'd hobnobbed. It was hard to sit still as my mind raced with fantasies of the opportunities the Year in Beer might bring. Alaska had certainly set a high standard for the trips to come. Chris and I looked at each other. Without a word, we knew we needed to brace ourselves for one heck of a year.

I closed my eyes in an effort to soothe my overactive imagination, reminding myself to slow down and breathe. When I looked up again, Shaun O'Sullivan was coming down the aisle. Without missing a beat, he pointed at us and declared in a loud voice, "Everyone beware of these people right here. You can't trust them. They're beer people."

Our faces flushed red as the entire plane turned to look at us. With his one comment, my calmed inner state whipped back into a frenzy. My heartbeat raced at a hummingbird's pace. One of the most popular brewers in the craft beer industry thought enough of us to make a scene.

The man seated to my left turned to me, "Oh, you're in the beer industry?"

"Well, yes, I guess we are," I replied.

When we arrived home later that day, I thought about Chris's comment regarding our mountain lion sighting five days before. I consulted the book *Medicine Cards* by Jamie Sams and David Carson. In it they write that the mountain lion is a symbol of leadership and that a sighting may signal "a time to stand on your convictions and lead yourself where your heart takes you." Chris was right. The sighting did signal something special. By following our hearts, the Year in Beer was now a reality.

FEBRUARY

LIFE IS BEST SHARED WITH FRIENDS

We drank beer and spread the word about the Year in Beer for five days in Anchorage. Once home, we planned on our lives returning to normal for the few weeks before our February trip to San Francisco. With only one Year in Beer trip under our belt, the full effect of our passionate undertaking had yet to unfold. Our lives had not yet been absorbed by the madness of nonstop travel.

The enthusiastic response we received in Alaska indicated that what we had previously considered to be a personal quest to follow our hearts actually went well beyond us. It interested our fellow craft beer lovers and their support increased our confidence to make something great of the Year in Beer. Despite all the positive feedback, however, we didn't foresee the interest growing and expanding as quickly as it did.

Before the Year in Beer started, Chris and I discussed the merits of sending out a press release. While I wasn't sold on the benefits, Chris insisted it was a good idea. It turned out that his foresight was far better than mine and in late January, the Associated Press posted a story about the Year in Beer. That's when our lives unexpectedly shifted into overdrive. We'd been told that the story was picked up, but not when it would hit the wire. Once the flood of emails and phone calls started, however, there was no question about our story being out there. Where all the publicity would lead was anyone's guess.

Chris, quickly becoming our public relations manager, received a steady stream of emails inquiring about the Year in Beer and requesting interviews. Each night after work Chris reported his contacts for the day. We coordinated our schedules and lined up interviews.

As beer lovers across the country learned about the Year in Beer, they emailed us with wishes of good luck. They expressed their longing to embark upon a similar adventure. People wrote to tell us about their local breweries and festivals. They offered to buy us pints if we made it to their neck of the woods. The Year in Beer resonated with the average craft beer drinker and they pledged to follow our adventures on the website. After all, we're average beer drinkers, too. Only we decided to blow our life savings on a dream. The words of encouragement and interest in our adventure further boosted our self-esteem and confidence. A whole host of friends and supporters from around the world stood behind us, including some we would actually meet in person during the year. And you know life is just plain better when shared with friends.

Each new day created previously unconsidered issues that needed a response. The heightened level of exposure required us to venture outside our comfort zone. Requests for live radio interviews started coming in. Print media interviews posed one challenge (like providing articulate answers worthy of quotation), but live media posed a whole host of challenges. My biggest nightmare included gonzo guy-focused morning shows where a high degree of sarcasm was sprinkled with obscene sound effects. To ease our anxiety, we brainstormed a list of possible questions interviewers might ask and prepared answers.

The radio interviews happened quickly, but required preparation on our part. Out of bed early, we pumped ourselves up and waited for the call, hearts racing with anticipation. During the interviews, we sat together with answer sheets in hand and pointed at each other to indicate who should answer the question. Each interview was 10 minutes of heart-pounding, breath-stopping excitement during which I felt like a celebrity. Being on the radio took me out of my regular life and I liked that feeling.

The interviews formed our public image and we took them seriously. Each one was critiqued and better responses discussed. Most often our debriefings degenerated into one or both of us whining about how lame we sounded. The first few interviews I joked about possibly gaining a few pounds from all the beer. I soon scrapped that topic, though, because it sounded too stereotypically female.

For the most part, I came to feel confident about my radio appearances. I articulated my answers and sounded reasonably intelligent. Chris, on the other hand, tended to ramble. It didn't take long to discover that I performed better in live interviews and Chris appeared better in print media. Newspaper writers often favored the angle of Chris as a lucky guy with an indulging wife. They portrayed me as a sidekick who tagged along.

Despite my best efforts, my quotes would get chopped up and I sounded like a blithering idiot. That is, if my quotes made it into the article at all. One writer called Chris the "Hugh Hefner of the beer world." In an attempt to figure out what exactly that meant, I ran a comparison. Hef: mansion, millionaire, and multiple girlfriends. Chris: nice home, barely a savings account, and one wife.

A better analogy might be Chris as the Sonny to my Cher. Sonny could hold his own but with Cher, he became one half of a great duo. Not that I want to be a Bob Mackie-wearing gay icon or anything, but it works a heck of a lot better than Chris as a smoking jacket-wearing porn icon. I admit the sidekick label is *my* issue. Chris and I each consider our self to be one half of *thebeergeek.com*. However, even today public misperceptions about women and beer linger. Although it's getting better, it's still hard to convince some people that I'm not a sidekick.

For February's trip, we planned to stay the first two nights in San Francisco then head east across the Bay Bridge to spend the next two nights in Oakland. I had faith that on this trip I would be seen as more than Chris's junior associate. Oakland, where we lived for seven years, served as both the base camp for our earliest beer adventures and the epicenter for the growth of our beer knowledge. There, people view us as the inseparable pair that we are. Our fond memories and sentiments about the Bay Area run deep and this trip would bring us back to our beer roots. It was an opportunity to retrace our steps and re-connect with old friends.

Unlike Alaska, San Francisco offered the familiar comforts of home, something that diminished the trip's feel as a special Year in Beer event. It's easy to take for granted that we lived in the birthplace of the post-Prohibition craft beer movement. But even if it didn't feel like it, San Francisco was a real trip.

For the Year in Beer, our weekend focused on a series of events collectively known then as "Beerapalooza." The precursor to San Francisco Beer Week, Beerapalooza encompassed dozens of beer-related events all around the greater San Francisco Bay Area. Our agenda included functions such as a special release party, a chocolate beer dinner, a barley wine festival, and an anniversary celebration.

We started our long weekend on Thursday with a two-hour drive to City Beer Store for a beer tasting. This bottle shop/tasting room is located in San Francisco's colorful South of Market district. Originally, SoMa was an industrial area filled with sweatshops and housing for lower class European immigrants. Today, it's known for its diversity, including Folsom Street, the heart of San Francisco's gay bondage and discipline community and home to City Beer. Rainbow gay pride flags fly in front of places called The Stud, Stormy Leather, and Wicked Grounds, a "kink café and boutique." Barely noticeable amongst the other businesses, City Beer's sandwich board on the sidewalk identifies its location.

Opened in 2006, we first visited in 2007 when a friend told us we *had* to go there. That friend couldn't have been more right. Descending the steps into the store, owners Craig and

Beth Wathen greet customers like old friends and the selection of beers is nothing short of amazing.

The small space[3] with a concrete floor reminds me of a basement turned rec room. Coolers and shelves filled top to bottom with bottles of beer line the walls. Two overstuffed chairs separated by a side table offer a comfortable spot to relax while a few bistro tables and stools at the kegerator bar create a pub feel. Behind the bar an Ikea-esque demonstration kitchen is staged, complete with a microwave, dishwasher, and sink. In all, it's a very comfortable place to be.

It was actually during our first visit to City Beer that I started to understand my identity as a beer traveler. Up to that point, I judged a person's beer knowledge by their level of ability to discuss the nuances of specific beers. With that as a measure, my untrained palate and average memory for flavors left me with low beer self-esteem. Many beer geeks strive for the ability to identify the subtle characters of particular beers. City Beer helped me understand that Chris and I go beyond the beer itself. Only then did I start to appreciate and accept that we were beer *travelers*.

During that first visit, I browsed the shelves. Beers from an Italian brewery, Birrificio Le Baladin, caught my eye. Le Baladin is located among the famed vineyards of Barolo wine country and in 2003 we took a five-hour detour on our drive from Switzerland to Provence to visit. I had never seen their beer in the U.S. before. Given how out of the way it was for us to get there, I always considered it one of the more remote breweries we've visited. "I've been there," I thought to myself when I saw it. Admittedly, my surprise turned to slight smug-

3 In October 2011, City Beer Store expanded, doubling its size. Included in the remodel was a new bar and slightly different décor.

ness as I wondered how many other people in the shop had actually been to Le Baladin. In that moment the lengths to which we went to visit breweries became clear.

Chris and I define beer travel as: "experiencing the diversity of beer throughout the world by drinking it at its source." Enjoying a beer where it's brewed, whether at the brewery itself or at least in its home country, is an experience you just don't get sitting in your living room or even your neighborhood pub. It's nearly impossible to fully grasp the communal conviviality of a German beer hall or the family feel of an English pub without actually being there. Through our travels we have come to understand not only beer cultures in other parts of the world, but also the people.

The first night of February's Year in Beer trip fell on a Thursday, which is Special Event Night at City Beer. It also happened to be Valentine's Day. In honor of this special occasion, City Beer offered a special tasting of Chocolate Indulgence from Brewery Ommegang in Cooperstown, New York. We became part of a romantic, 50-person Valentine's Day gathering.

We squeezed our way through the throng of cheerful beer drinkers and up to the bar. The volume created from the capacity crowd made conversation challenging. People stood close together, sharing the limited floor space with kegs stored against the walls and in the corners. Cases of beer stacked in the nooks and crannies around the shop served as makeshift tables. Beth's face lit up when she saw us. She shrugged her shoulders and made an inaudible comment about the large turnout. I held up two fingers to order our glasses of Ommegang Chocolate Indulgence.

Along with our glasses of beer, Beth passed me a small plate with two chocolate truffles. While most people stood conversing, Chris and I retracted into our introverted shells and shared one of the easy chairs.

In spite of the failure of Chris's Alaska beer drinking survival strategy, he tried again. For San Francisco, he planned to take it easy the first night. "It's going to be a long weekend of beer drinking," he told me. However, Chris in City Beer reminds me of Halloween as a child: you ate all your candy until you either became physically ill or your mother took it away. Chris followed his Chocolate Indulgence with beers like Anchor Bock, Avery Out of Bounds Stout, and Russian River Redemption. Six beers later, I took him away. I wasn't going to wait until he got sick. Such is Chris's concept of "taking it easy." After February, he didn't make anymore Year in Beer trip drinking strategies. There was no point.

We returned to City Beer the following afternoon to meet up with our long time friend, Rowdy Corrick. We first met him as the bartender at Barclay's, our neighborhood pub in Oakland. Our fledgling interest in craft beer had already brewed when Barclay's opened in 1991, but it was there that our passion fully developed. For Rowdy's part in our beer education, Chris calls him our Yoda.

As bartender and beer buyer at Barclay's, Rowdy formed friendships and business relationships with the brewers. Brewing industry contacts invited Rowdy to private parties, river cruises, and special events. As his friends, we went along for the fun. Rowdy introduced us to the perks and inner workings of the brewing business.

Chris Devlin[4]—our friend and writer of several Seattle-based beer blogs—was in town for the festivities and he planned to join the three of us at City Beer. We first connected with Chris D during the 2007 Oregon Brewer's Festival media tasting where his rants about the oft times overly serious act of beer drinking held our attention. We found a kindred spirit in Chris D. His sarcastic wit is lost on some and unappreciated by others, but we enjoy his company.

A master storyteller with an infectious laugh, Rowdy gave an account of the Bay Area beer scene that captivated the three of us. His stories offered history and insight that left us fascinated. Rowdy stood to make a point, his deep voice drowning out Chris D's attempts to get a word in. There was no interrupting Rowdy as he pounded his fist on the table to make yet another point. The few others in the shop seemed unaffected by our animated discussion. Craig, who was busy stocking the shelves, laughed and shook his head at Rowdy's diatribes. An afternoon spent laughing and drinking beer with friends. Life can't get much better than that.

For a change of scenery, the four of us decided to take a cab to 21st Amendment Brewery. Located near AT&T Park, home of the San Francisco Giants, the brewery was only a mile and a half away. The cab ride took about five minutes, but in our buzzed state, it would have taken us much longer to walk there.

February is Strong Beer Month, as presented by 21st Amendment and Magnolia Pub & Brewery, another San Francisco brewery. Started in 2002 as a way to beat the winter blues, every February the breweries each brew six strong beers. Drink

---

4 Chris is a recurring character in our Year in Beer story, so for clarity, I will identify him as "Chris D" from this point forward.

all 12 beers in the month and the reward is a commemorative glass. Chris wanted to try a few of the special brews while he had the chance.

Chris, Chris D, and Rowdy ordered a vertical tasting of 21st Amendment's barley wine, years 2006-2008. Chris also ordered a pint of Hop Crisis, a beer measuring 11.8% ABV. Not particularly interested in partaking of such high alcohol content beers, I ordered a Claudia's Kölsch. A light and refreshing beer style that originated in Cologne, Germany, Kölsch's lower alcohol content makes it a much more drinkable beer. I didn't want to be left out of the Strong Beer Month celebration altogether, though, so I took small sips of each of the barley wines in order to cast my vote. Our group named 2006 as the strongest, 2008 the smoothest, and 2007 the best.

Chris D had plans with friends, so we parted for the evening. Rowdy, Chris and I headed to the Cathedral Hill Hotel for the chocolate beer dinner presented by our friend Bruce Paton, aka the "Beer Chef." The chocolate dinner was one of Bruce's most popular and we knew there would be many familiar Bay Area beer community faces. Plus, a few of our new Alaska friends had told us they would be down for several of the weekend's events, including the beer dinner.

The appetizer course was presented cocktail party style, so we mingled with 150 other craft beer lovers and journalists and chatted with various friends as we ate our chocolate-covered foie gras hors d'oeuvres. It looked like a peppermint patty and I popped one in my mouth without even asking the waiter what it was. Swigs from my glass of Urthel Hop It helped wash the taste out of my mouth. I much preferred the shot glasses of chocolate lobster bisque.

When the first course was ready to be served, Chris, Rowdy, and I made our way to one of the large banquet tables. Glasses for each course's beer were placed at the formal table settings, sparkling in the light of the chandeliers above. The first course of roasted quail didn't entice me but I fiercely guarded my lobster cake with a milk chocolate beurre blanc sauce in the second course.

The beers that accompanied each course were styles like Bock, Trappist Quadruple, and Belgian Dark Strong Ale. Although they were perfectly matched to the entrees, I personally could not keep up with these potent, bold-flavored beers. Half empty glasses of beer were abandoned as I switched to water.

I was almost full before the final course, "Ménage au Quatre in Chocolate," arrived at the table. The top button on my pants was already undone, but I did my best to finish them all. After that I was officially stuffed.

In our wallflower days, Chris and I would have attended an event and left, too shy to join others out for an after-party. This night, however, we resisted the temptation to dash back to our hotel and instead accepted an invitation from Ken Pajak (owner of Café Amsterdam in Anchorage) to join the Alaska contingent across the street at Tommy's Joynt.

Tommy's Joynt is a San Francisco institution dating back to the 1940's. The exterior's colorful murals intrigue passersby to step into the dimly lit, no frills cafeteria-style hofbrau. Once inside, the smell of roasted meats is absolutely mouthwatering. Carvers at the smorgasbord serve roasted turkey, brisket, and ham to hungry customers. Fully satisfied from our decadent dinner, however, we passed by the carving station, took our beers upstairs and found a table.

Ken, Jim "Dr. Fermento" Roberts, and Alaskan home brewer Dennis Urban had been invited to San Francisco to judge the Toronado Barley Wine Festival. Beginning in 1993, the world famous Toronado Pub has hosted this annual festival, which includes dozens of the best barley wines from around the country. A select group of beer judges, including members of the Alaska contingent, determines the best of the lot, an honor coveted by many brewers.

Joined by Dennis's wife Lisa, we talked over pitchers of Anchor Steam. Chris and I spoke about how much we'd enjoyed Anchorage the month before and mentioned that we'd like to return during the summer to hike and bird watch.

"That would be great! We'll take you fishing…and hunting…" Lisa said excitedly. As nice as her offer was, Chris and I prefer to watch birds, not kill and eat them.

The unusually sunny February weather thawed this group from the cold north. They partied all weekend. As we called it a night, the Alaskans left for another bar.

We dragged ourselves down Market Street the next morning to meet Chris D at Toronado for the Barley Wine Festival. A major thoroughfare, Market Street frequently bustles with a colorful cast of characters, including street musicians, business people, and the homeless. On Saturday mornings, however, the only bodies out in the mid-Market Street area are the leftovers from the night before, which usually means prostitutes and junkies. Unfazed by our gritty surroundings, we enjoyed having the wide sidewalk mostly to ourselves as we made our way to the Lower Haight.

Toronado is one of the premier beer drinking establishments in the country. From the outside, it looks like any other dark Haight-Ashbury dive bar and it is. Inside, the twenty-plus years of patina easily distracts one's eye from the menu of nearly 50 world-class beers, but not for long. Toronado's bartenders are perfectly matched to the pub's messy, tangle of décor, which includes beer memorabilia, empty bottles, and a collage of stickers on the walls. "Potheads against drugs." "Work sucks." "Guns don't kill people, people with mustaches kill people." And in case you didn't think those public displays of opinion were useful, a sign on the register read "Tip, you bastards." Now, that's about as succinct as you can get.

Long and narrow, the natural light in Toronado is limited to the front door. The further you delve into the pub, the darker it gets. Around the corner in a small lounge area at the back, one can escape sight of the front door altogether. It's good for those who want to disappear, aren't interested in knowing the time of day, and vampires.

Chris D greeted us at Toronado's door. In spite of the 70°F weather, he covered his lanky figure in his usual black hoodie and black jeans. Together, the three of us planned to make our inaugural appearance at the 15th annual Toronado Barley Wine Festival.

This festival is organized differently than the Great Alaska Beer and Barley Wine Festival we attended in January. Here, Toronado replaces its varied beer menu with over 50 barley wines. Each beer is numbered and two sizes (3 ounce and 6.5 ounce) are available. No cost to attend, you simply purchase the beers you want to try. Toronado's festival is quite popular and table space is limited, even with its side room open. The line to get in starts forming several hours before the doors open and often stretches around the block.

By the time of our mid-day arrival, the barley wine geeks had already made their way inside. There was no line, but activity around the front door bustled. Smokers on the sidewalk engaged in animated discussions. VIPs darted back and forth across busy Haight Street to the Peacock Lounge–the site of the judging. Muffled sounds of an over-capacity crowd filled the air. The three of us stood dumbfounded by all the commotion.

I took a look inside and hesitated. Entering a loud crowded party once it's started is a daunting prospect, but like getting into a cold pool, you just have to jump in feet first and hope you make it out alive. I turned back to the two Chrisses and raised my eyebrows. "Are you guys sure about this?" I asked.

I led the way with a primary goal of finding a seat. It was five deep at the bar, so I gently nudged people from side to side to create enough space to keep moving forward further into the pub. Slow going, it was a challenge to get through the crowd and look for a seat at the same time.

We ended up at the back of the pub without having found a seat. Our only choice now was to scramble to the left through the lounge toward the side room that had been opened up for the festival. With that area open, the capacity of Toronado is doubled, but that didn't translate into available seating, just twice the crowd.

We passed from the dark pub through to the brightly lit side room. A group gathered around a makeshift bar, keeping the one bartender moving constantly. The two Chrisses followed me down the narrow aisle, where people looking for seats and those trying to get beers jostled past each other to get through. The lucky ones with seats happily tasted away, scarcely paying attention to the plight of those still standing.

We navigated the entire length of the pub and doubled back through the side room. Following a horseshoe-shaped path, we found ourselves at the side room's door to the sidewalk. It was the end of the line and we had two choices: huddle in the small spot where we stood or go back outside and make a second pass. We unanimously agreed to stay put. Now all we needed was some beer. Chris, Chris D and I decided that each of us could carry three beers. One at a time, we braved the mob and ventured toward the closest bar.

"If I don't come back in 30 minutes, send a search party," I said as I disappeared into the crowd.

Reunited after gathering our beers, we packed together like sardines, glasses of barley wine clutched to our chests. The challenge became keeping track of which beer was which as we shared our samples.

"What beer is this?" I asked.

"That's the Big Woody from Glacier Brewhouse," Chris informed me.

Chris D held up a glass, so he could see the color. "Is this the Abacus Blend?"

"I'm not really sure," I said. "Chris, which hand did you get this one from?"

"That's the Abacus," he said pointing at the beer in question.

After twenty minutes of this, we politely asked the nearest group for a sliver of their table space. Surprisingly, they paused to think about it. After much hesitation, however, they eventually gave in.

Some participants came prepared with their Beer Judge Certification Program beer style guidelines, picnic snacks, water, and activities to keep occupied in between tasting (one woman was knitting). All business, these were the people who planned to sample each and every one of the 55 barley wines available.

Through observation, first time festival goers learn a lot about how to survive this event. Here's what we learned:

1. A table or other hard surface is critical. Otherwise you hold your glasses as you taste, increasing the chance of confusion regarding which beer is which as you pass them amongst yourselves.
2. There is strength in numbers. A group of people provides better defense of the aforementioned hard surface.
3. Order beers by size and number only. This is important as the tap handles are numbered and the bartenders won't know the names of the beers. Ordering by name guarantees an exasperated bartender who will skip to the next person until you figure out how to do it right. Remember, Toronado bartenders are surly by nature and you can triple that on an insanely busy day like the festival. Here's an example of how to order: "Small number 19 through 21, please."
4. Six-pack holders serve as the perfect beer carriers. Veteran attendees bring empty six-pack holders, so they can order six beers at a time. The sample glasses fit perfectly in the slots and it's easy to carry.

A man returned to our adoptive table with his six-pack of samples. He methodically removed one beer at a time and called out the number. The woman who brought her knitting retrieved the beer and placed it on the corresponding circle on her placemat. Like most groups, this one did not start tasting until all the beers were collected. When they had a sample on every circle, we congratulated them at achieving a complete set. It took them an hour and a half, a record time of which they were particularly proud.

After only an hour, the strong beers and Toronado's cacophony of beer drinkers left us with headaches and claustrophobia. The aftermath of the previous night's revelry further decreased our tolerance for a stuffy room. Plus, the warm, sunny day compelled us outside.

Chris wanted to try a few of the featured beers at Magnolia—the second brewery involved in Strong Beer Month, so we walked 10 blocks up Haight Street. We passed through a string of houses and eventually came to a stretch of businesses. The smell of incense wafted onto the sidewalk as we passed a shop full of imported items from India. We noticed the glass bongs and pipes in a smoke shop window. Every other storefront had an array of items with marijuana leaves and Bob Marley's face. This is the Haight-Ashbury of the Summer of Love fame and Magnolia Pub and Brewery is right in the heart of it.

The corner brewery was busier than we anticipated, but seats were readily available and the noise inside the tile-floored dining room was a fraction of what Toronado had been. After the 20-minute walk, Magnolia offered a chance to rest and calm the nerves frayed by the chaos at the Barley Wine Festival. We sat at a dark wooden table and the Chrisses ordered strong beers: Promised Land Imperial IPA and Old Thunderpussy Barley Wine. Once again, I opted for something lighter and ordered the Kalifornia Kölsch.

Magnolia is cozy and funky, projecting a modern 1960's Haight-Ashbury attitude. "Reduce, recycle, and reuse" could easily be their motto. Water is brought to the table in old Dickel Whiskey bottles, the napkins are washable flour sack kitchen towels, and even the old menus are cut up and used as doilies. The black and white photos of a young Jerry Garcia on the wall celebrate the Haight's heyday. The three of us sat quietly enjoying our beers.

Sanity restored, we decided to continue down Haight Street to check out Wunder Brewing Company. Wunder was the most recent brewery incarnation in what Chris calls the "cursed location." The space on 9th Street had been home to two previous breweries, neither of which survived. We had been to one of them, Golden Gate Park Brewing, which wasn't very memorable but made The List nonetheless. Eldo's (brewery #2), however, never made The List because the time we tried to visit, it was closed for a private party. Chris joked that at this rate, we could keep adding to The List by returning to this location every few years. We hoped Wunder would break the curse.

Inside, Wunder looked like its two predecessors–long and narrow with the brewery at the end. A balcony along one side offered a bird's eye view of the entire establishment. Sitting at the bar with our shared taster set, Wunder was the quietest place we'd been all day. We sunk onto our stools and let out big sighs. "It's just nice to be able to hear ourselves think," Chris said.

The taster set included both a barley wine and a chili beer. With all the strong beer from the day, a barley wine seemed too much, so that one was saved for last. The bartender suggested tasting the other five samples before the chili beer. Just to be oppositional, we all tried it first. A chili beer is just as the name implies, a beer brewed with chilies, and is almost always a difficult style to drink. Wunder's version hit the back of your throat and burned all the way down. Afraid that it might burn coming back out, we left that sample mostly untouched.

After a quick visit, a notch on The List's bedpost, we moved along[5]. We rode the N Judah Muni train to the end of the line to the Beach Chalet Brewery and Restaurant.

The Beach Chalet, down the road from the famed Cliff House, is situated on the top floor of an historic Spanish-style building dating back to 1925. The Golden Gate Park Visitor's Center occupies the bottom floor, where faded WPA-commissioned frescoes depict the culture of 1930s San Francisco. The Beach Chalet was already on The List, but on such a beautiful day, we decided to take time out to gaze at the amazing view. Large windows running the length of the restaurant offer a panoramic view of Ocean Beach when it isn't shrouded in the infamous San Francisco fog. This day, it was clear as far as the eye could see.

After a few beers, we took a quick walk across the street to the recreation trail before boarding the N Judah back into the Haight.

We made a pass by Toronado to see how the Barley Wine Festival was progressing. Now in the early evening, the crowd numbers had not changed, but the group had lost some of its energy. A few festival goers had crossed over the happy drunk line and were now headed toward passing out. The second wave of arrivals jockeyed for position, prepared to pounce on

5 Unfortunately, Wunder did not escape the kiss of death and folded like its two predecessors. The location is currently home to a 4th brewery, Social Kitchen & Brewery.

any void left by someone falling off their bar stool. One of the keys to a successful (and relatively sober) day of beer drinking is to travel by foot and drink taster sets. So, despite our trio's long hours of beer drinking, our senses were intact enough for a quick taste of the winning beers. We still didn't have seats, but at least this time the slow, droopiness of those around us made for a lot less jostling.

Discussion soon shifted to a newly opened Belgian beer café in the North Beach district. Praise for La Trappe had been circulating in the beer community since its opening two months before. The thought of exploring a hot new beer bar interested us far more than listening to inane barley wine-induced babble. We assumed that the further away from Toronado we got, the better chance we had of escaping the raucous beer geek crowds. All in all, it seemed a nice way for the three of us to end our long, beer-filled day.

A long walk to North Beach seemed like a good idea when we started out, but halfway up Russian Hill, one of San Francisco's most brutal hills, I wondered what I was thinking. My thighs burned and my heart jumped out of my chest. "This walk surely justifies a beer," I managed in between heavy breaths. The Chrisses concurred.

An hour later, we approached a brightly lit bistro on the corner. Through the large windows, an open kitchen and a few small tables with crisp white tablecloths could be seen, but no beer taps. Upon entering, however, we noticed a narrow staircase leading downstairs.

The staircase curved around, revealing brick walls and exposed beams awash in an orangey glow. Groups of people sat at large wooden tables talking in whispered conversations and sipping beers in glasses of all shapes and sizes. On the right near the base of the stairs, bright lighting illuminated a row of tap handles at the bar. This was definitely the place. The Alaska contingent was already firmly established at the bar. Our unexpected meeting altered our plans from a quiet escape to a fun little party.

La Trappe offers hundreds of bottled beers, in addition to 19 rotating taps. With classics like Orval, Rodenbach Grand Cru, and La Chouffe, the bill adds up quickly, prompting Chris to call it "the land of the $10 beer." Belgian beers tend to have big flavor and often have high alcohol contents to match. They are made for sipping and enjoying, not for chugging. Chris D feared that the increasing popularity of Belgian beers would create a negative trend.

"Strong beers have become the new shots for idiots," he groused.

Ken Pajak got a kick out of that quote and vowed to write it on the chalkboard at Café Amsterdam when he returned to Anchorage. Dr. Fermento thought it equally quotable and later mentioned it in his blog. The mood in La Trappe's cellar was mellow and mature, yet still conducive to lively and interesting conversation. It swept us away late into the night.

The culminating event of the weekend was the *Celebrator Beer News* 20th Anniversary Party, held across the San Francisco Bay in Oakland. With the event starting later in the afternoon, we had the morning to spend in what locals call the East Bay, including Oakland and Berkeley. Now in our old stomping grounds, the birthplace of our craft beer development, the opportunity to come full circle with our personal beer history was upon us.

The Year in Beer was the biggest, most ambitious beer travel adventure we'd ever embarked upon. It ushered in a whole new attitude toward our beer travel. The weekend thus far had been an homage to our personal beer history, so we continued our retrospective by taking a walk down memory lane. Barclay's in Oakland was a big part of our early beer history. However, we went there frequently during our visits to the Bay Area. A place we revisited much less often was Triple Rock Brewery and Ale House, brewery #1 on The List.

To be honest, Chris and I aren't altogether positive what brewery was our very first. Over the years, we've narrowed it down to two possibilities, one being Triple Rock in Berkeley. The other possibility has long since been defunct, so years ago we agreed to deny its possible claim as brewery #1.

Chris D hitched a car ride with us across the Bay Bridge to join us at the brewery. As a frequent patron of Triple Rock's sister brewery, Big Time, in Seattle, he was especially interested to see how the two compared.

Triple Rock became only the fifth brewpub in the United States when it opened in March 1986. The founding owners, brothers John and Reid Martin, still maintain ownership and operate the original equipment used for their very first batch of beer brewed on Christmas Day 1985.

All of the pub's originality is evident the minute you walk in. Grooves in the dull wooden floor reveal the thousands of beer lovers who've set foot in there. Without shiny varnish to shield it, the floor has absorbed its share of spilled beer. A faded vertical lunch sign from the Allen Hotel dominates the room. The walls are decorated with vintage metal signs and beer trays from breweries with names like Knickerbocker, Yuengling,

Blatz, and Hamms. The Chrisses and I pulled up some stools at the antique bar.

"I hate to tell you guys this," Chris D said, "but this isn't the mirror image of Big Time."

"Really?" Chris responded.

"It looks similar, though."

Based on a trip to Seattle years ago, both Chris and I mistakenly remembered Big Time as the mirror image of Triple Rock. Instead of the bar being on the left, Big Time's was on the right. We remembered the kitchens being on opposite walls, as well. The thought of my memory being completely wrong was rather embarrassing. We'd been telling people for years that the two were opposite…and they'd believed us.

The bartender served our pints then turned his back to us, attending to his cleaning duties. Chris D took a sip of his IPAX IPA and remarked how it tasted just like Big Time's Bhagwan's Best IPA.

"Blasphemer," the bartender accused without turning around.

The comment took us by surprise and we turned to look at him. The bartender explained that IPAX served as the model for Bhagwan's, not the other way around. Chris D re-phrased his observation, "Bhagwan's tastes just like IPAX." With a nod of satisfaction, the bartender went back to cleaning.

"I remember coming here in like 1986, 87," Chris told us. "Triple Rock's original beer lineup included two beers; Red Rock and Black Rock. Red and Black mixed together created a third beer; Orange Rock."

Once again, the bartender—a longtime Triple Rock employee—interrupted his cleaning, this time to sort out Chris's false memory.

"Triple Rock originally served three beers," he informed us. "Red Rock, Black Rock and Pinnacle Pale Ale. A mixture of Pale and Red created 'Orange' and a mixture of Red and Black created 'Checkerboard'."

"Really?" Chris responded. Like a boy who was just told there is no Santa Claus, Chris just couldn't fathom that what he'd believed wasn't true. "I don't remember it that way."

"You've told that story so many times, you believed it," I laughed.

Even I believed it; a family story told and re-told so many times that it became truth in our minds. Discovering the facts debunked one of our frequently told stories about our early beer adventures. If there's anything to be taken from this visit, it's 1) the countless retelling of a story does not make it true, and 2) the memory of a craft beer enthusiast cannot always to be trusted.

Later that afternoon, the *Celebrator Beer News* 20th Anniversary party was well underway by the time Tom Dalldorf, editor/publisher, led Dr. Fermento and other *Celebrator* writers in a Mardi-Gras parade. Dressed in a white tuxedo and oversized top hat, Tom used a plunger with streaming ribbons like a bandleader's baton. They danced to the sounds of a Dixieland jazz band. Once on stage, Tom officially opened the celebration.

A decade earlier, we'd attended the 10th Anniversary party at Pyramid Brewing in Berkeley with Rowdy. Eighteen breweries poured their beer at that party. Ten years later, 700 people helped celebrate the longest running "brewspaper" in the country by sampling beers from over 40 breweries. During its 20 years of publication, the *Celebrator* had changed its name and publishers, but for us, it has remained a sentimental favorite. Before the internet and social media, the *Celebrator* served as an important source for openings and closings of breweries around the country. Chris used it as his primary tool for organizing some of our first beer adventures. It was also the inspiration for the many regional publications that now exist.

A glance around the convention room provided a snapshot of the growth of the craft beer community. Among the hundreds of craft beer faithful present, the originators of the movement almost went unnoticed: Dean Biersch, co-founder of Gordon-Biersch in 1988; Judy Ashworth, the ex-publican of Lyons Brewery Depot, one of the first bars to support and promote craft beer; and Pete Slosberg, who in 1986 founded Pete's Brewing Co., maker of Pete's Wicked Ale. It was a privilege to mingle with these founding fathers and mothers. Sharing beers with old friends was another perk; some, like Rowdy, we planned to see at the party, others came as a pleasant surprise.

Halfway into it, the event had become a whirl of beer, laughter, and craziness. There were friends to see and beers to taste. The noise level rose as the celebration progressed and I needed a breather. Chris and I sat at one of the round tables set up in the middle of the room; a pleasant escape from all the action.

Through the crowd, I spied a familiar figure across the room. It was Ted, one of my regulars from Barclay's. It had been a dozen years since I last saw him.

As I approached, a broad smile flashed across Ted's face. "It's Merideth!" he exclaimed. Turning to Chris, he continued, "And Mr. Merideth!" Big hugs all around, Ted introduced us to his wife. The perfect match, she seemed like a female version of Ted. She was a craft beer drinker, too, and together they radiated an eternally sunny disposition. Ted laughed frequently when he spoke and his eyes nearly disappeared as his smile filled his boyish face.

For over a year, I waited on Ted and his two friends every Sunday. It was noticeable when they didn't show and when one was absent, the others explained why. Nostalgic thoughts flooded my head as I thought about the "good old days" at Barclay's. Regular customers like Ted made the experience more than a job. It was life in our neighborhood.

The group from Alaska arrived and I spent some time with Lisa Urban. Lisa is a beautiful, unapologetic extrovert and a homebrewer. This combination makes her very popular at beer events. The more beers I drank, the more I tried to keep up with Lisa's outgoing personality. Whatever Lisa asked for that afternoon, she received: beer swag, posters, Mardi Gras beads and my appearance on the Brewing Network's live broadcast.

The Brewing Network broadcasts live from beer events, as well as a weekly show on beer-related topics. They have a huge following, the "BN Army," and at the time, I knew little about them. At Lisa's insistence, I was thrust up to the table and told to put the headphones on. Tom Dalldorf was the guest of the moment. Anyone who knows Tom, knows that he is a whimsical eccentric who loves to talk. I sat quietly self-conscious getting redder in the face with each passing second. A large crowd had gathered around to watch and listen.

After a few minutes, host Justin Crossley asked Tom to introduce his guest. "I didn't know I had a guest," he said. Stunned and holding my breath, the pause as Tom looked in my direction seemed like forever. We had crossed paths for years, but didn't know him very well. It was highly possible that now, in all the excitement of the celebration, Tom might not remember my name. Much to my relief, he did. I seized the moment and quickly described the Year in Beer. Justin politely interjected as soon as there was a pause and moved on to the scheduled programming. In my one-minute appearance on the Brewing Network, two goals were accomplished: get our name on the air and not sound like a dork. Okay, that second one is debatable, but *thebeergeek.com* definitely made it onto the broadcast.

Several hours later, the event wound down and the afterparty moved around the corner to The Trappist, a beer café. Like La Trappe in San Francisco, The Trappist serves high-end beers to a craft beer-savvy clientele. We entered to find it several people deep at the bar. Chris, Chris D, and I squeezed through and, in an accomplishment that is just shy of a miracle, found seats at the end of the bar. The place to see and be seen, everyone from beer writers and sales reps to brewers and prominent local pub owners were there.

The night ended as a blur.

Prior to the weekend, it was hard for me to consider February's Year in Beer trip special. We had lived in the Bay Area for many years and still traveled there frequently, so it was hardly going to be the exciting new experience that Alaska had been the month before. But by Sunday, I realized that we *had* done exciting new things: the tasting at City Beer, the Barley Wine Festival, and La Trappe. These experiences had breathed new life into an old, familiar place.

San Francisco wasn't our only trip in February. While in Alaska, our friend Matt Venzke told us about having entered Wynkoop Brewing Company's Beerdrinker of the Year contest for the third time. The contest name was familiar due to seeing ads in the *Celebrator*, but beyond that it was a mystery to us.

Matt explained that the first step is to submit a "beer résumé"—a curriculum vitae of beer geekiness. His beer geek accomplishments included several collections: 3,569 unique bottle caps carefully organized in binders, 3,389 beer coasters cataloged and cross-referenced, and 286 brewery glasses. In Alaska, he had expected to hear any day if he made the cut. "This year is my best entry," he told us. "I have a good feeling about it."

Shortly after returning home from Alaska, Matt emailed us with the good news: he was one of three finalists headed to Denver for the contest. While in Alaska, Chris had told Matt that if he made the finals, we would go to cheer him on. Arrangements were immediately made for what Chris called a Year in Beer "side trip," an impromptu addition to the year's calendar. Just one weekend after San Francisco, we were in Denver supporting Matt in his quest to be the 2008 Beerdrinker of the Year.

Between our Monday return from San Francisco and our Friday departure to Denver, I developed a sinus infection. For several days, my participation in this side trip was hotly debated. I didn't want to be left out. No matter how bad my condition, I was determined to go—sinus infection in a pressurized cabin be damned. In one of the most excruciating moments of my life, my head almost exploded on the descent into the Mile High City.

Even with a throbbing head, I did my best to be a trooper and keep up with our usual beer travel activities. Our weekend started with a short walk from our hotel to Great Divide Brewing to meet Matt and Michelle.

Great Divide didn't always have a taproom and our first visit in 2001 entailed standing at a bar set up in a corner of the brewery. During this visit, we were pleasantly surprised to find that they had been successful enough to expand. We walked the length of the narrow bar to find Matt and Michelle at a bistro table. Now late in the afternoon, we left it up to Matt to set the evening's agenda.

Matt had heard a rumor that the finalist who stayed out the longest the night before the contest always won. He informed us that he intended to test that rumor, so we'd better prepare ourselves for a long night. First on Matt's agenda was a judges/finalists meet up at Falling Rock Tap House.

The four of us walked the half-mile over to the Falling Rock. Along the way, Chris kept asking me how I felt. "Okay," I told him. The truth was I felt awful, but for Matt's sake, I did my best to project an image of health.

Falling Rock Tap House, whose motto is "no crap on tap," is a beer lover's buffet. You want everything, but can only have so many in one sitting. With a selection of over 75 taps, it's a must stop for any beer geek visiting Denver. It's also a favorite of the locals.

When we arrived, Falling Rock was filled with the regular Friday after-work crowd. The pub displays all the charms of Toronado (including snarky bartenders), but is three times the size and serves food. Thousands of beer bottles line the brick walls. Beer signs of all shapes and sizes cover the room and tap handles stick out from the walls. The bar area was already standing room only.

We followed Matt through the pub. He wasn't clear on what he was expected to do and no special table for the meet-up had been reserved. He checked downstairs and found nothing, so we wound up at the end of the bar.

Once Marty Jones, organizer of the contest, and a few of the judges arrived, Matt decided he better mingle. Lisa Morrison, a beer journalist from Portland, Oregon and a contest judge, was seated with her husband. Chris and I went to say hello.

"Yeah, I'm not really sure what I'm supposed to be doing either," Lisa admitted, "but it's Falling Rock, so enjoy! Cheers!"

Several glasses clinked together in a group toast. I had decided to save my beer drinking for the actual contest the next day and my clear water looked out of place amongst the various colors of amber in the other glasses. I offered a weak smile and sighed. A stuffy head was bad enough, but to be drinking only water in an amazing beer place like Falling Rock only added to the misery. An hour later, Matt suggested we leave for Wynkoop Brewing Company where he was expected at a judges/finalists dinner.

Meeting Matt in person for only the second time, I was struck by the difference in his personality. In Alaska, Matt and Michelle tagged along with us while we met prominent beer people for the first time and attended special gatherings. Now in Denver, Matt showed his confident side. Any anxiety about the contest was hardly noticeable as he networked with judges and extended friendly interactions to his fellow contestants. In a complete reversal from our first meeting, we were now the reticent ones riding on the coat tails of a Beer Drinker of the Year finalist.

Chris and I quietly joined the table of judges and finalists. The dinner wasn't extended to friends and supporters of contestants, but we were welcomed all the same. As Matt's guest,

I tried my best to look alive, but the walk from Falling Rock had left me in a cold sweat. A corner seat enabled me to prop myself up against the wall. My eyes struggled to stay open and my body longed for a bed. We listened as Marty Jones, dressed in a plaid cowboy shirt, welcomed the eight judges and three finalists in his pronounced southern drawl.

As a long time brewery front man and craft beer promoter, Marty's winning smile and gregarious nature made him well-suited to host the dinner as well as emcee the Beerdrinker of the Year contest. Throughout dinner, Matt and Michelle socialized with great ease. Even Chris managed to engage in polite chitchat. I, on the other hand, sat mostly quiet.

The party returned to Falling Rock for a nightcap. This was where Matt's stamina needed to shine if he was going to test the myth of the last finalist standing. We had vowed to give him as much support as we could, so our stamina needed to kick in, as well.

The vibe of the group had changed and it now felt a bit formal as people sat quietly drinking their beer and conversing. Matt pressed on and did his best to keep himself involved with the judges.

One by one, people departed until eventually Matt was the last finalist present. He wondered how much longer he would be expected to stay out. We had no idea, but by now I was pale, sniffling, and barely able to keep my eyes open. Our commitment to the cause had been fulfilled and Chris decided to get me home to bed. It was 11 P.M. Matt and Michelle stayed for another few hours.

On Saturday, Chris and I arrived at Wynkoop an hour before the contest. The small number of people present surprised me, but then again, I really had no idea what to expect. We found Matt and Michelle at the bar. Despite looking every bit of cool, Matt admitted that he was really nervous. Chris, Michelle, and I all offered Matt our reassurances and encouragement.

Prior to the contest, organizers sent Matt a list of preparations, so he had a fair idea of what to expect. He had packed his bribe for the judges and had a short skit practiced and ready to perform. Matt studied beer trivia and reviewed beer styles in anticipation of the question and answer portion and the blind beer tasting. He was as ready as he ever would be.

The banquet room where the contest was set up was a lot smaller than I expected and I told Matt so. It was easy for me to say, he told me, because I wasn't the one who had to go up there.

Chairs were set up in lecture-style. Three podiums with maroon-colored skirts were arranged at the front, each one with a sign listing the finalist's name. A long table for the judges sat opposite. The banner behind the emcee's stand read, "The Beerdrinker of the Year National Finals."

Shortly before the contest started I ordered my first beer of the trip, a Rail Yard Ale. I may not have felt 100%, but it would be just plain wrong to drink anything other than a beer while watching the Beerdrinker of the Year contest.

The event commenced with the entry of the judges. Beer media and past winners comprised the esteemed panel. Dressed in ill-fitting judicial robes with English solicitor wigs resting slightly askew their heads, the judges filed in and took their seats. Little did we know, the contest would last for several hours.

At times, the contest dipped to the level of the Gong Show. The finalists were asked to sing their favorite beer jingle. Matt needed little coaxing to get going. "Schaefer is the one beer to have when you're having more than one." He waved his hands to beckon the crowd to join in. By the second verse the audience of 100 spectators, friends, and media burst into song. Matt bobbed his head from side to side in time to the jingle.

One judge asked the finalists, "If you were a beer, which beer would you be and what kind of glass would you be served in?" Matt was asked to answer first.

"Well, let me examine myself," he paused. "I look kind of conventional. I can be boring at times and I'm kind of corny, so I guess I'm an American macro-lager." The room erupted into laughter as Matt continued, "And do they make elastic beer glasses because I'm slowly expanding." The crowd laughed harder and applauded his response. Even the other finalists chuckled.

At other times, the contest took on the esoteric quality of Jeopardy where it helped to be an encyclopedia of beer knowledge. Judges asked serious questions related to beer knowledge and solicited opinions about issues like the Transportation Safety Administration's ban on liquids in carry-on luggage. Matt chose a humorous response to the question.

"I would like to start a petition asking brewers to start packaging beer in 3 ounce containers," Matt answered. This response received whoops and hollers from the audience, some of whom had undoubtedly experienced the inconvenience of the regulation.

Next came the bribing of the judges. Year after year, finalists resorted to bringing bottles of home brew and rare specialty beers. Matt, however, showed exceptional creativity.

"I really respect the esteemed panel here today and to me you're kind of like the royalty of the brewing world," he said.

Matt reached into a plastic grocery bag and pulled out gold crowns adorned with bottle caps. The judges clapped with approval and a woman behind me exclaimed, "Wow!" Cameras flashed from all directions as photographers captured the moment. The other finalists each had a look of defeat.

Michelle assured me that Matt had designed and created the crowns on his own without any assistance from her. He thoughtfully color coordinated each one. Red caps looked like rubies and green caps emeralds. Black caps created an especially dramatic look. The judges proudly placed the crowns on their heads.

After the short intermission, Matt faced the portion he had most worried about: the blind tasting. The other two contestants held Beer Judge Certification Program (BJCP) credentials. This meant that they had completed courses in style guidelines, tasting, and beer evaluation and passed a written and practical exam. BJCP credentials meant they were experts in beer tasting. Matt was not BJCP certified, so he compensated for his layman's palate with humor. The beer name was revealed to the audience as the finalists received their sample of beer.

"Okay, Matt. What does that beer say to you?" Marty asked.

"It says 'drink me,' " he quipped.

The last few bits of laughter drowned out the beginning of Matt's serious response. When he was finished, Michelle and I worried. His answer seemed to be way off. Much to our surprise, however, the other contestants offered similar answers. The third finalist to answer, J. Mark Angelus from Nehalem, Oregon, went so far as to punctuate his flavor assessment by also naming a specific brewery. A collective gasp filled the room. While J. Mark misidentified the brewery, he correctly identified the beer as a black lager.

In the end, Matt's bribe, self-deprecating humor and extensive knowledge of beer trivia won the day. Named Beerdrinker of the Year 2008, Matt won free beer for life at Wynkoop Brewing Company. The legend of the last finalist standing the night before proved true.

After a few beers at Wynkoop, we continued the celebration at Great Divide Brewing. Regulars, Beerdrinker of the Year judges and J. Mark, the finalist with the amazing palate, filled the taproom. Focused on Matt's performance during the contest, it was easy to ignore my throbbing sinuses and stuffy head. It wasn't until we reached Great Divide that I remembered how ill I really felt. The sickness seemed to advance by the minute. I quietly watched as Matt reveled in his victory.

We walked to Rock Bottom Brewing on the 16th street mall for dinner. Matt's black t-shirt with "The Beerdrinker of the Year 2008" in bold yellow announced his achievement. Random people stopped to congratulate him. Some inquired how he became Beerdrinker of the Year. Others asked how many beers he had to drink in order to win. The question highlighted the widespread portrayal of beer drinkers as hedonistic stein-chugging binge drinkers. Matt answered with the annoyed grace of a person who considered himself much more that.

"It's not a beer drinking contest," he clarified. Most people lost interest at that point and walked on.

After a quick bite of dinner, Chris–a concerned and loving husband–escorted me back to our hotel. Before my head hit the pillow, I heard the hotel room door close. He left to drink more beer with Matt and Michelle. Grave illness prevented me from being angry at his departure. Sleep found me before jealousy reared its ugly head.

The next day, Matt and Michelle's flight back to Virginia left around the same time as ours to California, so we went out to the airport together. Good-byes were said with a bit of sadness. We had new friends to share our beer adventures with, but they lived across the country. Without immediate plans to get together again, we'd have to keep in touch via computer.

Sufficiently ill, travel worn, and partied out, I had less than two weeks to recover, go back to work, and prepare for our second Year in Beer side trip: Philadelphia.

MARCH

GOOD "CRAIC" KEEPS YOU WARM

When I contemplated the Year in Beer schedule, I envisioned 12 events in 12 months with a few weeks in between each trip. Thus far, Year in Beer activities had kept me busier than expected. Overnight work trips and appearances at the office filled what little time I spent at home. Fleeting moments of rest and relaxation fell in there, too. I longed for those "few weeks in between" upon which I had previously planned.

In early February, during the height of our promotion frenzy, the Greater Philadelphia Tourism Marketing

Corporation invited us to be part of a media group covering the inaugural Philly Beer Week. Chris, somewhat naïvely, responded that he needed to consult with me and review our finances. They informed him that we were their guests. We had thought about a visit to Philadelphia many times, but it never fit into our travel schedule. With an invitation this good, though, we made the time. We barely suppressed chuckles of amazement each time we thought about it. Bewildered, and to a certain extent envious, our friends also shook their heads at our incredible stroke of luck.

"Philadelphia officially makes us beer media," Chris observed one day.

"I don't know. I don't feel like beer media…" I answered. "Although I guess some people do consider us 'big beer people'."

"Well, it's about time we got some recognition," he concluded.

I brushed it off, but also pondered whether Chris's proclamation merited serious consideration. Maybe the truth lay somewhere between Chris's self-assuredness and my humble hopefulness. Nonetheless, someone was paying for us to go drink beer. That was just plain cool.

We left the house at 4 o'clock in the morning and arrived in Philadelphia at 4 o'clock in the afternoon. The schedule permitted us a quick clean up before diving into a 3-day whirlwind tour of the Philly beer scene. When we arrived, Chris and I were exuberant with child-like anticipation, but also filled with anxiety about our ability to live up to expectations. We were determined to show the organizers that they had made the correct choice to invite us. The last thing we wanted to do was expose our inexperience with a major faux pas.

The first assembly of our group eliminated any doubts, however. Of the eight other people invited to Philadelphia, we knew 3 of them, including Lisa Morrison, who we'd just seen a few weeks before, Bay Area-based beer journalist Jay Brooks, and Rick Sellers, who at the time worked for *Draft Magazine.* It was like a meet up of West Coast beer journalists. Chris and I relaxed; we were in good company.

For Philly Beer Week, the city partnered with the beer community to encourage travel to the area. They pulled out all the stops to show off Philadelphia as a worthy beer destination. The mention of our first engagement—dinner at Monk's Café—sent a ripple of excitement throughout our group. For good reason, Monk's is one of the most notable Belgian beer cafés in the United States.

Monk's proprietor, Tom Peters, is a Chevalerie du Fourquet des Brasseurs—a Knight of the Brewers's Mashstaff. It's a great honor to be chosen by the Belgium Brewer's Guild to be a member of this elite group and only people who demonstrate exemplary service to the brewing profession are included. Monk's is also designated an Ambassadeur Orval, a title bestowed upon establishments that promote Orval with good presentation and service. There's nothing like starting the tour off with a bang.

Tom greeted us at the door of Monk's. His big smile and warm personality revealed little about his lofty status in the beer world. Several in our group were seasoned beer media and well aware of Tom, if not already personally acquainted with him. Chris was familiar with Tom Peters and Monk's Café. At the time I was relatively clueless, but even so, the enthusiasm was catching. Tom's presence generated a heightened level of excitement as we prepared to dine at his world famous beer establishment.

We followed Tom single file through the restaurant to a private room at the back. People sitting at tables turned to look at us, undoubtedly wondering about the identity and significance of our group. Inside I was thrilled, but also felt slightly undeserving of such royal treatment. It seemed like a dream. How was it that a couple of average beer drinkers who aspired to be a part of the beer media core had found themselves at Monk's having a private dinner with Tom Peters? Luck, I would say.

The private back room, with its dim lighting and cluttered antique bar, brimmed with European romance. The romance faded quickly, though, as the frequent flashes and rhythmic clicks of cameras from the local media created an atmosphere more like the Fourth of July. The attention surprised me. First of all, I really had no idea what to expect from a media tour. I thought maybe they'd show us a good time around the city and give us a sales pitch about what makes Philadelphia a great beer destination. In turn, we'd be expected to plug both the city and Philly Beer Week on our website. However, there was more to it than that. Not only were we going to be wined and dined (or in this case brewed and wooed), but also an integral part of Philly Beer Week's publicity campaign. The discovery that local television stations and newspapers viewed our group's presence as a newsworthy story was startling to say the least. Chris basked in the glory of it all. I wished I had worn a better outfit.

The camera flashes continued as the room quieted down to hear Tom welcome us and introduce the first course: a turbot roulade stuffed with spinach, pine nuts and bacon, paired with a gueuze that Tom blended at Brasserie-Brouwerij Cantillon several years before. The best way to describe gueuze to a non-beer person is to liken it to a tart Champagne. It's an acquired taste that I have yet to acquire. Taking the tiniest of sips, the tangy effervescence of Tom's gueuze put a tickle in my nose.

Several more courses of fancy food with French names arrived paired with more Belgian-style beers. It was a world-class feast and we were the guests of honor. The jubilant mood at the table was dizzying. Laughs and chatters swirled around the room from the many conversations going on at the same time. As unimaginable as the invitation to this trip was to begin with, now that it was actually happening, it felt absolutely surreal. Whether or not we actually were, at that moment I felt a part of the beer media cartel.

Our philosophy on beer travel has always been to engage in activities any beer traveler could enjoy. We don't seek out special treatment simply because we have a website. The lavish attention we now experienced flew in the face of that philosophy. Worlds away from our regular life, it was both exhilarating and bemusing.

With the last course served, the chef came out to join us. Tom poured a special surprise, Rochefort 8° Cuvee, a beer bottled in magnums and designed for aging and sharing. Available only at the holidays and not imported, Tom had personally brought the beer back from Belgium. Those around me salivated as they waited for their glass of beer. I, on the other hand, had not yet developed the knowledge of, or a liking for, Belgian-style beers so I was relatively detached from all the fuss.[6]

Today it deeply disappoints me that I lacked full appreciation of my dining experience that evening. Now that I'm more aware, I hope the chance comes around again someday.

---

6 It wasn't until our very last Year in Beer trip in December that I understood Belgian styles and developed an appreciation for them.

Our time with Tom continued after dinner with a guided pub tour of nearby beer establishments, including an unexpected addition to The List. Nodding Head Brewery and Restaurant, located just around the corner from Monk's, was the second stop of the trip. Walking up the stairs, I marveled at the feat of transporting kegs up and down this second floor brewery.

Our group scattered to explore. The bobble head doll collection lining the walls made me laugh. Walking by, several disproportionately large heads with broad smiles nodded up and down while others remained remarkably steady. I jumped up and landed hard on the floor in an effort to get all the heads shaking. The journalist from Toronto laughed at me as he passed by.

We found Lisa Morrison sitting quietly at a table with her dark beer.

"What'd you get Lisa?" I asked.

"The Vibrator. It's a doppelbock," she said. "I couldn't resist asking for a Vibrator in a bar."

"We'll come back when you've finished it and see how happy and relaxed you are," I joked.

"Oh, I miss my husband," she laughed.

Friday started off with a walking beer tour of the city with Richard Wagner, founder of the Pennsylvania Brewing Historians. Dressed in a waistcoat and short breeches with black buckled shoes and white stockings, he looked like Benjamin Franklin. Almost anyone in period dress would look like Benjamin Franklin to me, but Richard's long graying hair and broad-brimmed hat made the comparison easy. We followed as he led us to the Liberty Bell. Despite being out for only a short time, my sweater provided little warmth against the nippy weather.

Before going indoors to view the bell, however, we had to negotiate the airport-level security. Our small video camera was allowed in without question. Not so for two members of our group, Fausto Fernós and Marc Felion from the Feast of Fun gay community lifestyle website. They got a more thorough screening. Security required them to unpack their camera equipment, show their media credentials and explain the nature of their work. Up to that point, I had been envious of their big camera and Fausto's roaming microphone. They looked much more like a legitimate media outlet than we did. However, after watching the grilling they went through, I was content with our small handheld camera.

A group of school children assembled around the bell listening to the docent's presentation. He explained the bell's crack and engaged the 8-year-olds with questions. Every few minutes, a dozen arms shot straight in the air for a chance to dazzle the docent with their knowledge. It was hard not to smile at their eager faces. We made a loop around the bell, eavesdropping on the docent's talk as we did so. Just as my body became comfortably warm again, we were told it was time to move on. Thus, our 10-minute visit to the Liberty Bell concluded. In the short time we'd been in Philadelphia, the pace had been quick; something that would not slow during our visit to the city.

We walked the streets of Philadelphia occasionally stopping on street corners where taverns once stood to listen to our tour guide. Buildings remained in a few spots, but mostly we viewed historical markers or had to use our imaginations.

"As the largest seaport in the colonies, Philadelphia was shipping beer around the world from its early days and quickly developed a reputation as a first-class brewing center," he explained. "With the influx of German immigrants in the middle of the 19th Century, lager made its first appearance in America in Philadelphia in 1840."

The information was fascinating, but in short order I was once again covered in goose bumps, making it difficult to pay attention. Also, a walking tour didn't go well with jet lag and beer drinking from the night before. A more passive sightseeing bus tour with beer-related commentary would have suited our group better, but we trudged along.

We passed A Man Full of Trouble tavern, established in 1759. As the only surviving tavern building from pre-Revolutionary Philadelphia, it is the last remnant of the city's once thriving tavern trade.

"It's no longer open to the public," Richard told us, "but take a look at the sign. The tavern signs often said a lot about what type of establishment it was."

The brick building had been restored and in an effort to preserve it, the public was not permitted inside. We studied the sign out front; a man escorting a woman on one arm with a parrot on the other and a monkey perched on his shoulder. A kitten poked its head outside the woman's basket. Any man who juggled a parrot, kitten, monkey and a woman might very easily have been full of trouble. No wonder he needed to get to the pub.

We continued on to City tavern where we went inside for a beer talk and tasting. The original City Tavern, completed in 1773, had served as the unofficial meeting place for the First Continental Congress. The current building is an exact replica of the original structure, which was demolished after a fire in 1834. Today, the historical site offers the experience of authentic 18th century cuisine, including beer. Even though the concept seemed a little cheesy, the history was remarkable.

We gathered together and listened to Tom Kehoe from Philadelphia's own Yard's Brewing Company as he introduced their Ales of the Revolution series. Based on the original recipes of America's founding fathers, the beers contained traditional ingredients. Since barley and hops were not readily available at the time, the ingredients used were a bit surprising to our group of modern beer drinkers. The Poor Richard's Tavern Spruce Ale, brewed with spruce tips and molasses, tasted like Christmas smells. The sweetness blew me away, but so did the fact that it was based on Ben Franklin's recipe. "It's like drinking history," I told Chris.

Our server, dressed in a white mob-cap and an apron over her blue dress, brought us plates of cheese, crackers, and summer sausage with our beer samples. While most of us looked out of place in modern clothes, our tour guide, Richard, fit right in. He had even brought his own tin tankard for beer.

The George Washington Tavern Porter, also made with molasses, seemed more like a modern brew even though Washington himself had used the recipe hundreds of years before. It went nicely with the flaky duck sausage roll I popped in my mouth.

So far our guides, Cara and Morgan, from the Greater Philadelphia Tourism Marketing Corporation had maintained a tightly coordinated schedule. We stopped briefly at the modern Triumph Brewing (another addition to The List) before arriving at Tria Café for lunch.

We had the restaurant to ourselves as we mingled near the bar in the brightly lit café drinking Malheur Brut Reserve in champagne flutes and eating bruschetta with goat cheese and pesto. I was still a bit intimidated by the special treatment and being in such a hip, trendy restaurant didn't help my adjustment any. Our group was starting to relax and the pre-lunch hors d'oeuvres gave us time to interact and get to know one another. Among others, we met a food and beverage writer from Toronto and beer journalist Dan Rabin from Colorado.

When lunch was served, we sat in the compact dining area. Servers presented us with a Lancaster cheddar, chicken and truffle oil sandwich paired with an Italian Saison as owner, Jon Myerow, offered an overview of Tria's philosophy.

"We wanted to place beer and wine on an equal level," he said. "And create a place where a guy could bring a first date and actually get a second date out of it."

Focusing on specialty wine, cheese, and beer, Tria is serious about its business.

"Education is important to us," Jon said. "We focus on artisanal products and if you look at our menu, many of the items are foreign to most people."

He went on to say that if he didn't have an educated wait staff, most customers would walk out in frustration. Wait staff at Tria are expected to demonstrate proper serving techniques and are regularly quizzed on their knowledge of the three featured comestibles. This intrigued us all and begged the question: "What happens if a server doesn't pass?" Those who fail, it turns out, attend remedial courses at the Tria Fermentation School, where "you can satiate your intellectual curiosity while drinking and eating the syllabus." Not such a bad fate!

Throughout lunch, I contemplated how differently my life might have turned out if Barclay's had employed such a strict doctrine of beer education. The whole idea of being tested brought up insecurities about my beer knowledge. Working under such conditions, I might have quit altogether to avoid repeated failure. That would have meant no need for beer competency. No quest for knowledge. No beer travel. No List. No Year in Beer. Well, it's a good thing I was never tested.

Later that evening, we boarded a small bus to attend the opening celebration of Philly Beer Week. The gist of our media group's invitation to Philadelphia was to discover the city's beer culture and promote the inaugural Philly Beer Week. However, although dozens of beer festivities were scheduled around the city during the 10-day celebration, the opening gala was the only beer week function we actually attended.

The event was held at the Marketplace at East Falls, an enclosed bazaar similar to Pike Place in Seattle. Our group was ushered to the front of the line waiting to get inside. Without paying or waiting we were able to immediately join the party. By this point, I had begun to accept the exceptional treatment and even reveled in my V.I.P. status.

Inside, stalls selling flowers, fruits and vegetables, pastries, and meat lined the walls and filled in the center of the large space. The market was closed for the evening's event and local breweries had set up their stations in the gaps and vacant spaces. Along with a few hundred others who had purchased tickets for the event, we sampled our beer and poked around the indoor farmer's market. A half-hour after arriving, attendees gathered around to watch Mayor Michael Nutter tap the keg in grand Oktoberfest style.

"I do need to read the official proclamation, so all this beer you've been drinking already is outside the parameters of the official Beer Week. That means you just have to drink *more* after I make the proclamation because everything you've been drinking is outside the limits and doesn't count," he told the enthusiastic crowd.

As the mayor opened his folder to read the proclamation he said, "Oh, this is a long one. Good thing I didn't start drinking before I read this."

With his quick wit and casual demeanor, the mayor looked at ease amidst the crowd of beer lovers. The audience laughed as Mayor Nutter inserted quips into the reading of the formally worded official proclamation. To use the popular American political measure, he showed himself to be a man with whom I'd like to have a beer.

The live band provided a drum roll as Tom Kehoe from Yard's Brewing assisted the mayor in opening the ceremonial keg. Mayor Nutter pounded the spigot into the keg and beer started to flow. Cheers rang throughout the already jubilant crowd. Shortly thereafter, our guides ushered us out the door to another beer-paired dinner. The quickness with which we completed our visit to the opening ceremony was a little jarring, but perhaps a strategy of "leave them wanting more" was in effect. If we wanted to a more leisurely visit, we'd just have to make a return trip to Philadelphia.

Saturday was yet another busy day with a bus tour of several breweries located in the Philadelphia suburbs. Before we hit the road, though, we all wanted to do one thing: run the front steps of the Philadelphia Museum of Art *a la Rocky*. Unfortunately it started to rain, so instead of running Chris and I slowly climbed to the top to avoid slipping and falling. Besides, have you seen the number of steps there are? Even taking our time we huffed and puffed our way to the top.

The famous Rocky scene has become an iconic image of an underdog's resolve to win, something that definitely applied to us. A modest website with dreams of becoming big, we wanted to forge our way to the top and make a name for *thebeergeek.com*. With limited time to daydream at the top of the steps, however, we snapped a few pictures of the amazing view and descended to rejoin our group at the Rocky statue.[7]

Drinking cans of Sly Fox Pikeland Pils, we waited our turn behind the other tourists to snap a photo with the 10-foot tall Rocky. Add beer to a thoroughly touristy activity and the inner goofball in all of us came out to play. We laughed at ourselves, teased each other for being dorky, and patiently waited as everyone got a chance to get their picture taken. More and more, the outing was feeling like a school field trip.

Back on the bus, the group was in high spirits for the 45-minute drive northwest to Sly Fox Brewery and Restaurant in Royersford. At this point, people were more comfortable with one another and our individual personalities were starting to emerge. The media tour had put together people from all walks of life, from the popular self-assured beer writers to the more reserved established ones and from bright-eyed beer media newbies to gay podcasters. It was like high school all over again.

We arrived at Sly Fox where, aside from tasting beer, the purpose was to view their canning line. Sly Fox Brewing is one

---

7 The 2-ton bronze sculpture of the famed boxer that appears at the top of the steps in Rocky III is now more conveniently located at the bottom right of the steps.

of several breweries promoting cans as a superior alternative to bottles when it comes to packaging. In general, proponents say cans are softer on the environment, better for the beer, and more convenient for the consumer. Neither Chris nor I had ever seen canning in action and we were excited.

Stepping into the brewery, vague memories of a 5th grade class trip to a garden hose factory came to mind. I did question, though, if the memory was real or I had incorporated a *Simpsons* episode into my own history. It's sometimes hard to tell. In any case, we gathered around the canning line as Sly Fox Brewmaster Brian O'Reilly explained the process. Unlike the manufacturing of garden hoses, the canning process is really quite fascinating. I mean, come on, who hasn't thought about how drinks get into the can? In a nutshell, here's how it happens: Topless cans funnel into single file where they're purged with CO_2 before getting filled with beer. Lids are then placed on top and sealed. Voila! A can of beer is now ready for that backyard barbecue.

We enjoyed a brewery tour and lunch at Iron Hill Brewery in Phoenixville before heading back into Philadelphia. A day full of beer and food had rendered our group sleepy and the bus was quiet. Luckily there was a short time to rest before our final dinner together.

The respite livened us up a bit, but the conversation at dinner remained mellow. Chris and I offered each other a toast. "We survived our first media tour without making any rookie mistakes," Chris whispered to me. I smiled back. Maybe Chris had been right. Maybe Philadelphia did officially make us beer media.

Toward the end of the evening, I thanked our hosts and fellow media group members.

"I want to say thank you so much to our hosts, Cara and Morgan. I'm glad to meet the new people I haven't met before and to hang out with the people I have met before. So, thank you. It's been a great couple of days." Cheers and clinks of glasses rang out. Short on eloquence, but long on sincerity, no one seemed to mind that it wasn't the greatest thank you speech ever.

Chris and I stayed home after Philadelphia just long enough for our household routine to return to normal and the dogs to think we were staying for good. Four days later, however, we callously yanked that security out from underneath our unsuspecting little doggies.

As I said my good-byes, Porter sat still and refused to look at me. Stout bounced around the couch. We knocked teeth as he jumped up to lick my face. Poor little dog, I thought. Ignorance is bliss. I dragged my heavy heart full of bad dog-mom feelings out of the house and back to the regularly scheduled events. March's Year in Beer trip to Boston was our fifth St. Patrick's Day visit in six years.

Beginning in 2003, Chris and I started a tradition of going to America's most Irish city for St. Patrick's Day. The best reason for our repeated visits is that Boston offers good "craic." Whether you believe this expression to be an authentic Gaelic word meaning chat or an adaptation from the English word "crack" (also meaning to chat), the feeling is the same–time spent laughing and joking with friends warms you from the inside out. It's the perfect cure for Boston's chilling March days.

In fact, Boston's St. Patrick's Day spirit inspired our original concept of the Year in Beer as a television show. The area's heritage provides plenty of things to do and see throughout the year anyway, but when it's St. Patrick's Day, the city comes alive with festivities and events. It's more like a weeklong celebration and by the time the day actually arrives, Boston is awash in shamrocks, Guinness and everything green.

St. Patrick's Day is a major holiday to Bostonians. Many people either take the day off or work only half a day. The celebrating starts early and lasts all night. When we planned the 2008 Year in Beer calendar, there was no question about March's destination.

Besides being a great St. Patrick's Day destination, Boston also had a sentimental allure for Chris. His parents grew up in Manchester, a small town north of Boston, and as a child he often visited his grandmother who lived near Boston Common. Chris had lived in California since the age of 15 and Boston took him back to his childhood.

For the Year in Beer, we flew a red eye to Boston, arriving at 6:00 A.M. Friday morning. Our plan included a drive to Portsmouth, New Hampshire to visit three new breweries before the start of our St. Patrick's Day festivities. Always on the hunt to add breweries to The List, we had visited all of the Boston breweries on previous trips. In order to add a few more, Chris planned an excursion outside the city. Along the way, we made a breakfast stop in Manchester at the home of a childhood friend of Chris's parents. Despite never having met Woody and his wife, they welcomed us with open arms, bacon and eggs, and plenty of nostalgia. Afterwards, we continued north to Cape Ann Brewing in Gloucester, Massachusetts.

The 2004 movie *American Beer* documents a group of friends taking a 40-day 38-brewery quest across the United States. In it, Jeremy Goldberg talks about opening a brewery. Four years later, Cape Ann Brewing opened with Jeremy at the helm. We viewed him as a fellow beer traveler and went to Cape Ann hoping to meet him.

Jeremy served us samples of Cape Ann's Fisherman's Brew and talked about the brewery. It surprised him to hear that Chris and I had seen the movie and made a special trip to Gloucester to visit the brewery. I happily told Jeremy about the Year in Beer as we stood in front of the newly lacquered boat-shaped bar.

The pride of Gloucester's fishing tradition was alive and well at Cape Ann Brewing. The pine wood-paneled walls and low ceiling felt like being below deck. A large fishing net hung on the wall along with a large blue banner picturing an image similar to the Gorton's fisherman behind a boat wheel. Combined with the crisp March air, the feel at Cape Ann seemed quintessentially New England, at least to a West Coast girl like myself.

You don't visit hundreds of breweries by staying in any one pub for very long, though, so after a few more samples of beer we purchased a six-pack of Fisherman's Brew and moved on to Smuttynose in Portsmouth, New Hampshire for a noon-time brewery tour. The last to arrive, we joined four other people at the tasting room bar. I tried to get out of the tour and just drink beer but our volunteer brewery guide quashed that idea.

In all our years of beer travel, we have toured hundreds of breweries. With little variation, the brewing process is basically the same everywhere and all brewery tours offer the same dog and pony show. I started the Smuttynose tour like a teenager being dragged around a museum by her parents. However, even with my best efforts to remain disgruntled, I actually saw something new and different: two fermentation tanks that had been painted to resemble a black eight ball and a bright colorful sun. I admit, the sight of them made me smile.

We frequently say that beer brings people together and makes the world smaller. On the tour, we met Harry, a transplant from Santa Rosa, a city located just a few hours from our house. He explained that he had moved to Boston to be an opera singer.

"If someone told me, 'You will someday meet an opera singer,'" I told Harry, "I would have thought the person nuts."

He laughed and said, "Yeah, I get that a lot."

I would have never guessed Harry's aspirations. One, because I don't generally think about opera and two, Harry, a bespectacled young man of average build, possessed few of the stereotypical physical traits of an opera singer.

Harry not only hailed from Santa Rosa, he also worked at The Publick House in the Boston suburb of Brookline. The Publick House serves over 25 draught artisanal beers and an extensive menu of bottled beers. We like the warm and cozy atmosphere and the beer list offers us a chance to taste East Coast beers we rarely have the opportunity to order. Another of our must-stops in Boston, Sunday's agenda already included a visit to The Publick House. Harry told us he'd be working that night, so we knew we'd have a chance to talk to him again.

At Smuttynose, we had received a coupon for a free pint at their sister brewery, Portsmouth Brewing. Not to be cheated out of a free pint, all six of us on the Smuttynose tour converged on Portsmouth Brewing a few miles away. Chris and I enjoyed a 10-beer taster set. As much fun as we were having, though, self-preservation dictated we make it an early night. We walked around the corner to our hotel. So far, our trip had been just a warm up for the big show: St. Patrick's Day weekend in Boston.

On Saturday morning, a light veil of snow fell outside. The surprise of it added to the romantic charm of New England in the late winter. A notion that is, admittedly, easy to embrace from the warmth of a hotel room. A quick look at the weather forecast the night before would have eliminated the element of surprise, but where was the romance in that? Chris was decidedly less excited about the snow. "I don't know why I'm surprised," he said. "It snows every time we come out here for St. Patrick's Day." That was true. No matter what the weather had been like before we arrived, by the time we entered the city the snow was either forecasted or falling already.

Normally the snow had little impact on our visits because we didn't have a car. However, this morning's plan included an hour's drive south into Boston. Chris's anxiety rose quickly at the thought of snowy driving conditions. My anxiety rose at the thought of repeating our Alaskan cab ride. We sped up our morning plans in order to hit the road as soon as possible.

In spite his concern, Chris drove us safely back to Boston. We both heaved a sigh of relief at the return of the rental car. But, we relaxed a little too soon. The Boston style of driving combined with the international cabbie code of conduct meant white knuckling it in the back seat as a cab took us into the city. Let's just say that Bostonians are eager to get where they're going and you'd better not get in their way. Our Alaskan cab ride seemed like a Sunday drive in the country by comparison.

Happy to arrive at our hotel in one piece, we dropped off our bags and pushed out into the brisk March air. The sky was dry for the time being, but the air smelled damp from earlier snowflakes. The release of our anxiety and stress from the morning was almost palpable. A calm, content feeling enveloped us as we walked along the familiar sidewalks. Not even the hurried hustle and bustle of an East Coast city or the impatient driving style of the average Bostonian could penetrate us. Bundled up tightly, we were warm and happy inside.

We're creatures of habit, gravitating to the same places and activities year in and year out. Boston brings this out in us like few other cities do and like stable-bound horses, we instinctively followed the streets to one of our favorite places, Boston Beer Works, for a pint before attending the Boston Bruins game at the TD Banknorth Garden. There is nothing better than watching a live game of hockey in the legendary Garden and what goes better with hockey than beer.

Conveniently located near the Garden, Boston Beer Works is a natural part of our Boston ritual. Because it's so close to a sporting arena, I always anticipate the pub being packed before the game. Every year open seats at the bar welcome us. I still haven't figured out why the place isn't crowded, but I'm not complaining.

The industrial décor of the brewpub reminds me of the men having lunch atop a skyscraper girder immortalized in Charles Ebbets' famous photograph. From the bottle cap logo to the diamond plate details and metal stools at the bar, the pub gives off a workingman's vibe.

Despite this manly blue-collar feel, however, the best selling beer at Beer Works is their Bunkerhill Blueberry Ale. We avoid the beer served with a spoonful of frozen blueberries in the bottom and order our go-to Beer Works beer: Curley's Irish Stout. A brewery that truly understands the beautiful relationship between beer and sports, the other Beer Works location in Boston is situated across the street from Fenway Park.

Along with hordes of Boston Bruins fans, we left the Garden in good spirits after the 2-1 win over the New York Islanders. We then hightailed it to another favorite Boston locale, the tasting room at Harpoon Brewing. At the time, tastings were offered in short one-hour increments, so timing was critical. Our past experience told us not to worry about a crowd, so we didn't. That was a mistake. We climbed the stairs of the second floor tasting room to find that the beer was flowing to an already packed house. "This crowd has got to be because of our promotion of Boston as a St. Patrick's Day destination," Chris said. I scoffed and mockingly agreed with him.

We made our way in and found floor space near the side of the bar. Figuring it would be awhile before Chris came with our samples, I settled in to watch the swarm around the bar. The upstairs tasting room overlooks the brewery, so visitors have a bird's eye view of operations. However, it's easily forgotten when the beer is flowing. Not one person in the crowd looked out the large windows into the brewery. Instead, dozens of people vied for the attention of the two bartenders.

Without batting an eye, the bartenders masterfully served the mob. With a glass in each hand, one bartender used the brim of his baseball cap as a third hand to turn off the tap. He handed beer out to the crowd and immediately picked up two more empty glasses to fill. I turned around to find Chris right next to me. Now I had a beer in my hand, as well.

"That was quick," I said.

"Yeah," Chris replied, "It didn't take nearly as long as I thought it would."

"I've been watching the bartenders. They're amazing. You've got to get them on video."

One reason for the extraordinary popularity of the tasting hour is that the beer is free. The catch is that you have to listen to their timeshare pitch about the brewery. In the middle of everything, the female bartender stopped pouring and prefaced her brewery spiel.

"Now, if you'll allow me, I'll tell you a bit about the brewery. I'll do it as quickly as possible and the faster I can get through it, the sooner you'll all be back to tasting beer," she said. "Harpoon Brewery was started by Dan Kenary and Rich Doyle in 1986 because they wanted to bring a fresh local beer to their hometown..."

The room remained relatively quiet until she finished ten minutes later. "And, lastly, the orange tap handle is the Harpoon IPA. It's the number one selling IPA in New England. It's our interpretation of the classic English-style beer using American hops and malt."

The tasting stopped a half-hour later and the shop opened for purchases. Lucky for us, our small bit of floor space happened to form the head of the line. We were able to quickly pay for a couple of six-packs and left the building before most people had even picked out their beer, t-shirts and pint glasses.

In the quick hour we spent at Harpoon, our comforting sense of calm turned into buzzed giddiness. The loud, lively atmosphere awakened our excitement at being in one of our favorite cities. From there, we walked to the Barking Crab where bowls of lobster bisque and baskets of fried clams awaited. We also planned to meet up with our friend Brad Ruppert who was also in Boston for St. Patrick's Day.

Chris and Brad had been internet friends before coincidentally both becoming finalists for the Chief Beer Officer position in 2007. We met Brad in person the evening after Chris's interview. Going out to a pub with him that night, our first impression of Brad was that of someone with a ridiculously severe case of ADHD. Either that or he was on speed. Scarcely a moment of silence, we barely got a word in edgewise that night. Brad is a fun-loving party guy who isn't afraid to make his presence known. You can always rely on him for a good time and we looked forward to meeting up with him and his friends.

We passed a large sign advertising Anthony's Pier 4. "That place was our big treat when I was little," Chris said. "When we would visit my grandmother we'd come here for dinner. My sisters and I loved the Shirley Temples."

We arrived at the Barking Crab, a ramshackle structure located along the edge of the Fort Point Channel. I readied myself for my 4-day lobster love fest. Seafood shacks are Boston institutions and serve some of the best seafood in the city. To fully enjoy and appreciate the seafood shack mentality, however, all pretenses must be left at the door.

The interior of the Barking Crab is casual and functional with picnic tables, paper napkins and plates, and food served in plastic baskets. The place is perfect for us. We love fresh seafood, but dressing up for a fancy restaurant is not our style.

Large blue fiberglass tanks filled with lobsters and crabs sit against the wall behind the bar. If you pay attention, you can watch the kitchen staff pluck your order out of the tank. Previously only open in the summer, the addition of a wood-burning stove now allowed the Barking Crab to operate year-round. The stove definitely makes it cozy and warm, if not a bit smoky, inside during the cold days of March. We like the Barking Crab not only for the great food and fun atmosphere, but also because they serve good beer and have been known to play Flogging Molly now and again.

We chose seats at the bar where the briny smell of salt water and the oily scent of fried food mingled. Chris enjoyed fried clams with his Harpoon IPA. I polished off a cup of lobster bisque before moving on to my main course: a lobster roll. When my sandwich arrived, Chris and I reverently gazed at the over-sized hot dog bun packed with red and white lumps. The quantity and quality of the meat in a lobster roll is always a talking point, but the bun is what really separates the good from the great and the Barking Crab's is the best of the best. I average 3-4 lobster rolls and 4-5 bowls of bisque on our trips to Boston. Lobster is not something I eat at any other time, which makes it all the more enjoyable when I visit.

With a full Irish accent, our bartender greeted some new arrivals. "Hello there laddies," he said. Figuring it to be a group of his friends, I didn't bother to turn around. But then a familiar voice spoke up. Our friend Brad and his entourage of five had arrived. We turned around.

"Hey there kids!" Brad said with a broad grin.

"Look at you in your kilt," I said.

"Commando style. All of us," he said motioning to the other two men in the group. The whole restaurant surely heard his personal disclosure, but Brad didn't care. He was as free of shame and modesty as he was of his Fruit of the Looms. I shook my head and laughed. If only I could be that carefree, I thought.

Brad introduced us to his wife, as well as his brother and a friend and their respective wives. As we joined his group at a table, all I could think about was the fact that, according to Brad, the men had nothing on underneath. Flushed with embarrassment at shaking hands with guys I believed to be sans underpants, I completely missed their names.

Chris and I sat quietly self-conscious. Having spent more time with Brad, his companions were better able to match his pinball pace. Now we had a whole group of Brads all vying for attention. Commando kilt wearing was a frequent joking point, but once the food came, it was a whole new ballgame. Errant lemon juice squirting in someone's eye, bits of crab and shell in people's hair, it was a good thing they all wore bibs. I did my best to stay out of the line of fire. Don't get me wrong. We like hanging out with Brad. He takes us out of our quiet, subdued comfort zone.

When the shell buckets were full and the bibs were wadded up on the table, it was time to continue the party elsewhere. Chris suggested Cambridge Brewing, yet another regular stop during our trips to Boston.

Leading six happily inebriated people on a multi-train ride to Cambridge challenged us like never before. Wrangling a herd of feral cats would have been easier. But by the time we reached Cambridge Brewing, the energy level dropped from college frat house to more relaxed and adult-like. I drank a Charles River Porter and ate a bowl of ice cream made with Cambridge Brewing's stout. It was the perfect way to end the night. Forget warm milk. Beer and ice cream make the perfect nightcap. We would need a good night's sleep for our big day ahead: the Boston St. Patrick's Day parade.

Sunday morning, Chris and I rode the train out to South Boston (a.k.a. "Southie") to watch the parade for our second time. Far from the Macy's Thanksgiving Day parade, this is an honest-to-God neighborhood affair attended by a half million people.

While people from all over the city and beyond attend the parade, the theme of the day (besides St. Patrick, of course), is definitely Southie pride. The parade is Southie's day to shine and the neighborhood folk treat it like a huge block party (or "pahty," if you want to go native). As we walked from the train station to the parade route, I overheard a guy talking on the phone. "What kind of trouble do you think I'm gonna get into? It's not like I'm going to the bah [bar]." The young boy in the stroller who accompanied the man looked happily oblivious as he took in the sights.

Neighborhood residents celebrated out on their porches and up on their balconies. Everyone is in green. From the comfort of her porch, a woman sat next to a child lounging in a child's size lawn chair. With a yard-stick-sized fruity alcohol drink in one hand and a cigarette in the other, she offered happy greetings those on their way to the parade. A few years previous, we even passed a two-story-tall beer bong.

People freely walked the sidewalks with cases of beer, but if you prefer to drink in a more civilized manner, the bars are open. However, the lines outside are long. I have never understood people's willingness to wait in a line out in the cold for the opportunity to pay $20 to get into an already packed bar. I do a lot of things in the name of beer, but I refuse to wait in line or pay a cover charge to get it. The liquor stores also have lines to get in. There's no cover charge, but even if there were people would probably pay.

For most St. Patrick's Day celebrants, the compulsion to wear absurd outfits completely overrides any iota of rational thought. Inhibition and self-consciousness have no business on St. Patrick's Day and are tossed aside with just as much disregard. As we scouted a good parade-watching spot, I speculated about the proper apparel for carrying a case of beer down the street. Gold hot pants? Maybe, but not really my style. Huge feathery pimp hat? For a guy perhaps. Fake eyelashes with shamrocks on the end? Too distracting. The thought of that combination alone confounded my senses, but the actual sight of it was downright nauseating. My reserved green turtleneck, on the other hand, was an understated show of support for the holiday. Rational thought, modesty, and self-consciousness are strong in this one.

We eventually set up camp in one of the so-called "family zones" —relatively quiet and drunkard-free areas where the kids could be safe. For the *beergeek.TV* episode, we sought footage a bit more tame than *Girls Gone Wild*, so it worked out perfectly.

The Gaelic Day Spa Salon across the street posted a large "closed for the day" sign in the window. Over the years beer spas have popped up in Austria, Germany, and the Czech Republic. Would the Irish version be a Guinness body wrap or a Harp facial scrub?

Some of the parade participants perplexed me just as much as the Gaelic Day Spa Salon and I was hard pressed to picture the Irish Prison Service Pipe Band members guarding convicts. One would have to be highly skilled to quell a prison riot in a kilt. Now maybe if they went commando style…

Local politicians in convertibles waved as they drove past. Others worked the crowd on foot shaking hands with the populace. Civic groups, Irish dancing schools, and marching bands also streamed passed. The Fanad Accordion Band from County Donegal marched along in their purple uniforms with white shoes and tall plumed hats. Now there's a visual of hell on Earth: a group of teenagers dressed in the most God-awful outfits possible playing accordions. I can imagine nothing more mortifying, especially for a teenager. On the other hand, adults might consider it quite brilliant. It's certainly one way to quell raging teenage hormones. No one looks attractive in purple polyester. "That has got to be the cruelest thing ever," I told Chris. Surprisingly, they each wore the content face of a consummate professional. "This one time at band camp..." Chris replied.

The mayor from a town in County Donegal also found his way into the parade. As he passed by, Chris dashed out into the street and very proudly introduced himself as a descendant of great grandparents from Donegal "City." The mayor politely noted that they consider it a "town." Despite numerous visits to Ireland, countless hours spent reading Irish history books, and family lineage from Donegal, Chris still made the mistake. He was deeply embarrassed, but it impressed me that he even made the effort to introduce himself to the man. I snapped a picture of the momentous encounter after which Chris came slinking back to the sidewalk. "I feel like such an eejit," he said.

But not everyone that took part in the parade hailed from Ireland. The local Star Wars fan club also marched. Storm Troopers donned green plastic hats, shamrocks on their uniforms, and waved St. Patrick's Day flags. This hardly fit the fierce image of Darth Vader's army that I grew up with and the sight of this group completely deflated my childhood fantasy of battling the Empire as Princess Leia.

In 2008, Easter occurred early and March 17 fell on the Monday of Holy Week. The Catholic Church prohibits celebrating a saint's day during Holy Week, so in all its wisdom, the church officially moved St. Patrick's Day to the previous week. The decision effectively created two St. Patrick's Days.

Memories from Catechism classes made the parade's occurrence on Palm Sunday feel odd to me, but years in Catholic recovery made me indifferent. At least I wasn't flaunting my blasphemy like the girl in the ultra mini skirt with the green garter belt and feather boa, but something tells me she really didn't think twice about it anyway. I did see an older couple go by with a palm in one hand and a beer in the other. So, perhaps the two events weren't so mutually exclusive after all. Catholics do have the right idea: party tonight, confess tomorrow, all is forgiven, repeat the following weekend.

Later in the afternoon, Chris and I traveled 40 minutes on the Green Line out to Brookline, a suburb southwest of Boston. As we walked up the street to the Publick House Beer Bar, we were excited not only because it's an amazing beer café, but also because we would once again see Harry. Meeting an opera singer was so far out of the realm of our imagination that we questioned if that's what he really told us. As important as ordering a beer, we would have to confirm that we really heard what we thought we did.

From past visits, we knew that the moderately sized pub filled up fast and the wait for a table could be long, so we planned our arrival for close to opening time. We hoped for a mellow stress-free visit where we could drink excellent beer, play Scrabble, and eat some tasty frites. And that's exactly what we got.

The interior of the Publick House is somewhat dramatic with its black ceiling and mustard-colored walls. The wooden features and dim lighting give it a cozy European feel that we enjoy. Shortly after settling at an open table, Harry came over to greet us. Before any beer was ordered, Harry confirmed that he was, indeed, an aspiring opera singer. Beer has provided us the opportunity to meet a lot of interesting people over the years. Meeting an opera singer still ranks high on my list of cool encounters. After spending the afternoon in the Family Zone, we ordered our first beers of the day. It was 5:30 P.M.

We'd been partying for several days and the parade was now behind us. St. Patrick's Day had finally arrived. Along with the masses, we headed straight for our favorite Irish bar in Boston: the Black Rose. The Black Rose is *the* pub to go to any time of the year, but on St. Patrick's Day, it's packed all day long. It didn't matter that it was Monday, the start of the workweek for most people.

The key to finding a seat at the Black Rose on St. Patrick's Day is to arrive early. They serve a full Irish breakfast, so early literally means first thing in the morning. Throughout the weekend, the lines in front of the Black Rose had been long. We braced ourselves for the worst as we rounded the corner. Much to our relief, the only people standing outside the front door were smokers satisfying their nicotine habits. However, inside the first floor was already at capacity when we arrived at 9 A.M., so we headed up the stairs to the second floor bar. Looking down, a chaotic sea of green swayed and moved. At that moment, I felt woefully unprepared for the long haul. The day had barely started and the jubilant noise was already making my body vibrate.

Upstairs, we nudged our way passed people who appeared to be several rounds into their day. My heart sank as I realized we might have arrived too late to get a seat. I was hungry and I wanted breakfast. Just as it seemed too early to be drunk, it was too early for me to get cranky. The luck of the Irish must have been with us, though, because we found an empty table in the corner.

Our fondest memories of hours spent at the Black Rose had occurred downstairs in the thick of the action. The bartenders are usually Irish and speak with melodic accents. The music from the live band is traditional and everyone sings along. Conversation inevitably turns to Irish politics. It's all the things we love about being in Boston on St. Patrick's Day.

Now sober and tucked away in the corner on the second floor, it was hard not to feel a bit disappointed. Chris and I sat quietly observing the comfortably numb who were firmly established in conversation. We had a few more Guinness to drink in order to catch up with the rest of the party. In the meantime, we took solace in the people watching. As might be expected, it was of the highest quality, especially the t-shirts.

A young man propped himself up against the bar and prepared to ignite his Irish Car Bomb. His shirt read, "Irish today, shitfaced tonight, hungover tomorrow." His buddy announced his intention to get lucky with the slogan, "Drink until she's Irish." No pick up line needed there, I guess. Then there was the girl who stumbled by with a tight green shirt: "Everyone loves a drunken Irish girl." Her friend trailed behind her laughing and spilling her Guinness as she went. With two shamrocks strategically placed on her breasts, her shirt said, "Touch my lucky charms and I'll choke your little leprechaun." Hopefully some drunk guy didn't mistake her for the one with the shirt that read "Rub my shamrocks for luck."

It was really quite responsible of us to eat a big breakfast before a full day of drinking beer, especially a hearty one. A traditional Irish breakfast is a plateful of eggs, toast, bacon, sausage and pudding, both black and white. White pudding is a sausage-like food made with grains, spices, and lard. The addition of blood creates the black version. Often served fried or grilled in its skin, we don't like pudding at all and always ask for it to be omitted from our meal. So, more accurately, our breakfast was a not-so-traditional almost full Irish breakfast.

After breakfast, we talked about what to do next. Our agenda was free until a punk show later in the night. A newly arriving group of people looked for an available table. With breakfast remnants on our plates and pints half full, we looked like a good prospect for vacating the premises soon. They stood nearby, ready to swoop in. We assured them that we planned to leave soon and invited them to join us now so they could at least get started on their beer drinking. Several hours later, Chris and I had yet to see the front door. In the meantime, a small band set up in the corner.

Chris often talks about the concept of "friends for a day." Everywhere in the world, beer culture lends itself to meeting new people. For however long you know them, they're your friends for that time. Friends make beer travel experiences memorable.

We learned that our new tablemates, a group of co-workers from Toronto, Canada, had driven all night in order to participate in the day's festivities. With additional people at our table, I was able to let go of my self-consciousness. No longer feeling like a wallflower, I relaxed and joined the party. Pints of

Guinness came and went from the table at a rapid pace. Empty plastic cups with dribbles of dark liquid in the bottom littered the table–proof of our good time. Conversation was lively and the video camera brought out the performer in everyone.

The combination of alcohol and Irish music always inspires at least one lass to perform moves she learned in her Beginning Irish Dance class 20 years ago. As silly as it may look, the brave soul's solo is always a crowd pleaser and today was no exception as a blonde-haired woman got up to dance a jig. It really didn't matter that she was off the beat of the bodhrán with less than polished footwork. She inspired other beer-filled people to dance, including one of our new Canadian friends. Dressed in a green polo shirt with the collar turned up, he danced a mean jig and helped create some of the best craic we've ever had the privilege to be a part of. It really doesn't matter where you're from or who you are because on St. Patrick's Day everyone is Irish.

Across the street a man dressed in a tie and white shirt worked at his desk. He tried desperately to avoid looking in our direction, but it was simply impossible to ignore the music and laughter of a good party. What sadistic boss would subject an employee to something as torturous as listening to the St. Patrick's Day revelry in the Black Rose? Surely it violated some employment regulation. My empathy for him was fleeting, though, as the waitress brought another round of Guinness to the table.

The constant influx of new arrivals kept the party's momentum in full swing. It was difficult to consider leaving, but we had a punk show to go to in a few hours. If we left immediately, I could get in a bowl of lobster bisque before the show, but we also knew that leaving meant not coming back.

By early evening, every pub in town would be packed inside and have a line outside waiting to get in. But punk show or not, common sense said that seven hours of beer drinking at the Black Rose was enough.

In January, Chris tried for two hours to get tickets for the Dropkick Murphy's show. A Boston-based Irish-inspired punk band, the Dropkick Murphy's exude pride in both their Irish heritage and their hometown. Each year, they return to Boston in March to play multiple shows over several days. The local crowd, excited to have the band at home, moshes with heightened fervor. The band members' families and friends line the stage during each performance. This combination energizes the band and makes for an amazing time. The show's craic helps everyone to forget the nippy weather outside, at least for a few hours.

Already popular in the punk world, we'd seen the Murphy's multiple times in Boston. Though they became especially popular after the Red Sox won the World Series in October 2007, as their music had been blasted throughout the stands at games. This may have been one reason Chris didn't get through to purchase tickets and we were forced to break with tradition and make alternate plans. An important part of our Boston St. Patrick's Day ritual, not getting tickets to the show threw us off. Instead, we decided to see a band called Larkin Brigade at the Middle East Restaurant and Nightclub in Cambridge.

One might think that after seven hours of drinking, we could barely walk out the door. However, despite its reputation for being a thick and hearty brew, Guinness is surprisingly low in alcohol (4.2% ABV). Plus, as seasoned veterans of Boston's St. Patrick's Day celebration, we knew that the best way to survive the day was to drink a glass of water for every beer. Even with careful planning, however, I lost steam after leaving the Black Rose. I needed to either keep drinking where I was or call it a night. The lobster bisque I picked up at a stall in Fanuel Hall tasted fantastic, but didn't help much to revive me. The train over to Cambridge drained what little energy I had left.

With a short playlist, the show was over in an hour. Given their fast-paced, high-energy songs, that was probably a good thing. One of my favorite Larkin Brigade songs is "The Upscale Downtown Irish Pub" and its lyrics demonstrate the band's understanding of the importance of good craic.

"Pints in glasses. Raise a din. They never shoulda let us in. We're all wicked liquored up at the upscale downtown Irish pub"

That more or less summed up our St. Patrick's Day in Boston. Cold, colder or coldest, there is no better craic than in Boston on St. Patrick's Day. As long as you have good craic, you're warm enough.

We took it easy on Tuesday, the final day of our trip. Chris wanted footage of the Black Rose "the day after," so we went there first. St. Patrick's Day at the Black Rose is crazy, but on a normal day, it's a place where Irish people gather and friends meet for pints. St. Patrick's Day plus one is a good time to go because it offers the chance to wander and get a good look at the place. The colorful flags bearing coats of arms that hang from the ceiling are visible regardless of the crowd size. However, the walls are also covered with miscellaneous pieces of Irish culture. Portraits of Irish revolutionaries and a copy of the Proclamation of the Irish Republic proudly hang behind the bar. Dozens of family crests line the walls around the restaurant. Road signs to places like Baile Átha Cliath and

Corcaigh fill in the gaps. The relative quiet and emptiness of the pub allowed us to calmly start our day. It was noon. With our pint glasses empty and video shot, we took one last trip out to Cambridge.

We sat at the bar in Cambridge Brewing Company, ordered our beers and started to film for *beergeek.TV*. The bartender came up to talk with us right in the middle of filming. Ever the professional, I continued the shot. She stood there for a moment, but eventually walked away. To show her that we weren't just being rude, I gave her one of my cards and explained what we do. She thought it was "cool."

Chris and I went about our beer drinking business when a guy walked up and asked, "Are you Merideth?" Taken aback, I admit that my first thoughts were, "Wow, I'm a beer celebrity. He must recognize me from *beergeek.TV*." He held up the business card I had given the bartender. With high hopes of being a beer travel celebrity clouding my head, I hadn't put two and two together. Our conversation with Will Meyers, Cambridge Brewing's Brewmaster, offered us a dignified end to a spirited trip.

The first three months of the Year in Beer exhausted me. Afraid to tell Chris that I felt like a nervous wreck, I tried my best to hide it. Inside, I questioned my ability to make it through the whole year. When we took on this adventure did we order a liter when we really should have ordered a pint? Just in time, we started a nearly one-month break from major beer travels. Three months down and nine to go.

APRIL

EVERYTHING DESERVES A SECOND CHANCE

One would expect that the few weeks at home after Boston would have provided much needed respite. However, as I learned, there is a point of exhaustion where relaxation becomes a challenge. Lying on the couch after work and on weekends seemed leisurely enough, but my mind was awash with thoughts of uncompleted chores; things like dusty cobwebs in the corners of the living room, bright green weeds sprouting throughout the yard, and the un-pruned limbs of our rose bushes that had grown long and twiggy. The guilt for not tackling my household chores now topped my already throbbing exhaustion. Even the creation of to-do lists, which usually comforts and focuses me, increased my confusion and inability to rest. The whole thing put me into a bit of a funk.

Thoughts of April's trip to Seattle did little to encourage me. It's not that enthusiasm for the Year in Beer had waned, but rather going to Seattle felt somewhat lackluster and, dare I say, uninspiring. In hindsight, Seattle was a nice change of pace—a no pressure, easygoing trip to visit friends. At the time, however, we viewed it as filler in between more fun and exciting destinations.

When Chris and I scheduled the Year in Beer calendar, we found that April offered little in the way of major beer events. We approached it as a free month, where we could choose any destination we wanted to explore. Washington and Oregon came to mind as hotbeds of the craft beer scene, but July already included Portland and the Oregon Brewers Festival. That left Washington.

When we first visited Seattle over ten years earlier, we'd left with the feeling that the city's beer reputation was overrated. However, over the years, the craft beer cafés and breweries popping up all over Seattle have helped the city emerge as a formidable beer force in the Pacific Northwest. Our friend and author of several Seattle-based beer blogs Chris Devlin (aka Chris D) spoke highly of the Emerald City's strengthening beer scene and he encouraged us to come visit. Maybe it was time to give Seattle a second chance. So with Oregon's elimination and Chris D's encouragement, we chose Seattle for April's destination.

We reached Seattle-Tacoma International Airport without any problems, but a few wrong turns and an encounter with construction prolonged our arrival at the hotel. By the time we pulled into the reception area, exasperation had burned our fuses almost to the end. We just wanted to get checked in so we could go get a beer.

I looked across the street as I climbed out of the car. A mural of the cover of Flogging Molly's album *Float* was painted on a music store wall. Sitting in an abandoned Irish pub, the seven band members stare straight ahead. A cat rests undisturbed on the table next to a silent fiddle. It's a snapshot of one calm moment in what I imagine to be the frenetic life of a band. I sung the title song in my head. "No matter where I put my head, I wake up feeling sound again. Breathe, it's all you can." It made a good theme song for my life at that moment.

After a quick check-in at the hotel, we left to meet Chris D as previously arranged. Acting as Seattle's good beer ambassador, Chris D took the afternoon off work to show us around. We certainly provided a good excuse for doing so and I'm sure he didn't have any problem sacrificing a workday to go drink beer. His presence and guidance were welcome additions to our visit. As an advocate of public transportation, he'd asked us to meet him at the downtown Metro Bus tunnel.

This was actually only our third time meeting Chris. We'd first met him at the 2007 Oregon Brewers Festival and the second time was just two months prior during February's trip to San Francisco. It was during our second meeting that we discovered that the three of us made convivial beer travel companions. Like us, Chris D doesn't cower at the thought of public transportation and considers walking an acceptable mode of transport. He also shares our relatively low level of tolerance for loud establishments and obnoxious people. As a fellow beer geek and a local, we trusted Chris D to get us to the best beer spots in Seattle.

With initial greetings out of the way, Chris D informed us of our first stop: Ram Restaurant and Big Horn Brewery at Northgate, a chain brewery. Upon hearing this, I feared that perhaps our trust in Chris D had been misguided. Chain breweries rank low on our opinion scale, partially because of the minimal level of creativity and freedom afforded to brewers. Plus, they count on The List only once. Chains often offer the same set of beers, with no variation. Therefore, subsequent visits to other locations offer nothing new. We had already visited a Big Horn Brewery during a trip to Fort Collins, Colorado six months before, so this visit would not be counted on The List. With little excitement in our hearts, we took the 20-minute bus ride to the Northgate Mall in north urban Seattle.

As we approached the brick building, Chris D implored us to give this stop a chance. We assured him we would keep an open mind. Having said that, the inside of the restaurant looked every bit the standard corporate eating establishment I expected. The enormous space was filled with table after table, all looking very uniform with matching chairs and table tents advertising specialty cocktails and happy hour appetizers. Dozens of high-backed chairs stood neatly tucked up to the bar in front of a long row of shiny tap handles. Televisions throughout played to an empty audience. The Chrisses each ordered the 71 Pale Ale and I chose the Total Disorder Porter. We sat down at a table to wait for a couple of Chris D's friends, Nat and Ian, both of whom had connections to Ram's brewer, Kevin Forhan.

Nat arrived first. An athletic sort, he walked in with his bike helmet still on his head and a fully equipped, professional-looking bike messenger bag slung across his back. While Nat unloaded his belongings, Ian showed up at the table. Together, Chris D, Nat, and Ian looked an unlikely trio. Chris, dressed head to toe in black, gave off a disgruntled, angst-filled vibe. While Nat, who had shed his outer layer to reveal a form-fitting, long-sleeved cycling shirt and small cycling hat, still looked like a bike messenger. And Ian in his red plaid shirt, tweed cap and thick-rimmed glasses belonged in the nerdy-hipster clique. However mismatched they looked, beer had brought these friends together. Chris D had met them as bartenders at some of his favorite Seattle hangouts. Nat worked at Big Time Brewery and Ian at Brouwers. We would be visiting both beer establishments during our trip.

Nat and Ian knew Kevin, Ram's brewer, through the beer community and once their presence was known, we were invited on a brewery tour. Kevin gave us each a taste of his IPA out of the conditioning tank and explained that he had recently gained more latitude to brew beers outside of the regular line up. Did increased variety necessitate a re-think of The List rule of chain breweries counting only once? I wondered. The sound of a wet splat interrupted my thought. I looked down to see a thick blob of brown-laced foam slide toward the drain in the tiled floor. "Oh, watch out for the wet," Kevin said. "That's the Buttface Amber fermenting away." I stepped aside, out of the way of the lava flow of dirty foam.

Listening to the excitement in Kevin's voice as he talked about having more freedom to brew new and different beers, as well as tasting some flavorful brews from the regular line up, forced me and Chris to reconsider our poor image of chain breweries. After all, we gave this one a second chance and it pleasantly surprised us. Any thought of changing The List rule about chain breweries was short lived, however. They still only count once.

From Ram, we embarked upon an urban beer hike around Seattle, with Nat on his bike and Ian joining us on foot. Chris and I walk and use public transportation whenever possible on our beer adventures. We never had a name for it, though, until several years ago when we met Dave Doran, author of a website called *urbanbeerhikes.com*. An "urban beer hike" is just what it sounds like: a trek on foot visiting an urban center's beer establishments. I love the term, as it captures the true character of the oft times long and arduous jaunts between breweries, making it a more accurate term than the less physically taxing pub (or, in our case, brewery) crawl.

Eventually, we boarded a bus and traveled several miles to one of Seattle's best beer spots, Duck Island Ale House. The Duck's dramatic red walls and dive bar vibe almost disguise the amazing beer selection. With everything from international beers like Affligem, Paulaner, and Franziskaner to the more local breweries like Baron, Hale's, and Iron Horse, it's tempting to characterize the Duck as Seattle's version of San Francisco's famous beer bar, Toronado. The depth of its beer rotation, as revealed by the number of tap handles affixed to the ceiling, certainly rivals that of Toronado, but the place is too bright and clean to pass as a dead ringer.

When we walked in, the guys immediately noticed the cute bartender. Wearing a black t-shirt and baseball cap, her tomboy attitude let everyone know that she could hold her own behind the bar. While that attitude was probably needed during night shifts, a Wednesday afternoon crowd of four guys and a girl didn't require much bravado. The fact that Oprah was playing on the television indicated the low level of toughness of the Duck's daytime crowd. Outnumbered by the guys four to one (six to one if you count the two guys playing a video game in the corner), my comfort with partaking in all-male conversation was unusually absent. I quietly sipped my Baron Brewing pilsner and turned to Oprah as she interviewed Maria Shriver.

In the course of exploring a city's beer scene, some establishments serve as quick stops. This can be due to a lack of time or sometimes a lack of enjoyment. In the Duck's case, it was due to Chris D wanting to show us as many places as possible. So before Oprah had a chance to broach the obligatory subject of what it was like to be married to then-California Governor Arnold Schwarzenegger, we left to continue our Seattle beer tour.[8] Nat, who we would see later at Big Time Brewery, departed for his bartending shift. Ian also left for work at Brouwer's, which was not on a stop on our night's agenda.

Judging by the weeds growing out of the cracks in the sidewalk, I guessed that foot traffic was not a common occurrence in this particular area. Cars sped by on busy Aurora Avenue North eager to get somewhere else. Chris considered a gander into Butch's Guns as we passed, but concluded that beer drinking and firearms made for a risky combination. A computer recycling shop with a collection of ancient machines in the window added to the dilapidated slightly oppressed ethos out on the street. Maybe there was a reason why foot traffic was sparse.

---

8 This was several years prior to published reports of Arnold fathering a child with one of his longtime household staff that led to the former-first couple of California's subsequent separation.

Within in a few minutes we reached Über Tavern. From the outside appearance, it fit nicely into the neighborhood. The large beer bottle-shaped sign jutting out the side and the "kegs to go" in white block letters across the top of the building created a ghetto liquor store look. Only the flower boxes out front hinted at the possibility of more than 40-ounce cans and Slim Jims.

Once inside the door, however, there was no question that we had entered a whole new level of beeriness. No longer in the down-and-out environ of the street, Über was clearly designed to attract high caliber beer drinkers. One might even say it appeared to cater to Seattle's beer douches (I'll explain beer douches later).

Über, with its periwinkle blue walls and a table with a lava rock fire pit in the middle, projected a posh beer café attitude. The cold cases lining the back of the bar sparkled with beer bottles in a variety of shapes, sizes, and colors. The difference in vibe between the Duck and Über was palpable. Duck Island was a come-as-you-are type of place, while Über was more of a designer jeans and collared shirt establishment. Some may refer to us as beer snobs and think we'd fit right in at Über. I prefer to think of us as non-snooty yet discriminating beer drinkers. Given the similar beer selections, we much preferred the casual attitude at Duck Island.

The Chrisses and I sat at the end of the bar closest to the door in front of the pink ceramic Delirium Tremens elephant. We ordered a round of beers and the three of us sat talking quietly.

Conversing with Chris D is always entertaining, especially when talking about beer. His cynicism and quick wit combined with his well-formulated opinions frequently make for humorous and lively discussions. We knew that Chris D had a long time girlfriend, Francesca, but we had never met her. As I got to know Chris better, I started to wonder what type of personality would best fit with his. Luckily, we would find out in a few days, as she planned to join us on one of our day's urban beer hikes.

Our visit to Über illuminated perfectly the method in Chris D's beer tour agenda madness. Every craft beer drinker has his/her own beer personality, including preferences for what they drink and where they like to drink it. The more places we visited, the more thorough our exploration of Seattle's craft beer scene. Chris D wanted to expose us to all that Seattle had to offer in the way of beer. And he still had more places to take us, so we finished our round and continued on.

Our urban beer hike took us on a half hour walk around to the other side of Green Lake, a glacial lake in the middle of Seattle's dense urban neighborhoods. As we strolled along the path, we mingled with Seattle's fittest. With walkers, joggers, cyclists, and rollerbladers criss-crossing by, it appeared that all of Seattle was happy and healthy. Even, the animals seemed happy, as the ducks pecked at the grass, squirrels bounced across the path, and dogs on leashes happily trotted along. It was a very idyllic scene.

On the other side of the lake, we made a pit stop at Latona Pub. The red brick building on the corner was walled with windows, offering a clear view inside. It looked like a breakfast café, but neon beer signs in the windows advertised their craft beer selection.

Although it was near capacity inside, there was still enough room to be comfortable. We stood near the bar to drink our pints. Everyone seemed to be having a good time as they laughed and chatted away. The camaraderie reminded me of living in Oakland and what it felt like to both work and hang out at Barclay's.

A real sense of community develops when people gather in close proximity, turning big city neighborhoods into worlds unto themselves. Neighbors meet at the corner café for coffee, bump into one another at the local market, and gather for pints at the pub. Not being from the neighborhood, I felt like a party crasher in Latona, but welcome all the same. Our urban beer hike had taken us to several of Seattle's neighborhoods so far and I was starting to understand the city a little better. I was definitely reminded of Oakland and it made me homesick for our old stomping ground.

The aroma of freshly cooking burgers and grilled cheese sandwiches smelled delicious and made my stomach grumble. Chris D recommended that we wait for the pizza at our last stop of the day—Big Time Brewery and Ale House, Seattle's original brewpub and the sister brewery to Triple Rock in Berkeley. I drank my pint as quickly as I could so we could leave for pizza.

Day had turned to early evening and Big Time's neon sign shown bright as we approached. The sign looked familiar, as it is the same shape and design as Triple Rock's. In February, Chris D had debunked our mythic memory of Big Time as Triple Rock in reverse. Upon entering the pub now, we saw for ourselves just how wrong we had been. The false memories about Triple Rock and Big Time lain to rest for good, a decade of being completely wrong had come to an end.

In our defense, however, the sign outside wasn't the only similarity. Both breweries are located near a university and are furnished in a dark wooden décor with an antique bar. Both have a raised seating area and large windows providing a view into the breweries.

We moved toward the bar at the back left side of the restaurant and Chris D's friend Nat served us pints as we sat down. Big Time was where he had cycled off to when he left us earlier in the day to go to work.

We ate our pizza dinner and drank Big Time's Trombipulator, a potent Belgian-style triple. The hazy golden beer with a sweet malty taste was dangerously drinkable at 10% ABV. Conversation started to dwindle and all three of us faded quickly as a full day of beer drinking and walking caught up with us. It was only day one, but even at this early stage, our opinion of Seattle had started to change. The varied neighborhoods offered something for everyone and all the beer establishments we visited were enjoyable in their own way. Seattle was shaping up to be better the second time around.

The next day, Chris D went to work at his job in a downtown law firm library. I only knew Chris in relation to his beer life and it was hard for me to picture him working among lawyers in suits. (Just as I'm sure many of my beer community acquaintances find it hard to picture me as a licensed psychotherapist.) Without our local guide, we were left to explore on our own. Chris planned a short brewery tour before meeting Chris D later that evening at Cooper's Ale House. Our friend Crista Prince, who we'd known since our early college days and now lived in Seattle, also planned to meet us. Until then, we started our day with an hour-and-a-half drive north to Anacortes in our rental car.

We had timed our departure from Seattle to arrive at the opening of Rockfish Grill and Anacortes Brewery, but we got there a half hour early. To kill time we took a walk around the nearby harbor. It was a quiet morning and the only other person we saw was a man preparing to launch his boat. Hundreds of sailboats bobbed gently in their slips. A Black-crowned Night-Heron stood in the shallow at the water's edge. I found it rather soothing, but all the while, Chris's anticipation of visiting the brewery was growing. In January, one of his highlights at the Great Alaskan Beer and Barley Wine Festival was a cask imperial IPA from Anacortes Brewery. Now, he looked forward to tasting it fresh at its source. By the time we circled back around to the brewpub, it was open.

It was bright and cheery inside with walls painted in a sunny yellow. The bartender served us a sample set and Chris enquired about the IPA he was so desperate to try again. Much to his disappointment, however, the imperial IPA currently being served was a batch that had been aged in bourbon barrels. As non-hard alcohol drinkers, barrel-aged beers often taste overwhelmingly boozy to us. Chris tried a sample of the IPA anyway and it tasted just as he thought it would—with a strong essence of bourbon. He sat on his barstool deflated and pouting. I, on the other hand, enjoyed a very tasty porter. The dark brew's flavor was the perfect combination of roasted coffee and chocolate. I was quite content. The rest of the afternoon Chris grieved the lost opportunity to have a great beer at its source and preached the need for a barrel shortage to curb the trend in barrel-aging beers.

After fish tacos in Anacortes, we traveled to the quaint waterfront village of La Conner, where we intended to make a quick visit to La Conner Brewing Company. To be honest, we didn't have high expectations of the place. Chris found it during an internet search, but it wasn't a brewery noteworthy enough to be talked about within the beer community. As people who must go to every brewery possible, we still give places a try even if we haven't heard much about them. We've found a number of great, yet unknown breweries that way. For La Conner Brewing, the plan was to dash in, add it to The List, and dash out. Unbeknownst to us, however, the annual Skagit Valley Tulip Festival—of which La Conner is a major host—was in full swing. La Conner's population of 1,000 doubled that day, as every tulip lover in the area descended upon the village.

The sidewalks were congested with 60-something aged women in gardening hats and sweatshirts embroidered with tulips. Like a town full of kindergarten teachers, each woman had a sweet, benevolent face. Judging by the looks of them, we concluded that the tulip-loving rank and file was most likely not a beer-loving bunch, so we anticipated few crowd issues at the brewery.

We came around the corner to find people milling about the entrance. This is never a good sign, as it usually indicates a wait. While the festival goers may not have been beer lovers, they apparently all wanted lunch at La Conner Brewing. We squeezed our way through the people waiting to be seated as we tried to find available space at the bar. One stool next to the server's station at the end was free. We did our best to not impede the bottleneck of hurried wait staff around us as we drank our five-sample taster set. Their brown ale was the most flavorful of the bunch, but not worth extending the chaotic experience of the busy establishment any longer by ordering a full pint.

Our quick visit to add a brewery to The List turned out to be a harried attempt to weave our way through a congestion of grandmotherly-types. By the time we reached the car to leave, we were stressed out. We let out a sigh and left town for Mukilteo, a city further south on the shore of Puget Sound.

From one end of the spectrum to the other, Diamond Knot Brewing & Alehouse in Mukilteo couldn't have been more different from La Conner Brewing. No longer in a quaint village with colorful flower boxes, we were now at a ferry terminal. Careful not to get in line for the boat to Whidbey Island, we parked across the street and dodged disembarking cars and bicycles on our way to the brewery.

Inside, Diamond Knot looked, fittingly, like it was located near a ferry terminal, not dirty per se but a bit gritty. Locals filled the small, nautical-themed pub and for the second time of the day, we felt out of place. At a table toward the back, a guy with a goatee down to his chest sipped on an amber-colored beer. Two men in dingy hooded sweatshirts and well-worn jeans hunched over their pints at another table. We had looked too edgy for prim La Conner and now too prim for edgy Diamond Knot. Even with over a dozen tattoos and piercings between us, fitting in with the regulars was tough to do. A linebacker-sized guy with a small barbell through his septum gave us a nod as we joined him at the bar.

Once we settled in, we had a chance to look beyond Diamond Knot's rough and tumble crowd. The floor littered with peanut shells was understandable, but a menu with stone-grilled meals seemed a bit trendy. Upon questioning the menu items, the bartender explained that management had wanted to offer more than deep fried mozzarella sticks and jalapeño poppers, but a small kitchen left few alternatives. Easy to heat up, the stones require little space. There's also no need for a large kitchen staff because the customers do all the cooking themselves. Shortly thereafter, we got to witness firsthand how it all worked.

The bartender delivered a scorching hot brick and a plate full of raw meat to the table behind us. We watched as pieces of meat and vegetable were placed onto the stone. A fantastic smell immediately wafted through the pub and all heads turned toward the hissing sound. Drinking beer to the soothing sound and smell of sizzling meat was intriguing, but unfortunately our agenda didn't plan for us to try it out ourselves.

However, we did get slightly off schedule after Chris discovered another notable feature of Diamond Knot. Returning from the men's room, Chris grinned from ear to ear.

"What are you smiling about?" I asked.

"The urinal," he said, "You have to check out the urinal."

"Uh, yeah," I replied. "Not sure how I'm going to do that."

Chris went back in to take a picture. An Anheuser-Busch keg with the side cut out served as the urinal. In all our macrobrew bigotry, we thought it the perfect usage. Chris went back yet again, but this time he took the video camera. Fortunately, our bar mate didn't have to pee. I hardly think that a man in the bathroom with a video camera would go over well in Mukilteo (or anywhere else for that matter).

We survived Diamond Knot and arrived back in Seattle in time to meet Chris D at Cooper's Alehouse for their annual IPA Fest. Cooper's, which touts itself as Seattle's original alehouse, is located in the Lake City neighborhood in northeast Seattle. It reminded me a lot of Duck Island from the day before with its red paint and black paneled walls. Cooper's offers something for everyone: dartboards at one end, pool tables at the other, TVs scattered throughout, board games, and of course great craft beer.

During the annual IPA festival, Cooper's rotates 50 different IPAs over the course of three weeks. A group of unidentified brews is also available for customer judging. On this Thursday night, IPA lovers packed the pub to take advantage of the bargain-priced sample trays. Chris D had arranged for us to challenge our taste buds in a blind tasting.

Outside our normal beer activity, a blind tasting was something we'd never done before. I'm not particularly confident in my tasting skills (other than to determine if I like the beer or not), but figured it would be an opportunity to try something new. I assumed the evening would consist of the three of us sharing an unknown flight of beer samples and it wouldn't matter if I made a wrong guess at every beer. However, we walked into Cooper's to find Chris D at a table with five men we'd never met before. A little taken aback, I shyly sat down as Chris D introduced us to the fellow beer enthusiasts Cooper's owner, Kirbie Predmore, had invited to participate. Like us, Chris D had not met the others before but having arrived before us, he was able to facilitate the exchange of names.

Introduced as having a website called *thebeergeek.com* and being the only female at the table, I felt the pressure to make a good show of it. I may have had the knowledge that comes with visiting hundreds of breweries, but confidence that I could pull off a blind tasting eluded me. My heart sank at the thought of bluffing my way through the evening.

Our first round was served and four small glasses of beer were placed on a numbered placemat. I sipped away, making notes on my placemat. After a few minutes, others at the table commented on flavor profiles and definitively stated which beers they liked and disliked. Our fun evening with Chris

D was turning out to be a test and proving myself worthy of attendance at this specially organized tasting was a daunting task. Luckily, by the time my turn came around, other opinions that I could agree with had already been put forth. I said a few remarks, most of which were lost as a table-wide discussion on the flight became fully engaged. The first bullet had been dodged.

Shortly after receiving our beers for round two, our friend Crista arrived. We'd first met Crista in the late 1980s as the girlfriend of a high school friend. She had grown up in a nearby city and had attended a different high school than us. While Crista and our friend had long been broken up and she had since moved up to Seattle and gotten married, she had remained our friend.

With her kids and husband occupied at home, Crista now had the rare opportunity to spend the evening with us. Naturally I found it more interesting to visit with a longtime friend who I hadn't seen in years than to focus on the beer in front of me. Crista, not being into beer to the same degree as us, was also more interested in catching up than participating in the blind tasting. While the Chrisses continued with rounds two and three, Crista and I chatted. After pinpointing the one imperial IPA in the first round, I had deftly hidden my blind tasting inexperience. With Crista's arrival, I was able to avoid future potential blunders and go out on top.[9]

When the tasting was over, Crista drove the Chrisses and me to Elysian Brewing Company in Capitol Hill. Elysian's large 200-seat dining room befits the most densely populated neighborhood in Seattle. With exposed beams in its high ceiling,

9 Chris performed remarkably well and correctly identified all thirteen samples in the tasting.

Elysian seemed huge. We had heard of the brewery best known for their Great Pumpkin Beer Festival, but had never been there. It was the fourth addition to The List on the trip.

Crista and I reminisced and filled each other in on happenings since we last talked. Over beers like the Zephyrus Pilsner, Avatar Jasmine IPA and Perseus Porter, we laughed until it was time for Crista to get home to her family. It wasn't nearly enough time to get fully caught up, but the time we did have was meaningful and important.

Throughout the years, our longtime friends have spread all over the country and beyond. Distance, children, and diverging lifestyles have all contributed to lost contact with the people who've played significant roles in our lives. Beer travel enables us to re-connect with these old friends and the invitation of "let's get together for a beer" takes on a much bigger significance.

Our friends often revel in stepping out of their everyday routine. They feel part of our beer travels when we get together, even if for them it means only traveling across town. Drinking beers with Crista reminded me that restoring connections with friends is just as important, if not more so, than meeting new friends during our travels. We'd known Crista for over twenty years, long before the development of *thebeergeek.com*. It was relaxing and even comforting to let go of being Chris and Merideth, the beer geeks and simply be Chris and Merideth, beer lovers, even if it was only for a few hours.

Late Friday morning we braved the hordes at Pike Public Market before meeting up with Chris D who planned to work a half-day. As touristy as it felt, a proper exploration of Seattle wouldn't be complete without a trip to the city's most popular destination. Plus, we hoped to get some good footage for the *One Pint at a Time* episode.

We walked down Pine Street toward the market and encountered a most beautiful sight: Beecher's Handmade Cheese shop. If there's one thing we love almost as much as beer (and each other), it's cheese. As we got closer, the pleasant aroma of cheese replaced the less appealing briny scent of the fish market. Chris couldn't pass up a taste of their "world's best" mac and cheese. The comforting smell wrapped around us like a warm blanket. We watched the cheese-maker through the window as he stirred a large open vat of milk.

Pike Place Fish Market's legendary fishmongers, however, were the ones to see in action. While PETA would disagree, watching a twenty-pound halibut being thrown across the counter like a rugby ball is just plain entertaining. The precise timing used to catch the slimy, scaly fish hurled at rocket speed is certainly a marvel to behold. The only flaw with this spectacle is if no one buys any fish, there's nothing to see. It then becomes just another smelly fish market.

Every once in a while, the fishmongers entertained us with a trick. With the pull of a string, a flounder in the ice moved. An unwitting woman nearby squealed and jumped with a start. It delighted the other tourists, as well as the victim. The man behind the counter tossed out a life-sized stuffed fish and his coworker failed to catch it. The fish landed at the feet of yet another unsuspecting tourist. The crowd erupted in laughter again.

Annoyed by the lack of sales, the fishmonger admonished the crowd of gawkers. "Come on. Isn't anybody going to buy a fish today?"

The group chuckled and he looked even more annoyed. Filled with impatience, I too wanted someone to make a purchase. We not only needed to get the stock Seattle footage and move on, but my ears could only take so much of the busker[10] on the sidewalk playing Appalachian-style music on his fiddle. Besides, the foul trout smell was making my stomach queasy.

Once Chris felt we had enough footage to get by, we headed downstairs underneath the market to wait for Chris D at Pike Brewing Company. Opened in 1989 by Charles Finkel, Pike Brewing beers won awards and received critical acclaim by notable beer writers like Roger Protz, Stephen Beaumont, and the late Michael Jackson (aka the Beer Hunter). However, the brewery suffered a decline in quality after Finkel sold it in 1997. Our last visit, which was shortly after the brewery had changed hands, left a mediocre impression on us. Even locals had confided that over the years, the beer had become average and the restaurant tourist-driven. Hesitant to order the beer, we reminded ourselves that this was a trip about second chances and ordered a taster set.

This time, the beer pleasantly surprised us. As we discovered later, the reason for the improvement was that in 2006 Charles Finkel purchased Pike Brewing Company back from the most recent owners. He then restored the brewery-restaurant to its original glory.

Chris and I quickly finished our pints of golden ale and IPA on cask when Chris D arrived. The second go round at Pike reminded us the value of revisiting places we'd been before. The experience added to our improving impression of Seattle's beer scene.

---

10 A street musician

Together, the three of us embarked on a whole new experience—one that required venturing outside the comforts of the city center. We rode the bus to Georgetown, an industrial area in the throes of redevelopment. The further out we traveled, the fewer passengers remained on the bus. I watched as, one by one, people got off and the bus emptied. The area appeared devoid of both businesses and houses. I couldn't imagine where they were going.

Further down the line, Chris D instructed us to get off at the next stop. As the bus drove away, I felt stranded. Looking down the street to the left and then to the right, I saw nothing but the back of the bus. With Chris D in the lead, we followed in the direction of Georgetown Brewing Company. Or at least Chris D's best guess of the correct direction. It was his first visit.

Even in its desolation, Georgetown emanates counterculture hipness—abandoned buildings with colorful graffiti and electrical poles wall-papered with concert bills and advertisements. We passed the odd business now and again. One retail shop displayed a t-shirt in the window with the phrase "Georgetown: not just for hookers anymore" across the front. The tourist-laden Pike Public Market seemed worlds away.

We encountered few other people on the street. With no one to ask, we trusted that we were headed in the right direction of the brewery. We spied an old red brick building on our left. "Malt House" was sculpted into the wall. Even with construction fencing along the sidewalk and boarded up windows, the old Seattle Brewing and Malting Company building stood proud and strong. Next to the Malt House, the front wall of a demolished structure refused to crumble and stood in defiance. This had to be it.

We walked along the side of the building labeled as the "Brew House" in search of Georgetown Brewing Company. Around the corner in the back, a white grain silo towered above us. "This must be the place," I said.

We opened the door to the brewery and entered a whole new world. Surrounded by the decaying remnants of Seattle's brewing history, Georgetown Brewing[11] was a pillar of renewal. The staff extended an enthusiastic welcome to the tasting room, which was basically a warehouse with a small bar area. As we sipped on our samples, locals popped in and out to get their growlers filled. The motto on their Manny's Pale Ale said it all: "Darn tasty beer." I liked it there and wanted to stay longer, but two more breweries anxiously awaited their addition to The List.

I felt isolated again as we waited for the bus. The quiet air sharply contrasted with the life bubbling inside the brewery. I stared down the street and speculated how long we might wait. We weren't exactly on the most active bus route. But we had entrusted our lives and thirst in the hands of our friend Chris D, so we waited.

The number 134 bus eventually arrived. After we boarded, Chris D admitted that he *thought* it was the correct bus. When I questioned him about the bus schedule, he said he hadn't really checked.

"I'm not positive, but I'm pretty sure this is the right bus," he told us in thinly disguised uncertainty.

A few left turns here and a couple of stops there, the bus veered in the opposite direction from our intended destination. Chris D immediately realized the mistake. Somewhat

---

11 Georgetown Brewing has since moved down the road to a larger facility on Denver Avenue.

panicked, we wanted off the bus as soon as possible but the next stop failed to appear. The bus rolled along, taking us further and further away from our destination. Finally, we arrived at the Olsen Meyers Park and Ride. Our shortsighted exit plan only went as far as getting off the bus. We stood there dumbfounded as the bus pulled away.

"Well, what do we do now?" I asked Chris D.

"Wait for another bus, I guess," he said.

The three of us milled about. I considered our options: walk or wait. The remote location eliminated walking and the absence of other people even made hitchhiking unlikely. Our best bet was to wait, but how long before another bus arrived? What if it wasn't the bus we wanted? I gave up and accepted the predicament.

Across the parking lot, four people dressed in yellow firefighter pants stared at a smoldering mound like hobos around a fire pit. The sign on the building read "Seattle Fire Department Training Center." I wondered about what lesson might be learned from staring at a pile.

Before we debated the ethical dilemmas of cannibalism, including which of us would be eaten first, a bus came. In the direction we wanted.

By way of bus and foot, we found our next brewery, Laughing Buddha[12], located in an industrial park unit. Breweries located in industrial parks drive me nuts. Often poorly

---

12 Laughing Buddha, now called Trade Route Brewing Company, changed its name shortly after our visit in order to resolve litigation regarding trademark infringement. The Lucky Drink Company of Australia objected to the name Laughing Buddha because it too closely resembled their U.S. trademarked Buddha shaped bottles and the name "Lucky Buddha." Along with the name change, the brewery changed locations and now brews a slightly different line-up of beers.

marked, I can never tell if we're in the right place or if they're even open. The three of us walked up to the solid door. The guys pushed me to go in first. I burst through the door with the Chrisses right behind me. Thrilled to have finally found the brewery, our raucous laughter disrupted the tranquility of the tiki bar tasting area. The only two people inside practically jumped with surprise.

The grass awning above the bar gave the impression of a hut on the beach. Bamboo partitions separated the public tasting area from the brewery. The whole thing induced a (very) fleeting urge to don a grass skirt and coconut shell bikini top. In the corner, a bright gold Buddha with a round belly rested on an intricately carved cherry wood hutch. Candles and offerings were placed on the shelf below. Standing in a whimsical pose holding a candle above his head, the Buddha's broad grin gave the sense of utter delight. What a blissful state to be in, I thought.

Despite our loud entrance, co-owner Chris Castillo offered us a friendly welcome as he served us up a sample of Pandan Brown, a sweet brew made with pandan leaf and palm sugar. He gave us a tour around the brewery, including a look in the refrigerator to see the cases of ginger root used in their Ginger Pale Ale. The tour commentary included information on the origins of the brewery's equipment. It was purchased from the now defunct San Andreas Brewing in Hollister, California.

San Andreas, a small-town brewery that catered primarily to locals, brewed good beer, including an apricot ale made with local fruit. Tricky to make right, most fruit beers end up tasting like candy. San Andreas Brewing succeeded in creating a refreshingly subtle fruit beer.

The spirit of San Andreas Brewing lived on in Laughing Buddha's Asian-inspired beers. Like San Andreas, Laughing Buddha brewed with unusual ingredients: a porter made with purple yams and an American-style wheat infused with mango. Apparently, even brewing equipment deserved a second chance.

From there, we walked around the building to our next brewery: Baron Brewing Company. Also in the industrial park, this establishment was clearly open. Through the glass door, we saw the unmistakable blue and white checks of the Bavarian flag. We expected to walk into a small tasting room. However, what we discovered was a handful of regulars with full pints of beer. With six people seated and the three of us standing, the capacity of this closet-sized tasting room had reached its limit.

The bartender, with a large breasted mermaid tattooed on his arm, was surprised when we asked for sample-sized beers. Despite being legally a "tasting" room, it was unofficially operating more like a pub. No one, except new comers, asked for sample sets and the regulars would never consider purchasing such puny beers. Everyone was very friendly and included us in the conversation despite our transient, out-of-towner status. While we stood with our small beers, the regulars were comfortably entrenched at the bar with full pints.[13]

After completing our day's mission of visiting three breweries, we meandered through Georgetown on Airport Way South. Even though the weather had been chilly all day, Chris had remained reasonably comfortable in his shorts. However, late in our outing, the weather took a turn for the worse. First it became cold. Then suddenly it started to hail. Chris D and

13 Baron later ran into legal trouble for operating what was essentially a pub out of their tasting room. They have since opened an official taproom.

I laughed hysterically at this apocalyptic change in weather. Through the laughter, cries of "Ow" could be heard. We looked at Chris. The hail was pelting his bare legs.

At that moment, we realized that we had stopped in front of a café. The three of us turned to look. A pair of women at a table near the window stared at us in shock. It's hard to say if they were surprised by the hail or by seeing Chris in shorts, but it was probably a bit of both. Cold and tired, we called it a day.

The first few days of the trip Chris had taunted Mother Nature in his shorts. He rarely wears anything else and it takes an act of God to get him to put on long pants. Weddings and funerals require some cajoling, but freezing cold weather will get him into long pants without question. During March's trip to Boston, Chris proudly announced that it would be the last time he planned to wear long pants until our visit to Belgium in December. However, the day after getting pelted in the legs with hail, he bowed to Mother Nature and wore long pants.

"I never realized that it would be 30°F in Seattle on April 19th. So here I am again in pants." Chris sounded dejected. "This really is the last day I'll be wearing pants until December."

"I wouldn't say that if I were you," I told him.

Together with Chris D and his girlfriend Francesca, we journeyed to Seattle's Fremont District. Across the street from the original Redhook Brewery is the famous Brouwer's Café.

The stark warehouse exterior did not prepare me for the impressive interior of Brouwer's. At night, Brouwer's is crowded with the hippest beer drinkers in Seattle, but our daytime visit made for a nearly empty establishment. The only sound to be heard when we walked in was that of jingling pocket change and squeaking shoes. We spoke in hushed tones as we crossed the cavernous space to the bar.

The bar spans the length of the restaurant and balconies loom overhead, creating a dramatic effect. The long row of draught beers and the glass coolers stocked with bottled beer filled me with dread. I can be fairly indecisive when faced with an extensive selection of beer. Add a slight hang over and my ability to choose is exponentially reduced to next to none. I finally decided upon Big Daddy's ESB from Silver City Brewing for my first beer, while Chris went local with Port Townsend's Hop Diggity on cask.

"Hey look, they even have one of those cool glass washer things," Chris said.

We watched as the bartender turned a glass bottom side up. He pressed it down on the washer and water splashed up inside the glass. This final rinse is said to clean out any residual impurities. Also, a wetted glass supposedly makes for a better pour of beer. All I know is that the longer I have to wait for my beer, the crankier I get.

Brouwer's is on many Top 10 lists of best beer bars in the United States. Now I understood why. With its comprehensive selection of bottled and draft beers, educated staff, and proper glassware (not to mention the glass washer) Brouwer's covers all the bases in creating the best possible environment for serving and drinking beer. For all its popularity, though, some reviews characterized it as grandiose and snobby. It's where Chris D first introduced us to the term "beer douche." In case he was wrong, Chris D hesitated to name Brouwer's as the birthplace of the term. However, he went ahead anyway and relayed the story of how he thought the term originated.

In June 2006, an unhappy customer posted a Brouwer's review on *BeerAdvocate.com*, a popular ratings website where a membership of a half-million beer fanatics review not only individual beers, but also beer establishments like brewpubs and beer bars. In part, the vengeful reviewer called an inattentive bartender a "semi-long haired douche." Regular patrons, including Chris D, knew exactly to whom the reviewer referred and thought it was hilarious. It is very possible that the bartender *was* acting pompous, but Brouwer's regulars characterized the reviewer as the one who was acting like a beer snob. From that point on, "beer douche" became a negative label for a pretentious beer drinker.

Akin to a wine snob, beer douches analyze beers and offer esoteric flavor descriptions. A beer douche in the group can greatly reduce the pure and simple enjoyment of drinking beer. Don't get me wrong, there's a time and place for displaying the skills of a beer douche—skills that I certainly do not have and would probably only learn with immense difficulty. But sometimes, you just want to savor the moment of drinking great beer with good friends. The term "beer douche" is now a standard part of the craft beer community's lexicon.

It didn't surprise me that Brouwer's could elicit a reputation as being pompous. Even without a full house, the attitude was aloof and even Goth. That didn't put me off, though. In fact, the thought of Morrissey brooding at the end of the bar or Robert Smith from The Cure lamenting his woes over a beer was kind of cool.

From Brouwer's, we followed along the Burke-Gilman Trail—part of Seattle's urban recreation trail system—to Hale's Ales Brewery. Luckily the rain had stopped, but the air remained chilly. The long walk helped us to not only stay warm it also gave me an opportunity to get to know Francesca.

A graphic designer by profession and crafter by hobby, Francesca is incredibly creative. Her ability to visualize beyond what is presented on the surface gives her the insight of seeing the artistry in everything and everybody. I was starting to understand how she and Chris D fit together. She saw Chris for much more than his beer obsession. As someone who likes beer, but is not a beer geek per se, she demonstrates a high degree of patience and acceptance of Chris D's love of beer, including his frequent nights out with beer friends and his solo trips out of town for beer events. By the time we arrived at Hale's, I had come to the conclusion that Francesca was the most perfect non-beer geek spouse a beer geek could ever have.

From the outside, Hale's is a plain gray building on the corner of Leary Way NW and 7th Ave NW, appropriate for a location formerly used as an industrial hose factory. However, the entrance–a wall of paned windows–is more dramatic than one would expect. We entered a foyer with the brewery on the right and the pub on the left. A smile came over our faces as we inhaled the sweet smell of malt. The aromas emanating from the brewing process are as comforting to a beer geek as the smell of freshly baked cookies to a kid.

The four of us found seats at the bar and ordered a few beers. My recall of our first visit to Hale's many years ago was faint and looking around the pub did little to jog my memory. The one thing that I did remember, though, was their motto: "Think globally, drink locally." Hale's was one of the first places to use that slogan and we've been incorporating it into our beer travels ever since.

The Hale's beer wasn't quite as we remembered. It wasn't bad, but it didn't invoke the "wow" factor Chris had recalled from our first visit. Had the brewery changed over time or was it us? One change I was certain about was that the tenacity with which we sought out new breweries to visit had intensified. Some might consider it our obsession, one that kept us on the move during our trips.

The mile-long route to our next brewery, Maritime Pacific Brewing Company, was the complete opposite of the tree-lined nature walk we took to Hale's. Instead, the area was starkly industrial, with little greenery to break up the bland monotony of warehouse buildings.

The brewery embraced their wrong side of the tracks location with the Jolly Roger Taproom. The most color we'd seen on our walk, the taproom's sign pictured a black tattered pirate's flag set against an orangey-red sunset sky. Below the Santa hat-wearing skull and crossbones, a group of skeleton hands holding metal tankards reached up from the bottom. They reminded me of zombies grasping for a live body. I could almost hear growls as they desperately begged for ale. We went inside to get our own thirst quenched.

For a pirate-themed establishment, I envisioned dark and seedy, but the windows in the front created an unexpected brightness inside the pub. The interior was decorated with the same red paint I'd seen in several other Seattle beer spots. It made me wonder if there had been some sale or exceptional deal on that particular shade of red. Or perhaps all the beer establishments had the same interior designer. I turned to Francesca. As the artistic one in our group, I thought for sure she'd have an answer for the phenomenon. She didn't. In fact, she said she hadn't noticed until I pointed it out.

Despite a good-sized crowd, the bartender served us a sampler set in a reasonable amount of time. We even had a chance to order a fried pickle and mahi-mahi sliders.

"Maritime is my 380th brewery," Chris announced. "It's a good day."

Chris D tipped his baseball cap to Chris and we all toasted his achievement. Despite my disappointment at trailing Chris by one in the brewery count, I had to admit that he was right. It had been a good day.

"Thanks for showing us all around," I said to Chris D. " I think you took us to every part of the city."

"Yeah, thanks," Chris added. "This has been a great trip."

"To a great trip," Chris D replied.

He raised his glass and the three of us followed suit. Together we toasted the end of four successful months of the Year in Beer.

Chris and I were in Seattle for only a short time, but each day was filled from morning to night with beery activities. In four days we visited twelve breweries, including nine new ones, and over a half-dozen beer bars. Yet it was our mellowest trip of the year thus far. There was no major beer event and no hoopla. It was simply a casual, good old-fashioned beer adventure.

Before this trip, we had taken to nonchalantly referring to Seattle with "Yeah, we've been there." Based on our initial visit, we were clinging to the assessment of the city's beer scene as overrated. As a result, we hadn't given much thought to another visit. With the prodding of Chris D, we returned after a decade and Seattle exceeded our expectations. The city's beer scene had definitely grown stronger, but having a friend as a guide made it all the more enjoyable. I'm glad that we heeded Chris D's call to come back. After all, everything deserves a second chance.

MAY

DARE TO TAKE THE ROAD LESS (TOURIST) TRAVELED

Our return from Seattle garnered the same frenzied welcome that had become our family's monthly routine. High-pitched whines that bordered on howling could be heard through the door. Intermittent barks warned of excited little dogs waiting inside. When we opened the door, Porter and Stout ran toward us, their nails clicking on the wooden floor. I dropped my bag and bent down to get a face full of dog kisses.

"Blech! Dog breath," I said as I scrunched my nose.

Stout whined as he wiggled around in circles. Porter ran to Chris and jumped up, putting his front paws on Chris's shins. Satisfied with a pat on the head, he grabbed the Christmas tree plush toy and ran outside to hide it. Not to be left out, our pet birds squawked. Ah, home sweet home.

One of the best things about returning home (besides being in our own bed with our own pillow) was that we always found it just the way we left it. Even though our housesitter Lilly stayed over night taking care of things, there was never any sign of her when we returned. So far Lilly had been an invisible Godsend and an essential part of the Year in Beer's success.

Chris seemed to enjoy the perpetual trip mode of the Year in Beer. For me, however, the nomadic lifestyle was more familiar, but no more comfortable. After four months, my need to feel grounded was intensifying. A few weeks holed up in the house like a hermit would have fit the bill nicely, but of course that wasn't an option. Establishing our name in the craft beer community meant bucking up and putting ourselves out there. There was just one problem with the idea of becoming part of the craft beer establishment: I didn't really know what that meant.

Those who have solid positions in the craft beer community write articles on the history of beer or offer tips on better homebrewing. They use flowery prose, witty comments, and words that I'm fairly certain are made up to write beer reviews. Videocast interviewers practically drool on camera as they hang on every word of their brewer interviewee. Chris and I walk down a whole different path, which makes it harder to conceive of our place in the craft beer community. As beer travelers who don't homebrew or review beer, how exactly do we fit in? Is there even a place for us in the establishment? Little did I know that May's trip to Germany would provide the answer—that the road less traveled would lead to self-realization and the confidence to continue efforts to make a name for *thebeergeek.com.*

May was one of the months we found easy to schedule. The year before we had attended the Bergkirchweih, a beer festival in Erlangen, Germany. A down-sized Oktoberfest, the festival left a highly favorable impression on us and returning for a second visit was a given. As luck would have it, Flogging Molly was touring Europe around the same time. Chris revised our weeklong excursion in Germany to conclude with three Flogging Molly shows in three different cities—Cologne, Munich, and Vienna, Austria. We were already excited about the first European trip of the Year in Beer. The addition of the Flogging Molly shows was simply head on the pint.

After what seemed like a few short weeks at home, we landed in Frankfurt. Before we could embark upon our latest adventure, however, we had to descend into the bowels of the airport.

The rental car agent pointed us in the general direction of the underground garage. She gave us a door number and a stall number. We didn't really understand this system until we started walking down what seemed like an endless corridor lined with a limitless series of numbered doors. We were tired, jetlagged and had our bags in tow. A long treasure hunt journey to the car was not what we needed. It felt like a nightmare where the hallway never ends. As we approached each door, I quickened my step with the hope that it would be the one. Every time my heart sank with disappointment, exasperation, and finally annoyance. Eventually we located our door and stepped into the garage.

Our eyes adjusted to the dim lighting as we searched for the stall number we'd been given. In the low ceiling and artificial light, the rows of cars reminded me of bats clustered together on a cave wall. Any issue locating our vehicle at this point would have been a problem with a capital "P" because we were a long way from the rental car counter. Before all hope was lost, however, a friendly employee appeared out of nowhere and led us to the car. Based on his American accent, I imagined him to be an American service man who had chosen to stay in Germany. It didn't matter where he was from, though. His help was much appreciated.

Once the bags were secured in the trunk, Chris and I took our positions up front. Our adventure could now begin. The car lurched and stalled down the aisles as we followed signs for the *ausgang* (exit). With great frustration, Chris struggled to familiarize himself with the clutch. He just needed time to get comfortable with the car, but my travel fatigue eliminated the filter on my mouth. A few unhelpful comments later, Chris finally had enough. "Come on, hon," he implored. Too tired to argue, he simply looked at me with pleading eyes. I felt bad because he was right. My navigator role required not only paying attention to the road, but also being a team player. So far, I scored low in that department. Within a half hour, however, Chris gained his driving confidence and I became comfortable with the road signs. We drove south toward Neuhaus.

Autobahn construction thwarted our efforts to obtain a much-needed beer as soon as possible and the two-hour journey we anticipated turned into four. We stopped only once to visit a brewery, Ochsenfurter Kauzen Bräu, in the town of

Ochsenfurt, but found it to be closed to the public. A nearby restaurant served the brewery's beer, as well as lunch, so the opportunity to revive ourselves enough to make it to our evening's destination was not totally lost. Exhausted, we limped into Neuhaus and to our *brauerei_hotel* (brewery hotel), Hotel Zum Löwenbräu, in the early evening.

Brauerei hotels are the best invention known in the beer traveling world. Usually family owned and operated, a brauerei hotel is just as the name states: a hotel with a brewery. Or, from our perspective, a brewery with a hotel. Our first choice for accommodation, the rooms are often some of the nicest and least expensive places to stay. Plus, good German beer and food are just a few paces away. As a bonus, it generally means adding another brewery to The List while getting great hospitality.

Our bodies ached for movement after the long flights and car ride, so after checking in, we explored the small town of Neuhaus on foot. No other restaurants or businesses in sight, we walked through quiet residential neighborhoods. The beautiful evening weather encouraged people out into their yards. Some looked up as we passed and offered a friendly nod and "*guten abend*." The carefully tended gardens were filled with colorful flowers and the front yard of each house was just as eye-catching as the next.

Along the way, we encountered several signs for the Hotel Zum Löwenbräu Felsenkeller. Felsenkeller was not a word we were familiar with, but we knew the "keller" part indicated a beer cellar. We hadn't seen a beer garden at the hotel, so we thought perhaps it was located somewhere else. We tried to follow the signs, but the trail always went cold and we were unsuccessful. In the end, we guessed that "Felsenkeller" was the name of the restaurant at our hotel and the signs were simply advertisements. It was the only explanation we could think of.

Chris and I wandered back to the hotel for dinner and beer. Sitting at one of the few tables set up out front, I took a deep breath and exhaled in relief at having arrived in Germany. The fresh evening air felt good after hours of climate-controlled conditions in the airports and planes. Three other guests sat at another outside table chatting away. Understanding very little German, their conversation served as background noise. Not much went through my mind as I strained to stay awake. Chris didn't say much either.

Jetlag is one of the first challenges of European travel. Our strategy for a smooth transition is to get on the local time as quickly as possible. On the final flight of our journey, we calculate the time at our destination. Usually that means it's very early in the morning. On the flight, while other passengers are reading and watching movies, we go to sleep. We get in at least a few hours of shut-eye and wake up in the morning just as the residents at our destination are arising.

The second part of that strategy is to stay awake as long as possible the first night. We aim for at least 9:00 P.M. An over-the-counter sleep aid before bed helps us sleep through the night, and the next morning we're more or less ready to go. A time-tested strategy, it has rarely failed us. As we sat at an outside table of the Hotel Zum Löwenbräu, Chris looked at his watch to gauge how much longer we needed to stay awake.

"Only two more hours," he said, eyes already half-mast.

"Two more hours? I can make it another hour at the most," I replied with a yawn.

Chris and I started a game of Scrabble to pass the time, but scrapped it half-way through. Nodding off in the middle of my turn didn't bode well for my winning the game. Chris's fatigue proved just as debilitating. Much to my surprise, I managed to maintain consciousness until our minimum self-imposed bedtime. Then, like zombies, we climbed the stairs to our room. Out like a light, Chris fell asleep only minutes before I did.

Our first morning in Germany, we walked the trails of a nearby nature area. Birds tweeted and small creatures rustled in the underbrush of the trees as we passed. Along the way, we actually stumbled upon the Löwenbräu Felsenkeller, which turned out to be a beer garden. Set back from the graveled country road, a large group of tables sat empty under a grove of trees. It hadn't yet opened for the day, so we couldn't stop for a beer. Instead, I pictured the forest beer garden filled with jovial drinkers and wished we had found it the night before. Our trip was starting out slow and that was probably a good thing. It would pick up soon enough and it was best to get in as much rest as possible at the beginning.

Chris became impatient to continue on to our next destination, so we checked out of the hotel and set off for Erlangen. Once on the road, however, he decided to take a short detour to Bamberg. On a previous trip there, we missed visiting two of the ten breweries in town. Chris thought we should try again.

Spared the bombings of World War II, Bamberg is one of the most well-preserved medieval cities in Germany. The historic town is also home to the world famous Aecht Schlenkerla Rauchbier from Brauerei Heller. Rauchbiers—brewed with malt roasted over an open flame—possess a distinct smoke flavor. Some specialty beer drinkers expound the virtues of the beer that tastes like bacon. As a general rule, everything tastes better with bacon. Beer served *with* bacon: good. Beer that *tastes* like bacon: not so good. Even our German friends Ute and Wolfgang, who'll eat and drink most anything, find it a hard style to drink. Chris likes it enough to finish a whole glass. How he manages it is beyond me.

We arrived in Bamberg around noon, the perfect time for beer and lunch. Or so we thought. The beer gods, however, had a different plan. One brewery opened at 2:00 P.M. and the other at 5:00 P.M. For goodness sake, why were these places closed mid-day on a Saturday? Chris admitted that a little research on his part might have been helpful. It amused us that both places listed an 11:00 A.M. opening time on Sundays. It seemed an unlikely day to have early opening hours.

Denied beers in Bamberg, we headed south to Erlangen for the main event of the trip, a beer festival called the Bergkirchweih. When we checked into our hotel, the woman behind the front desk wished us good luck when she learned of our intention to attend the festival. We assured her we knew what to expect since we had attended the year before.

What we didn't expect, however, was to find ourselves at 3:00 P.M. on a sunny afternoon in Germany having yet to drink a beer. Lucky for us, our hotel was located near the Kitzmann brewery and unlike every other place we attempted that day, Kitzmann had opened at 10:00 A.M. We threw up our hands. Go figure.

We washed down sausages and potato salad with our first beers of the day and basked in the sun. Our decision the previous year to take the road less traveled by tourists to explore the Bergkirchweih had been a good one. That first visit made such an impression on us that there was no doubt about its inclusion in our Year in Beer schedule.

Chris first learned about the Bergkirchweih in our local paper a few years before. A surprising source for such information, the story piqued his interest as something different to do in Germany besides the expected Oktoberfest. The Bergkirchweih starts on the Thursday before Pentecost[14] in Erlangen, a town northeast of Nurnberg. Over one million people—approximately 10 times the town's population—attend over twelve days, making it Germany's second largest beer festival. Most beer geeks dream about a trip to Oktoberfest, but how many know about "the Berg?" After reading that article, Chris vowed to one day attend.

The Bergkirchweih, which roughly translates to "Church Festival on the Hill," is located at the north end of town on a street alongside a hill. It includes a fair, complete with carnival rides, game booths, and food stalls. At the other end of the festival grounds is a series of roofed beer halls positioned on steep slopes. Permanent beer kellers nestle themselves into the hillside below. A *keller* (cellar) refers to the cool storage place where beer is lagered. The word keller in the name usually indicates an establishment that serves beer.

The main seating areas are located in the lower section of the beer halls, while the upper areas are canopied with trees, offering the feel of being in the forest. This gives the option of observing the festivities from above or being one of the observed down below.

We first visited the Bergkirchweih the year before during the last weekend of the celebration. The festival immediately struck me as a huge block party for locals and residents of the

14 The forty-ninth day after Easter Sunday.

neighboring towns. Families picnicked under the trees while small children swung like monkeys on the railing of a nearby set of stairs. I thoroughly enjoyed it. Without noticeable tourists, it seemed like a beer festival Germans would enjoy.

That first visit moved me to declare the Berg superior to Oktoberfest. Chris scoffed at my assessment as blasphemous because he considers Oktoberfest to be the penultimate beer event. For the Year in Beer, we attempted the Berg on the opening weekend. We wondered how the difference in timing might change the experience.

Finishing our sausages and beer at Kitzmann, we pointed ourselves in the general path of the festival. As we continued through the city center, the chaotic mix of people gave way to a steady stream of individuals all heading in the same direction. We arrived at the festival in the early evening, surveying the activity and reminiscing about our first trip to the Berg.

"We sat over there," Chris said as he pointed, "and listened to that Oompah band."

"Yeah and that guy told us we couldn't film. Then he made us move because we didn't buy a beer," I added.

We walked on and more memories surfaced.

"That's the tent where the mean waitress gave us the overly salted radish," I commented. Chris nodded his head in agreement.

Not quite ready to jump into the fray, we sat at an empty table away from the party. The music in the distance was quiet enough to allow conversation without yelling yet loud enough to create a festive mood. A family soon joined us. They unpacked their picnic of cocktail weenies and bread. A short time later, steins of beer arrived. The style of beer served at the Berg is a festbier, golden in color with a malty taste. Similar to an Oktoberfest beer, local breweries make it once a year for the festival.

The family of six people overtook our intimate party of two and our table soon became their table. I started to feel like a guest at someone else's family gathering. Our inability to speak German combined with the family's limited English compounded the awkwardness. But the slight unease was a small consequence of choosing the road less tourist traveled. Immersion provided the best possible opportunity to understand German beer culture.

The mother made a friendly comment or two in my direction. I looked at her with wide eyes, smiled, and shook my head slowly from side to side. She understood my body language for "I don't speak German." She smiled back and Chris initiated a group *prost*_(toast). Prosting works wonders when language differences prevent further conversation. Beer: the goodwill ambassador to the world.

I sat across from a fourteen year-old girl who drank a radler (a mix of beer and lemon-lime soda). Under the legal drinking age, her parents allowed her a modified version of beer. She understood some English and did her best to speak to us. Amongst the small talk, we learned that they came from Bayreuth— a town north of Erlangen—and that we shared a fondness for *The Simpsons*. Bart's exclamations produced the biggest laughs. "Don't have a cow, man" in a thick German accent is highly amusing.

Chris innocently asked if the girl's boyfriend was her brother. She giggled as she translated the misunderstanding to her family. They snickered and the boyfriend smiled politely. Although still an uncomfortable moment, it was a far less creepy blunder than mistaking a brother for a boyfriend. The encounter with this family broke the ice and we soon felt ready to join the flowing river of people passing by our table.

We ordered another beer at a nearby keller and wandered through the swarm of people. At the Berg, in addition to table service, you can purchase beer take-away style. The cost of walking around with your beer is a 5 Euro *pfand* (deposit) on the stein. When finished, you return the stein for your deposit or keep it as an inexpensive souvenir. We liked this system much better than Oktoberfest, where you have to be seated to order a beer and walking around the festival grounds with your beer is prohibited. Plus, at Oktoberfest bags are constantly searched for stolen steins, which is about as user-friendly as an airport security checkpoint.

The perfect weather during the Berg's opening weekend brought people out in droves. The festival buzzed with happy families and spirited young people. The steady clanking of steins rang in our ears as we walked from one end of the festival to the other. Each tent had its own band, so renditions of "Sweet Home Alabama" faded into a Four Non Blondes song. The crowd belted out the chorus with the singer: "And I said hey, ey, ey, ey, hey, ey, yeah. And I said hey, what's goin' on." Chris thought that the European Football Championship caused at least part of the upbeat mood because the Germans had high hopes for their national team.[15] If it wasn't soccer hopes, however, it could possibly have been the answer to our curiosity about the difference between attending the first weekend and last weekend of the festival.

It's easy to idealize the Berg as the complete opposite of Oktoberfest. That it's devoid of all the negative aspects of its

15 The German national team subsequently made the final game six weeks later.

big brother. In reality, however, it's still a large beer fest with a manageable family-friendly crowd during the day and a mass of drunken young people after dark.

Within a few hours of our arrival, the festival shifted into the nighttime mode, signaling our time to leave. However, before we left for the night, I engaged in the unique German tradition of drinking liters of beer and going on fast, whirling carnival rides. The ingestion of a large quantity of beer made it easy to overcome a fear of puking (due to the aforementioned consumption) on the ride and go for it. Chris thought it was a crazy idea, but his cautions were also easy to ignore.

I managed to keep my bodily fluids inside while spinning on the swinging centrifuge ride, but unfortunately, others did not. A few small wet drops landed on my cheek. Someone spitting? Rain? I could only hope. The ride came to a stop and I looked to my right. My hopes were dashed. If only I hadn't looked.

Before our 30-minute walk back to the hotel, we decided that a bathroom break would be a good idea. Earlier in the evening, the lines were short and uncomplicated. That all changed with the onset of the nighttime crowds. The woman in front of me shifted from one foot to the other and repeated "*Mein Gott!*" (My God!), while her friend laughed in agreement. By the time we finally reached the bathroom, they weren't laughing anymore. The forty-five minute wait proved to be a sobering experience for me as well.

By the time I returned to Chris, fatigue was rapidly approaching. I complained about the long line for the bathroom and he told me that he had a short exchange with another festival goer. Seeing Chris's t-shirt, which listed the year's schedule on the back, a man asked him about the Year in Beer.

"Some guy saw my shirt," he said, "and asked if I was traveling to all these places."

"Cool! Way to spread the word about the Year in Beer," I replied.

The quiet walk in the fresh air back to our hotel allowed us an extra half-hour to unwind from the festival. Just in time for bed.

The next day was Mother's Day—in both Germany and the United States—and another day to spend at the Berg. We had experienced the difference between the first weekend and the last, but we now wondered how an event like a beer festival would be affected by a holiday like Mother's Day.

We secured a table in the mid-day sun, purchased our beers and commenced the long practiced art of people watching. Mother's Day at the festival appeared much the same as the day before. Cheerful families filled the promenade. Dads walked with cotton candy-eating children on their shoulders—a beer in one hand, the child's leg in the other. Moms pushed strollers and avoided hits in the face from swaying balloons tied to the handles. Smiling couples strolled by arm in arm.

In general, people watching is both captivating and amusing. However, the entertainment value of sober people is far less than that of drunken ones. Without the fascination factor of alcohol-induced antics, the sedate daytime crowd became boring, so we brought out the Scrabble board. Soon we were fully engrossed in the game.

Breaking our concentration, a couple asked us in German about empty seats at the table. We used our usual hand signals to offer the seats to them. Motioning to others in the distance, the couple turned into a group of seven adults with a few young children. One by one they joined the table. With each new arrival, we shifted down until our butts were at the end of the bench. The introverted quietude of our Scrabble game disappeared.

One of the men addressed us in Spanish-accented English. "Your peace is over, with kids and Latins at the table," he said. I smiled and chuckled in friendly agreement.

Our tablemates laughed as they fired Spanish words at one another with dizzying speed. Before long an especially active youngster named Christian distracted me. The inner workings of this toddler's mind became transparent as he ogled the bite-sized Scrabble tiles like they were snacks. Any minute he was sure to make a grab for a handful of tiles on the board and shove them in his mouth. Fortunately Christian resisted the urge to do that. Instead, he encroached upon what little personal space I had at the edge of the bench by, for all practical purposes, sitting on my lap.

Leisure time over for the moment, Chris needed raucous crowd footage for *beergeek.TV*, so we packed up and moved on. After saying "adios" to our tablemates, we ventured down the promenade to the tent sponsored by Tucher Bräu and positioned ourselves near the music. Blasted at an ear-splitting volume, the most popular songs resulted in enthusiastic audience participation. The "Time Warp" from the Rocky Horror Picture Show got everyone up off his seat. It's not so easy to "jump to the left" in a crowded beer hall and the added challenge incited the crowd more. The tent roared: "Let's do the time warp again."

Another popular German beer festival song requires the crowd to sing, "Ooh, ah." With German lyrics, I have no idea what the song is actually about, but the tune is catchy. I quietly sang nonsensical sounds until the time came for the "ooh, ah." At which point I confidently yelled out the words while adding carefully timed hip gyrations. Luckily, Chris captured only a small portion of my rendition on camera before I stopped him. Allowing my full performance to be recorded would require a few more beers.

The band eventually took a break, much to the relief of our over-taxed eardrums. Chris and I looked at each other and shook our heads to stop the ringing in our ears. My voice was hoarse from competing with the music as I conversed with Chris. We were both grateful for the reprieve and used the relatively quiet moment to call our moms for Mother's Day. We may have abandoned the women who gave us life for world travel, but we weren't completely heartless.

With a lack of available seating at a table, Chris and I chose to stand at a counter near the aisle. It offered a good view of the whole scene. A group of middle-aged women in matching yellow t-shirts stood on the benches and prosted each other. Pretty girls in short-skirted dirndls giggled with young men in lederhosen. The Berg starts before the full swing of tourist season, so there aren't many foreign visitors. The only English that could be heard, other than our own, came from those who were confident enough to talk with us.

A group of guys in their twenties paused in the aisle to scan for seating. They all wore large, tinted 1970s-style sunglasses, shabby chic jeans, and fashionable European-style sneakers. They could easily have been mistaken for a boy band. From their arm punching, pointing and snickers, it was clear that they sought seats next to cute girls. The tallest of the group overheard Chris and I speaking English and asked us where we were from. The mention of California produced excited and interested responses. The group possessed a range of English language skills, with the tallest speaking most fluently. Slightly more reserved than the others, he separated himself from the chortles of his friends and made small talk with Chris.

In a side conversation, one of the guys with bright blue eyes used his best English to tell me that he played professional soccer. He uttered "Beckham" and a few other English footballer names. I knew it wasn't possibly true, but went along with it anyway and asked what team he played for. He threw his head back with laughter. In spite of his failure to fool me, he thought the attempt was hilarious. The music started up again, which made communication with the Justin Timberlake clones difficult. They soon continued on in their quest for seats next to available frauleins.

Left alone while Chris went to get beer, I was approached by a man of average height with a slight beer belly. He leaned in to be heard above the music and spoke a few words of German. Once again, I employed my deer-in-the-headlights-I-don't-speak-German expression. The wheels turned in his head as he searched for English words with which to respond.

"Where are you from?" he finally asked.

"California," I replied.

The answer impressed him much less than the boy band. With great determination, he mustered the words to say that he traveled to Minnesota once to see his grandparents. Grandparents living in America, let alone Minnesota, puzzled me and I considered it possible that he used the wrong noun. Then in slow, deliberate English I said that Chris and I were visiting Erlangen on holiday. My new friend noticeably stiffened at the mention of a husband and took a half-step back. His tone became more formal as he suggested that Chris might not like me talking with an unfamiliar man. The idea was ridiculous and I told him so, but that didn't seem to change anything. Then a light bulb went off in my head. Meeting Chris so young (we've known each other since high school), I had missed the exciting world of dating, including the delightful experience of pick up lines. When was the last time someone hit on me anyway? Admittedly, it boosted my ego to think someone had tried to pick me up.

As Chris returned with our beers, my friend departed with a high pitched "good-bye."

"Who was that?" Chris asked. Between the boy band and the Minnesota guy, Chris joked that I required a chaperone. He remained at my side the rest of the evening.

Whit Monday, a religious holiday in Germany, occurred the day after Mother's Day. Being a tourist in Europe during a religious or bank holiday poses some definite challenges. Unlike the States where everything is open and capitalism is at its peak, holidays in Europe often mean everything is closed. The notion of closed breweries preyed on our minds and caused an undue amount of distress. At check-out, the young receptionist at the hotel assured us that even religious holidays could not keep Germans away from their beer. We hoped she didn't give us false expectations.

Determined to visit at least one of the Bamberg breweries still missing from The List, we drove back there before heading to Cologne on Tuesday to connect with our friends Ute and Wolfgang. They live in Mannheim, a university town south of Frankfurt, and every time we travel to Germany, we make sure to swing through their city to visit. This time, we were meeting up with them in Cologne.

We first encountered Ute and Wolfgang in September 2005 at a punk show in Lindau, Germany. Among the 100 teenagers at the show, Chris and I noticed only one other couple that looked to be in our age range. We also noticed that the woman wore the same Flogging Molly shirt as I did. Like showing up to the prom in the same dress as another girl, I was somewhat embarrassed and pretended not to notice.

Waiting for the show to start, we sat at the bar and ordered a beer. When I turned around, the woman in the matching t-shirt was right next to me. She unleashed a torrent of German guttural sounds. Chris says my eyes went wide with lack of understanding. She paused before I could mime "I don't speak German." In lightly accented English, she said, "Oh. You speak English?"

She repeated her monologue in English and explained that she ran a European fan site for Flogging Molly. That interaction started a lasting friendship with Ute and Wolfgang.

We had made our first visit to Bamberg with Ute and Wolfgang and I thought about them as we arrived in the city for the second time. We approached our first stop, Maisel Bräu, with trepidation. From afar we saw a good sign that encouraged us, but we tried not to get our hopes up. Like a beacon, a sandwich board out front drew us closer. It read "*geöffnet*" (open).

A scan of the tree-shaded beer garden revealed only a few occupied tables. On a beautiful sunny day, we drank beer in utter bewilderment. A plausible reason for the absence of people was difficult to fathom.

With Maisel Bräu added to The List, we continued into the city center where we noticed a large banner advertising *Bamberger Biertage* (Bamberg Beer Days). It sounded like an event that's right up our alley, so we went in search of the celebration.

We walked from the parking garage to the Maximiliansplatz. Recalling previous visits to the tourist-heavy Bamberg, we pictured the Bamberger Biertage as a happy, chaotic scene with scores of people. However, after passing one closed shop after another, a ghost town is the best way to describe Bamberg on this particular day. The haunting fear of closed breweries on a bank holiday returned.

When we reached the site of the festivities, rows and rows of unoccupied tables filled the area. Buttoned up tight, booths from each Bamberg brewery circled the seating area. A sign informed us that the festival started at 4:00 P.M., four hours away. A woman stood in the lone open booth selling festival souvenirs, including bottles of beer. On the way home from our last visit to Bamberg, several bottles of Greifenklau had broken in our bag. Now we had the chance to replace the beer and finally bring it to our friends back home to taste. When we made our purchase, the woman made it very clear through her hand signals and tone that we were not allowed to drink it there. We assured her of our intention to leave. Beer travel sometimes comes with unexpected surprises from fortuitous timing, but also disappointments from near miss opportunities. We'd have to save Bamberger Biertage for another trip.

We made one more stop before calling it a day and visited the Alte Klosterbrauerei (also known as Brauerei Trunk), a secularly owned brewery on the grounds of the monastery at the Basilica of the Vierzehnheiligen (the Fourteen Holy Helpers).

From the parking lot, we made the long hike up the hill, passing through a gauntlet of shops selling every manner of religious object. We paid little attention to the ornate monastery buildings on our left and continued up to the beer garden. Filled with all the people we expected in Bamberg, older couples and young families sat at tables enjoying beer and the view. The warm air combined with the sounds of gentle chatter and birds chirping created a peaceful atmosphere. With the Year in Beer portion of our trip nearing completion, this was our last day of calm. After a night in the final brauerei hotel of the trip, the following few days would offer little in the way of tranquility: three Flogging Molly shows in three days in three different cities.

Chris had estimated a three-hour drive to Cologne to meet Ute and Wolfgang on Tuesday. Unfortunately, construction traffic on the A3 slowed our forward progress and sent us on a multitude of detours. The journey took us twice as long as anticipated.

After six hours in the car, it thrilled us to finally reach the city. However, the ordeal wasn't over. With roadwork on the city thoroughfares, numerous one-way streets, and an inaccurate map, another hour passed before we located the office to return the rental car and met up with our friends. No longer on the road less traveled, our stress levels rose. A visit to Früh am Dom to drink some Kölsch was in order.

Kölsch, the specialty beer of Cologne, is a refreshing straw-colored filtered brew. Served in distinctive small glasses, the name Kölsch is protected as a regional appellation similar to Champagne. One of the oldest and best known of the Cologne breweries is Früh am Dom. Located in the shadow of the imposing dual spires of the Cologne Cathedral, it's one of our favorite places to drink beer and is always our first stop when visiting the city.

Beer service in Cologne is swift and frequent, which suited our frayed nerves perfectly. Anxious to get beer and food, we sat ourselves down at the closest available outside table. We knew that Ute and Wolfgang's friend Tina, a fellow Flogging Molly fan, was going to be joining us and I looked forward to meeting someone new in Germany. But one by one the party grew into a spirited table of eight as more of their friends arrived. As the organizer of the European Flogging Molly fan club, Ute knows a lot of people. Everyone in European Flogging Molly circles knows Ute and Wolfgang and no matter what Flogging Molly show they go to, there is bound to be an entourage surrounding them.

The waiter arrived at our table within minutes of sitting down and deftly served each person a beer. The round tray with a tall handle in the middle holds a dozen beers in holes perfectly sized for the tall, narrow seven-ounce glasses. It clanked each time he removed a full *stange* (as the Kölsch glasses are called). After he delivered a beer to everyone at the table, he ticked Chris's beer mat eight times, the method used to track the number of beers served at a table.

Chris boasted that he could finish his glass in two gulps. Like a scene from *Name That Tune*, Wolfie quickly challenged Chris's statement. "I can do it in one," he said. Neither one of them lived up to their claim, but both came close.

With the waiter constantly weaving his way through the tables, the time lapse between an empty glass and a freshly tapped beer was minimal. I ordered *Schweinshaxe* (pork knuckle) to add the final boost I needed to fully recover from our driving ordeal. The large hunk of bone-in meat appears gluttonous and suitable for a medieval banquet table. It's one of the most delicious things I have ever tasted. Like a surgeon, I carefully removed the meat while our waiter replaced the empty glasses around the table. The agony of getting to Cologne was now long gone.

Dozens of ticks later, beer mats atop our empty glasses signaled that our table was finished and ready to cash out. The waiter came back around, counted the number of ticks and totaled up the bill. All paid up, it was time to walk to the concert.

It was the first time we had attended a Flogging Molly show in Europe and the enthusiasm of the crowd far exceeded what we had ever experienced in the United States. After a marathon night of loud music, refreshing beer, and good friends, we returned to our hotel at 1 o'clock in the morning. Five hours later, we were on the train to the airport for our flight to Munich.

Together with Ute, Wolfie and their friend Tina, we arrived in Munich. Airbräu—Munich airport's brewpub—provided us the opportunity to engage in the international remedy for recovering from a long night: more beer. We drank a quick round in the beer garden before boarding the S-Bahn into the city center.

Along the way I tired to make small talk with Tina. I spoke in short, simple sentences, as Tina had denied knowing English very well. As I was to find out later, she was shy. Once she felt comfortable with us, she was as chatty as the rest of us and her English was excellent.

Just under an hour later, we emerged from the underground train at the Marienplatz—the central square in Munich's city center. Much to the amusement of our group, Chris and I had logged more time in Munich than the native countrymen who accompanied us. As such, we all voted Chris the lead navigator during our excursion through the city. Wolfie would later praise Chris as an excellent Munich tour guide. Although he also admitted that he had never been on a tour in Munich.

Three times a day, hordes of tourists gather in the Marienplatz in front of the 19th Century gothic Neues Rathaus (New Town Hall) to watch and listen to the Glockenspiel (or corillon); something Chris and I had done numerous times before. Instead of guiding us towards one of Munich's most popular tourist attractions, however, Chris led us in the opposite direction to the Weisses Bräuhaus, the Schneider Weisse beer hall.

At Weisses Bräuhaus, the beer to order is not the large liter mugs of filtered brew, but rather tall glasses of cloudy, unfiltered hefeweizen. Although the light-colored building with dark windows has been a brewery for nearly 500 years, G. Schneider & Sohn Brewery wasn't established until 1872. The importance of this brewery in brewing history is that it revived the declining style of wheat beer.

Inside, Weisses Bräuhaus is a classic Bavarian beer hall with long dark wooden tables. At peak times, the noise level in the large open room can be deafening and the amount of people daunting for even the bravest of tourists. It's definitely not a place for the timid and a successful visit requires a certain degree of confidence.

When we first started visiting Germany, the abrupt no-nonsense manner of the wait staff put me off. I found the Weisses Bräuhaus waitresses especially scary. Often robust older women, they expect efficiency in ordering and pay little mind to those who hesitate. It's not unheard of for them to promptly walk away if a customer takes too long to order. In a packed beer hall, a botched attempt could mean a half hour before the opportunity to order came around again. Needless to say, visits to Weisses Bräuhaus filled me with anxiety. In past fits of nervousness, I was known to blurt out my go-to order, *Bratwurst mit Kartoffelsalat* (bratwurst with potato salad), whether I really wanted it or not. Not only the easiest menu item to remember, it's also easy to pronounce.

By now I was getting used to Ute and Wolfgang's friends joining us wherever we stopped and at Weisses Bräuhaus we met Felix, a 19-year old student living in Frankfurt and an avid Flogging Molly fan. Now that four Germans accompanied us, I was interested to see if our service would be any different.

At times, Wolfie can project that old-style German attitude: blunt, efficient, and stern-faced. In fervent anticipation, Chris predicted a showdown between Wolfie and the waitress. Much to my disappointment, however, our young waitress provided friendly, patient service. My whole story of woe and fear disintegrated. Sunshine and a beer garden is a great lifter of spirits—even for the Weisses Bräuhaus waitresses. Now accustomed to the service in German beer halls, and Weisses Bräuhaus in particular, the experience is less stressful.

The second stop on the Chris Nelson Munich Beer Tour was the Hofbräuhaus. At night and on weekends, it overflows with tourists seeking a rowdy beer hall experience. Here the iconic liters of helles abound and the dull clank of mugs rings throughout. On a sunny weekday afternoon, however, the tree-shaded beer garden offers a pleasant atmosphere to drink beer and chat with friends.

At the Hofbräuhaus we got a chance to talk more with Felix. He told us about plans to travel abroad to work when he finished school. He conversed easily and similar to Tina, spoke nearly flawless English. Felix's youth (he was half our age) and enthusiasm was invigorating. Before we knew it an hour had passed and it was time to walk to the venue for our next Flogging Molly show.

As a band, Flogging Molly is very accessible and several of the seven band members are known to hang out with fans before and after shows, especially when they're touring abroad. With the convenience of a beer garden attached to the venue, it goes without saying that the liters flowed freely before the show.

The mood was jubilant at the several tables filled with fans and band members. In Germany, Flogging Molly fans—usually teenagers and young people—loved interacting with the musicians they listened to incessantly on their iPods. No matter their level of English, fans chatted excitedly with Bob Schmidt, the mandolin/banjo player, as he snacked on a soft pretzel. The younger, more outgoing fans approached bass player Nate Maxwell, as he seemed to relate best to them. The more mature, subdued fans liked talking to Matt Hensley, who plays the accordion. In their own personalities, each band member received the fans with appreciation and a genuine interest in getting to know each one individually. Eventually Bob, Nate, and Matt left to prepare for the show and the revelry moved inside.

At the end of the concert, festivities in the beer garden revved up again. It was the second show of our mini-tour and our second late night.

The next morning we said good-bye to Tina while Ute, Wolfie, Chris and I continued on a train bound for Vienna, Austria. Felix, who was scheduled on a different train, would meet up with us again in Vienna. Our second country of the trip, Austria was also the last stop on our Flogging Molly tour. We all looked forward to the four-hour train ride, as it gave us an opportunity to get more sleep.

Following a band on tour is hard work. Hippies followed the Grateful Dead around for months at a time without problem, but in just a few days, my exhaustion manifested in laryngitis. Full nights of drinking beer and talking in loud, crowded atmospheres, combined with a lack of sleep was to blame. No more filming for *beergeek.TV.* The star had lost her voice.

We stayed in Vienna for a brief 24-hours, which isn't exactly enough time to see all the sites. However, it was enough time to visit two new breweries and eat *Wiener Schnitzl* in its namesake city. Ute guided us on a quick walk past the Spanish Riding School—the home to the famous Lipizzaner stallions—and the medieval castle Hofburg before going to our first Viennese brewpub, 1516.

Several more of Ute's friends, including Felix, joined us at 1516. My inability to project any sound above a squeak prevented me from participating in conversation with my new companions. On the plus side, they were spared the uncomfortableness of any beer-induced babbling. Drinking beer was all I had left. Well, that and the hope that the last of our Flogging Molly shows might relieve me of the frustration and boredom that stemmed from not having a voice.

A converted slaughterhouse, the location of the last Flogging Molly show exuded urban chic. The Open Air Venue—as it was so creatively named—included several buildings with five stages and multiple bars. A large grassy knoll spread out like a picnic blanket in front of the main outdoor stage. Tall, graffiti-covered walls surrounded the entire complex.

In no time, the sparse crowd that milled around the grass transformed into a still mob of people anxiously waiting in front of the stage. Once the music started, the mob became a swirling mass of controlled chaos. In other words, it became just another rowdy punk show.

We survived another night of great music and beer drinking to visit our second brewpub, 7 Stern Bräu, the next day. Our group tried to be lively, but traveling over 1,000 miles to watch three Flogging Molly Shows on very little sleep had taken its toll. The table was nearly silent as we quietly added 7 Stern Bräu to The List. Later that afternoon we parted ways with Felix. Ute, Wolfgang, Chris and I dragged our tired bodies to the airport to go home.

We arrived at Frankfurt airport and engaged in our goodbye ritual: a Bittburger at Terminal 2's bar. The taste of the English Ivy throat lozenges from the Viennese pharmacy that I had been sucking on since losing my voice conflicted sharply with the beer. Fatigue all around, the four of us hardly spoke. What little I did say could barely be heard anyway. Forty-five minutes later, hugs and "auf wiedersehens" were exchanged. Ute and Wolfie boarded a regional train back to Mannheim and we caught the shuttle to our hotel.

Within the hour, we were carefully maneuvering around the bed in our tiny hotel room. There was barely enough floor space for our bags and the scene became a comedy sketch as we tried to move around the room at the same time. Chris eventually settled at the desk to check his email before crawling into bed. With him out of the way, I completed the final, most important task of the trip: packing the beer we had gathered along the way.

On the floor surrounded by bubble wrap, plastic bags and dirty clothes, I sorted the beer into two piles, one for Chris's bag and one for mine. I smiled as I thought about how children distribute candy. One for you, two for me. Two for you, four for me. However, in this case, even distribution between the bags served two important purposes. One, it minimized the damage of a lost or destroyed bag because no one kind of beer was completely wiped out. Two, it helped to balance the weight of the bags, hopefully avoiding the charge for an overweight piece of checked baggage.

For thirty minutes I prepared the bottles for transport. Exhausted from the trip and feeling the pressure to get every bottle home safely, I started to sweat. It wasn't until the last bottle was packed away that I exhaled with relief. Chris, who had already fallen asleep, woke up long enough to put his book on the nightstand and tell me to come to bed.

Lying down, my nerves started to calm and the sound of my heart beating in my chest quieted. Thoughts of returning to our regular lives filled my head and a mixture of sadness and relief rippled through my body. Beer adventures are eventful and exciting, but the familiarity of one's own bed is peaceful and relaxing. Little dogs curled up at your side under the covers are very comforting, indeed. Home is the place to be.

I returned without a voice, but filled with memories of a great trip. I liked the idea that we engaged in atypical activities on our travels and that we dared to take the road less tourist traveled. Telling people stories about a beer festival they may not have known existed helped me to not only relive fun times, but it also gave me something to share with others. It dawned on me that *this* was our contribution to the craft beer community—to introduce people to new beer adventures and encourage them to create their own. Our May trip to Germany revealed what we had to offer and I took comfort in it. Satisfied with my self-discovery, sleep came quickly. The next morning, we headed home.

JUNE

DRINK OUTSIDE THE BOX

"Did you pack your umbrella?" Chris yelled from the living room.

"Yes," I yelled back.

"And your raincoat?"

Yes, mother…

It's hard to admit, but Chris's reminders did actually help because, more often than not, I either forgot to pack something or I failed to plan properly for the weather. As a result, I developed a checklist which included the mantra "meds, money, passport," —as long as I had those, I could survive anywhere and under any conditions. That being said, bringing the right clothes made one less topic for me to complain about, which benefited everyone. But this was Ireland, where two things are always guaranteed: rain and Guinness.

Ireland is one of our favorite places to drink beer and we've returned to the Emerald Isle numerous times since our first visit to Dublin in 1998. Our sentimental fondness for Ireland has developed not only because it was our inaugural trip across the Atlantic Ocean, but also because it's where we experienced the "aha!" moment that forever changed our philosophy about beer drinking.

It was late December when we tasted our very first sip of Guinness in a Dublin pub. With both the rain and a bitterly cold wind blowing outside, the warmth and coziness of the pub was especially comforting. It all seemed so quintessentially Ireland and from that experience we realized the importance of drinking beer within its own context. Nowhere else in the world could drinking a Guinness inspire such an emotional reaction. It is a profound encounter that every visitor, beer lover or not, should experience.

When it came to scheduling the Year in Beer, we knew that Ireland had to be included. The winter months had already been decided, so re-living that first experience was not an option. June was available and Ireland is a wonderful place to be during the summer solstice because it remains light out late into the night. Needless to say, very little discussion was needed to decide where Ireland fit into the Year in Beer.

As we've returned to Ireland year after year, we've started to long for a new experience. Craft beer made its first appearance in Ireland in the mid 1990s and has been growing ever since. The option of having an authentically Irish, non-Guinness beer experience is now easier than ever. Without an event to attend or friends to see, we felt we needed a theme for our trip to Ireland. So, we planned to drink outside the box by seeking out Irish craft beer wherever possible.

Chris was further inspired by a discussion on the Irish Craft Brewer website (now called *Beoir.org*) where he had learned that in some parts of Ireland, Guinness is served in room temperature pint bottles. Several people in the discussion believed "a bottle off the shelf" to be the true original way to drink Guinness. Uncertain as to how many pubs would serve Guinness in this manner, Chris welcomed the challenge. He planned to venture outside the norm and attempt to avoid draught Guinness as much as possible on the trip. I, on the other hand, had no intention of drinking outside that box or from any bottle.

We took the first flight of the day out of Monterey and headed to Los Angeles. From there, we'd catch an early flight to Chicago before taking a third and final leg to Dublin. Still half asleep when we boarded in L.A., the safety instructions passed in one ear and out the other. Most passengers scarcely pay attention to the pre-flight safety instructions anyway, let alone anything the pilot has to say once in the air. Some pilots drone on and on in a monotone voice about flight patterns, velocity and headwinds. Other times the pilot's announcement is so garbled you can't understand a word he says. All I, and every other passenger, really want to know is our estimated time of arrival and if turbulence is expected.

Chris and I try not to be too disgruntled when it comes to the trials and tribulations of travel. We earn vagabond karma credit that way. What goes around comes around.

For example, on Christmas Eve 2007, as we attempted to return home from Dublin, karma gave us our biggest reward yet. We arrived at the airport to discover that our flight to Chicago was delayed. This meant missing our connection to Los Angeles and, in turn, our flight to Monterey. Dublin airport is a zoo anyway, but the additional confusion of a 767-load of people trying to make alternative flight arrangements creates absolute bedlam.

The agent who assisted us offered an itinerary that departed Dublin several days later. We politely explained our desire to get home for Christmas. We then tried to suggest other nearby airports in California to which we could fly. The agent failed to grasp both our interest in spending Christmas with our family and our final destination suggestions, so we finally gave up and accepted the itinerary she gave us. We then immediately sought the assistance of a supervisor at the help desk. That's when we met Oliver.

Not only did Oliver understand that we wanted to get home, he also understood the options of flying into a neighboring airport. He spent close to an hour with us and when all was said and done, we were booked on a flight to San Jose where our nephew agreed to pick us up. In an incredible act of customer service, he even went below to the baggage handling area to re-tag our bags. Oliver really made our day.

It didn't end there, however. At the departure gate, Oliver found us and we thanked him again for helping us get home for Christmas. Much to our surprise, he handed us two business class tickets for the flight. It was the best Christmas present ever! We never forgot Oliver's generosity and to this day, we look for him each time we fly to Dublin. We also hope for a repeat windfall, but so far no luck. Maybe we spent our karmic allowance and haven't earned enough for another reward.

Of course we thought of Oliver when we packed for June's trip to Ireland. Chris wanted to take him a token of our appreciation, a bottle from our neighbor's winery. When we exited the plane in Dublin, the familiar round face greeted passengers on the tarmac. After a quick reminder to Oliver who we were, we told him a bottle of California wine was packed in our bag, a gift for his incredible customer service.

"Oh you have not," he said in a lilting Irish accent. That's when I got the first of many hugs from Oliver. A jolly round fellow, Oliver possesses the right disposition for managing an extremely difficult job. Herding flies would be easier than working as an airline supervisor at Dublin Airport. Security regulations prevented us from having the bottle of wine in our carry-on bag, so it was safely packed away in our checked luggage. We promised Oliver the wine on our way out of the country.

We survived baggage claim, customs and passport control and made our way to the rental car lot. Jetlag had diminished our problem-solving skills and we spent fifteen minutes trying to get the trunk of the car open. An embarrassing predicament to be in, seeking out the attendant's help would just be too much, but after Chris's agitated directive to ask, I did.

"To open the boot, you push the blah, blah, blah," the attendant instructed me.

I walked back to Chris. "Well?" he asked.

"I'm not really sure. I couldn't understand his accent," I answered. "But he called it a 'boot'." I giggled.

A few more minutes of fiddling based on what I thought the attendant's instructions were and the trunk popped open. Chris skillfully packed our baggage in the compact trunk and we hit the ground running or more precisely, driving. Landing at Dublin Airport at 9:00 A.M., forty-five minutes later we arrived at the gravesite of Arthur Guinness, the founding father of Guinness Brewery.

The previous week, Chris had finished a book on the history of the Guinness Brewery by Bill Yenne called *Guinness: The 250-Year Quest for the Perfect Pint*. In talking about the death of Arthur Guinness, the book vaguely mentioned his burial site. With a bit of research, Chris located the cemetery in County Kildare just outside of Dublin. He thought a visit to Arthur's gravesite would be the perfect way to start our trip. Armed with the name of the town and cemetery, Chris located its proximity on a map.

A navigational miscalculation resulted in us getting off at the wrong exit, which frustrated both of us. Tired and in need of a shower, the idea of driving around in circles lacked appeal. We backtracked down a narrow lane and I kept a keen eye out for the cemetery. Curiously, the resting place of one of the most well known Irishmen in history is not sign-posted.

"There it is!" I exclaimed. Difficult to notice, the entrance to the cemetery was set back from the road between two residences.

We parked the car a few doors down and walked thirty yards back toward the driveway. Focused on the wrought iron gate that identified Oughterard Cemetery in gold lettering, an older woman pinning laundry on a clothesline startled us. The exchange of morning pleasantries slowed our mission to visit Arthur Guinness's grave for only a moment, though, and soon we were squeezing through the small livestock-proof side of the wide gate. Up the gravel road, the cemetery sat on a hill.

Approximately 120 square feet, Oughterard Cemetery contains graves, as well as the remains of a round tower and burial vault that stand tall above the stone wall boundary. We had no information regarding where within the cemetery we might locate Arthur Guinness's resting place, but luckily, the small area made a random search feasible. With deep dips and large mounds, the cemetery was far from flat. Up and down, I wandered among the waves of green grass, weaving past both modern marble headstones of the recently departed and tilting slabs marking the graves of people who died hundreds of years ago. Names like O'Malley, Meaney, and Read were chiseled on headstones, but the name of Guinness was nowhere to be seen.

Initially I assumed that the large stone vault was the remains of a medieval church. But after making a thorough search of the cemetery grounds and not finding what we came for, I decided to step down into the roofless structure to take a look.

"I found it!" I hollered, breaking the silence of the countryside. Score two for Merideth. First the cemetery then the gravesite itself. I mentally high-fived myself.

Chris joined me and together we examined the three-foot high gravestone built into the right hand wall. I fiddled with my hair, trying to minimize my just-off-the-plane appearance and look more presentable for filming the introduction to the *beergeek.TV* episode. While Chris prepared the camera, dialogue ran through my head.

"There's probably only one name more famous in Ireland than St. Patrick," I started, "and that's Arthur Guinness. We're here at his gravesite to kick off June's episode of the Year in Beer. Welcome to summer solstice in Ireland."

After an off-camera nod to Arthur and a request for his blessing of a good trip, our June adventure began.

We hopped back on the road toward Roscommon, home to the Galway Hooker Brewery and the town where we'd spend our first night in Ireland. We had been introduced to Galway Hooker Irish Pale Ale six months earlier at the Bull & Castle, a gastro pub in Dublin. The Sierra Nevada-inspired pale ale had blown us away. In a country dominated by a single brewing company, to imbibe craft beer was to truly drink outside the box. With this trip focused primarily on Irish craft beer, a visit to Galway Hooker took high priority. Prior to leaving, Chris had arranged a brewery visit with Aidan Murphy, one of the two co-owners/brewers. A welcoming host, Aidan agreed to interrupt his brew day for our visit.

At the industrial park location, Aidan offered a warm greeting as he invited us into the storage unit-sized brewery. Like his beer, Aidan seemed to be California-inspired. With his rosy cheeks and unpretentious attitude, he nodded his head in approval as we explained the Year in Beer and our aim to drink Irish craft beer on the trip.

"Wow!" Aidan said. "That's really kewl."

His Irish-accented pronunciation of the word 'cool' made him appear all the more boy-like and endearing.

Aidan led the way past the conditioning tanks to the brewery. The floor was wet, making it necessary for us to skip across pools of water. Aidan, on the other hand, easily sloshed around in his rubber boots. The lighting from above reflected off the brewing vessels, but with few people seeing the brewery, there was no need to polish the copper to sparkling clean.

He poured us a pair of full pints of the Irish Pale Ale (the only beer they produced at the time) right out of the conditioning tank. Not quite ready, the under-carbonated brew possessed all the flavor of the finished product. Conversation with Aidan required little prompting on our part, which allowed us to sip away at our beers. While rolling up thick hoses, Aidan chatted effortlessly about American craft beer and its influence on his own country's brewing. Aidan said that he planned to attend the Great British Beer Festival in August, so we told him that we would look for him.

After our quick half-hour visit, Aidan apologized for not having more time and sent us off with two Galway Hooker pint glasses. As a thank you for his time, we left him with the second bottle of wine we had packed. It may seem odd to give a brewer a bottle of wine, but unlike us, almost every beer person we know also enjoys the grape-based beverage. We departed the industrial park for our Bed and Breakfast in Roscommon town.

Saturday morning, we headed two hours southwest to Doolin, a coastal village on the coast of County Clare. We especially enjoy Western Ireland and Doolin is one of our favorite places to go. Although, getting there can sometimes be a challenge.

The roads in Western Ireland are little more than country lanes with no shoulders. Even with the occasional threat of livestock blocking the road, drivers come barreling down like they were on the autobahn. As the driver, Chris is closest to the cars passing in the other direction. Imagine the nerve-racking sight of a lorry that shows no sign of slowing down coming straight at you on a road that seemingly won't fit two cars side-by-side. It's a moment of truth that gets the heart racing, adrenaline rushing, and the instinct to swerve to the left kicking in. However, this brings me to the harrowing experience of being a passenger on an Irish road. It's terrifying to be literally inches away from the stone walls that often line the roads. Over the years, I have learned to tuck in the side mirror and look straight ahead, so as not to get freaked out by the lack of available wiggle room along the side. While these things have been helpful, there remains the issue of hearing the thorny brambles scrape the side of the door. It's like fingernails on a chalkboard, only more dangerous and potentially deadly.

In spite of these brief moments of terror, driving in Western Ireland is a breathtaking experience. In between the quintessential Irish towns and villages, the area includes beautiful stretches of coastline, green pastures with white sheep, and vast fields of craggy landscape. Doolin, like the area as a whole, offers all of those things.

A well-known travel show host once called Doolin "touristy." It's true. Commonly considered the capital of traditional music in Ireland, Doolin attracts a steady stream of tourists each year. It's also a launching point for ferries to the Aran Islands, a set of three starkly rugged limestone islands that are steeped in history going back thousands of years. Rather than being touristy, however, Doolin to us is an international gathering place where backpackers, cyclists, and older visitors all come together to enjoy the scenery, clap along to Irish music and of course, drink Guinness.

Doolin is a fishing village with around 200 residents and three traditional pubs, each of which serves Guinness on nitrogen. I like it this way, as do many others. What most people don't know is that this signature serving style is a thoroughly modern dispensing method that was launched in 1964 to boost slumping sales.

According to the book Chris had recently read on the history of Guinness, during the 1950s, half the Guinness sold in Ireland was on draught. However, in the United Kingdom, sales were primarily in bottles and represented only 5% market share. With lagers gaining popularity, Guinness sought to increase draught sales outside of Ireland. However, up until the late 1950s Guinness on draught was poured by mixing beer from two casks—one above the bar and one below. Pouring a proper pint required a skillful bartender and maintaining consistency and quality while expanding was going to be tricky. The process they eventually developed was a two-gas system that dispensed the beer from one metal keg using a mixture of carbon dioxide and nitrogen. Achieving the perfect blend of gases created the thick, creamy head that gives Guinness the aesthetic appeal we see today.

That evening, we started out at Gus O'Connor's, the most popular pub in Doolin and our sentimental favorite. Without the option of a craft beer, Chris took his first crack at ordering a bottle of Guinness off the shelf. His request took the bartender by surprise and required her to break from the usual routine of pulling pint after pint of Ireland's famous brew. She left the set of taps, went into a small back room behind the bar, and returned with a large bottle and a glass. As Chris served himself, I patiently waited for my smooth, nitrogen-infused pint. Poured from the tap in stages, it's a process that takes several minutes to complete.

That night we intended to play Scrabble, down a few pints, and enjoy the European Football Championship match between Russia and the Netherlands. However, Gus O'Connor's would not be showing the match because the manager thought it would interfere with the dinner crowd. The bartender suggested we try McDermott's, located in the "upper village" about a 15-minute walk away.

We ventured out into the unsettled weather and down the road. A winter-type storm had hit the area earlier in the day and still lingered into the evening. Gale-force winds blew almost the entire day and during the occasional cloudbursts, the rain came down in proverbial buckets.

We arrived at McDermott's windblown, but dry to a standing room-only crowd of football enthusiasts. After weaving our way around the pub, we joined a couple from the Czech Republic at a large table.

When the game was over, we managed to leave McDermott's in between cloudbursts and arrived back at our room minutes before an earth-shaking downpour, accompanied by thunder and lightening. Just one month ago, I sat in the Bavarian sun drinking a refreshing German lager. Now, we were experiencing the damp isle of dark, robust stout. Several locals had told us that the storm was the worst they'd ever seen.

Throughout the night, heavy rains brutalized the area with even more intensity. The storm not only kept us awake, it washed anything and everything down hill, including into a gift shop unfortunate enough to be located at the base of a small slope. Filled with several feet of water and mud, the next morning the fire brigade worked to pump the place out. The shop was still closed when we left Doolin a few days later.

At breakfast on Sunday an Irish guide aimed to quell the fears of her American group. She assured them that the ferry ride out to the Aran Islands would not be too rough and they could put their worries to rest. She compared it to a bumpy car ride.

That was the biggest understatement I had ever heard. Chris and I once took a ride out to the Aran Islands in weather that paled in comparison to the current storm. Even then, the boat had rocked from side to side and up and down. I don't get seasick, but on that day I was as close as I have ever been.

Staying firmly planted on land, we braved the weather and drove thirty-minutes to Biddy Early Brewery in Inagh. Our Biddy Early experiences were hit or miss at best, so we set off with a wait-and-see attitude. Our first trip to the area since the start of *beergeek.TV*, we needed footage to include in the next episode.

Our inaugural visit to Biddy Early occurred during our second visit to Ireland in 1999. Without a car, we spent twenty Irish pounds (approximately $30 at the time) each way on a cab ride from Ennis, a distance of only 14 kilometers. At the time, Inagh—a crossroads village on a well-traveled route between Ennistymon and Ennis—consisted mostly of two buildings, Biddy Early and a small convenience store/gas station/post office. We took one sip of the house beer and immediately asked the bartender to call us a cab back to Ennis. It tasted awful. The limited number of customers in the pub at that moment combined with the slow response of the cab made the whole experience very awkward. No crowd meant our presence (and dislike for the beer) was highly conspicuous. In the forty-five minutes we were there (a majority of which was wait time for the cab's return), we downed maybe one-fourth of our pints and the only reason we even drank that much was because of all the nervous sips we took trying to assuage our discomfort.

We dashed out the pub door the minute we saw the cab pull up, leaving two almost full pints on the bar.

Years later, we mentioned this experience to some fellow patrons in Dublin's Porterhouse Brewing Company. They knew the brewer and insisted that we give the brewery another chance. We did, and enjoyed the beer much better the second time around.

On yet another trip, we stopped in for a quick beer and noticed a hand-written sign taped to the wall. "Tomorrow 3 P.M. Taoiseach Bertie Ahern here." Excited, Chris and I planned to return the next day to catch a glimpse of the Irish politician. The Taoiseach (pronounced 'tea-shock') is equivalent to a Prime Minister. We roughly knew the job of a Taoiseach, even though pronouncing the title completely escaped us.

We returned the next day to discover that the sign had been written the day prior to our seeing it. The previous day, we left the pub around 2 P.M., an hour short of Bertie's arrival. The bartender handed us a local paper with a picture of Bertie pulling a pint. A fine tasting Biddy Early beer helped drown our frustration and disappointment on that visit.

"Fourth time's a charm," I told Chris during the drive over.

"We'll see," he replied. "Get your jazz hands on because we need to film here."

A little on the tired side, I needed the energy of what Chris and I call "jazz hands." A reference to the movie *Showgirls*, it's our way of gathering energy for spirited on-camera delivery. Chris often reminds me to have jazz hands before he turns on the camera. Any thoughts of the delightfully bad movie that won seven Razzie Awards and inspired a drinking game make us burst into laughter. The intonation of Chris's voice and his dramatic hand gestures crack me up every time, effectively giving me the requested level of enthusiasm.

As we arrived in Inagh, Chris and I were surprised to see how much it had grown. A decent-sized parking lot was now situated across the street from the pub and the convenience store/gas station/post office had separated into three distinct businesses.

We entered Biddy Early to find three lads drinking at the bar. Their beverages of choice should have been our first clue to the calamity waiting to unfold: a glass of Bailey's, a can of Heineken, and a bottle of Bud poured into a glass with a straw. Besides them, a few occupied tables in the restaurant area rounded out the daytime crowd. We drank our pints near the turf-burning stove and took some time to get a feel for the atmosphere. Actually, the relative quiet of the pub made for prime filming, but after a few minutes observing the young men at the bar, I feared that the sight of a video camera might invite their attention. I had little interest in engaging with them in conversation.

We drank our pints and watched and waited, hoping they would leave soon so filming could begin. Bereft of meaningful conversation, they listened to sound bites and music on their phone. One clip sounded pornographic, which made us wonder about the recording's origin as it played over and over. But the thrill of orgasmic moaning soon wore off and they moved on to their next sound. We listened to "Eye of the Tiger" for what felt like a hundred times or more. "It's the eye of the tiger, it's the thrill of the fight, da da da something of our rival." If I thought about what Hell might sound like, an endless loop of that song could easily be it. Once the chorus sticks in your head, it never lets go. Getting it out of your head is about as painful and frustrating as separating fingers stuck together with Crazy Glue.

Initially entertained by the antics of the three lads, irritation and annoyance ultimately set in. As if the situation hadn't gone far enough downhill, the straw sucking Bud drinker decided to dunk bread in his beer and eat it. He followed this with the use of air freshener as both a deodorant and a breath freshener then spent the next twenty minutes furiously wiping his tongue trying to get the taste out of his mouth. That was actually funny. At that point, hope for their exit so we could film still existed, but in the end, we surrendered. They won and we left. "It's the eye of the tiger, it's the thrill of the fight…"

The lack of footage meant Biddy Early's absence from the episode, which was probably for the best because the beer tasted a little off. The brewery had been for sale for over a year and we wondered if the owner had lost interest altogether.[16]

That night, Chris devised a brilliant solution to our lack of footage for the episode. His idea also addressed feedback we frequently received about *One Pint at a Time*. Chris, who on camera possesses the emotional range of Mr. Spock, generally presented as stiff in the episodes. His answer? Kiss the Blarney Stone and gain the gift of gab. We had engaged in this centuries-old tradition many years before, but Chris obviously required a booster lip lock with the stone. He decided to stop at Blarney Castle the next day and sacrifice his dignity by engaging in one of the most touristy things to be done in Ireland.

Monday's weather remained unstable throughout the three-hour drive south to Blarney. Light rain followed us with peri-

16 Shortly after our visit, Biddy Early stopped brewing. It's now the Biddy Early Pub.

odic heavy downpours, but mostly the skies were just cloudy. Luckily, the rain held off throughout our visit to Blarney Castle, including filming Chris's explanation for why we were there.

"I realize that I'm sometimes less than articulate on the videos," Chris started, "and I've decided to maybe try to fix that. I'm calling on a higher power now to help me be a little more talkative."

Chris and I marched straight to the top of the castle to the famed bluestone. We waited in line behind a dozen others for our turn to kiss it. I went first. As I sat down, an elderly gentleman in an Irish cap held me around the back and guided me in bending backwards to the stone. As he did so, he quipped, "We know how she kisses at night, but how about during the day?" The waiting crowd chuckled.

Chris went next. "And down and down and down," the man said, "and a kiss there. Easy coming up and there you go." He gently moved Chris along and immediately turned to the next person.

Prior to the assistance of safety bars and a cheeky old guy, a person literally risked their life to kiss the stone. Apparently one had to be dangled by the ankles to reach their lips to the stone. Now, there is little risk, save the occasional grope.

When the deed was done, I turned to Chris with the camera running.

"I feel a lot more talkative now. I just don't have anything to say, so let's get going," Chris said. A woman nearby giggled.

"Maybe it takes a little bit to kick in," I responded.

As we continued on our journey, the clouds disappeared to reveal a clear sky. It's said that Ireland has two seasons, rain and no rain, and we got both in two days. The improved weather dried out the soggy air and encouraged us to ramble leisurely along the coast. Sailboats gently rocked on the calm blue sea and the beautiful views made it difficult to resist stopping at vista points along the way. The bright day even offered us the opportunity to do something rarely available in Ireland: enjoy a beer outside in the sunshine.

We arrived in Cork City in the mid-afternoon and immediately headed to Franciscan Well, one of the original Irish craft breweries. We had first visited Cork City and Franciscan Well during our 1999 trip to Ireland and loved it. At that time, Irish craft brewing was young and our travel experience was limited. Now, craft brewing in Ireland had increased in strength and we were seasoned travelers. It interested us to know how things might look now.

Cork is a bustling city, but across the River Lee, where Franciscan Well is located, the surge of people relaxes and the pace slows. We followed along the North Mall of the river until we came across an archway with a large sign above that marked the entrance to the brewery. Set back from the street, we walked down the alley and turned into the dark pub. It looked more or less how we remembered, except for one addition: a beer garden. A slow time of day, there were few other customers. We ordered a Rebel Lager for me and a Friar Weisse Wheat for Chris from the bartender and walked out to the patio. In the bright light and fresh air of the beer garden, we enjoyed beer other than Guinness. Not the usual Ireland experience, the scene truly encapsulated the concept of drinking outside the box.

Our time at Franciscan Well invigorated us, a previous experience reinvented to feel fresh and new. People often wonder why we go to Ireland year after year. "Haven't you seen it all?" they ask. But the adventures we encounter in between visiting the familiar alter the way we experience that place in subsequent visits. On that day, we saw Irish beer culture in a whole new light. While our idea of drinking beer in Ireland had already begun to change, it was our experience in the beer garden that day that solidified our opinion that it didn't always have to entail a deeply flavored stout in the coziness of a traditional pub. The growing craft beer scene in Ireland created choices and it's certainly easier to see things in the natural light of the outdoors.

Content with rediscovering the old, we readied ourselves to explore the new. Further proof of Ireland's evolution out of the Stout Ages lay in our next stop: the Bierhaus, one in Ireland's growing trend of specialty beer bars. Chris had exchanged emails with the owner, Dave O'Leary, prior to our visit. Despite his awareness of our impending arrival, Dave greeted us in a quiet, reserved way. We quickly realized, however, that Dave's low-key demeanor should not to be confused for a lack of hospitality.

The Bierhaus reflects Dave's personality in that it possesses a humble character, one that appeals to locals aiming to escape the city center. It boasts an impressive array of international beers, including a banana beer served in a plastic half coconut shell. Staying true to our mission, however, I opted for Carlow Brewing's O'Hara's Stout. We sat at the bar enjoying our beer while observing the locals.

The Bierhaus Bierfest, a summertime celebration of beer, had taken place over the previous weekend and, as Dave explained, business was slow because the regulars were home still nursing their aching heads.

A man with a Slovak accent popped in to show off his pictures from the weekend's festivities. Dave allowed him to present his slideshow on the flat screen TV hanging on the far wall. A group of young men gathered around. Picture after picture formed an endless parade of smiling tipsy faces. It looked like we had missed one heck of a party. At the end of the entertainment, the men moved on to a game of Wii bowling and we brought out the Scrabble board.

Behind us, men animatedly flung their arms toward the TV screen. Their voices cheered or jeered the latest play. The frequent craning of our necks to watch the action greatly reduced our ability to concentrate on our own game. Noticing Chris's interest, the bowlers invited him to play. Chris politely declined. He hadn't consumed enough beers to overcome his shyness and accept the offer.

I regained focus on the Scrabble game and intently stared at my letters. Vocabulary words scrolled through my head and potential word scores were calculated. A familiar sound broke my concentration. "Whoop whoop. Whoop whoop." It was the red alert signal of the USS Enterprise from *Star Trek*. I turned around as a Wii bowler fished in his pocket for his cell phone. It was hardly surprising given that he wore a shirt adorned with the Starfleet insignia, something I had failed to notice before.

After a few beers at Bierhaus, we walked arm in arm back across the river to our hotel. Thanks to the summer solstice, at 11 P.M. the sky was barely on the dark side of dusky.

"I love that it's so light out," I said.

"That's why I wanted to come here in June," Chris replied.

Giving Chris a kiss on the cheek, I thought about the Blarney Stone and wondered how long it would take for the effects to kick in.

On Tuesday, the skies once again filled up with clouds and we dodged the rain while attempting to accomplish our main task for the day: tour the Beamish Brewery, producer of one of two stouts brewed in Cork City.

At the time of our visit, there was wide speculation that the brewery's days of operation were numbered, a tragic prospect that could end over four centuries of brewing history on the site located in the heart of Cork's medieval city.

Earlier in the year, Beamish's parent company, Scottish and Newcastle, was acquired by a joint effort between Heineken International and Carlsberg. In the deal, Heineken (which already owned Murphy's Irish Stout, the other beer brewed in Cork) would receive Beamish. During our visit to Cork, the Irish Competition Authority was in the process of reviewing whether or not it was a conflict of interest for Heineken to produce both stouts. Observers of the deal predicted that if the acquisition were approved, one of the two breweries would be closed. Heineken already had established operations at the Murphy's brewery, so any approval of the new merger meant a certain death for the Beamish Brewery. With so much riding on the outcome of the Irish Competition Authority's decision[17], we knew that this trip to Cork might possibly be the last opportunity we had to visit the Beamish Brewery.

The man at the gate advised us that Beamish no longer offered "tours," due to insurance reasons, but instead offered "visits," which consisted of a hosted audio-visual presentation in the hospitality room and beer tasting.

17 In December 2008 after six months of review, the Irish Competition Authority approved the deal. Within weeks of assuming operations, Heineken International announced that the Beamish Brewery would close.

When we returned to the gatehouse 30 minutes later, a handful of other visitors had gathered. Shortly thereafter, an older gentleman dressed in a black v-neck sweater greeted the group. "Okay, welcome everyone." he said. "Are you ready?"

A few excited people responded with a resounding, "Yes!" but most of us just nodded our heads.

"Please follow me. For safety reasons, you must stay within the marked area. No wandering off," he warned.

A red and white rope helped to keep us within the white lines painted on the asphalt of the yard. As we walked in a mostly single file line behind our host, people whispered in confusion about the need for such safety precautions. The yard was wide; no trucks were driving in the area and the overhead was clear of anything that might fall on us. Nonetheless, our host's instructions were heeded as we followed him to the basement-level hospitality room.

The group scattered as everyone took their seats at one of the numerous oak tables. To begin, our host played a ten-minute video telling us to be mindful that the area is a working brewery, which came with accompanying safety risks. "Visitors should avoid smoking in these areas as there are flammable materials nearby," it said. "Please use the ashtrays located at the designated smoking points."

When the video finished, Chris and I both thought that may have been the extent of the presentation, but then our host cued the next, more interesting video explaining the history of the Beamish Brewery.

There had been a brewery on the Beamish Brewery site since the early 1600s, with Beamish being founded nearly 200 years later in 1792. William Beamish and William Crawford purchased the site from an existing porter brewery and by 1805 their Cork Porter Brewery had become the largest in Ireland. A position it maintained until Guinness passed it in 1833.

Our host, a retired brewery employee, explained the brewing process and showed us jars of the different malts used in creating the deeply dark Beamish Stout. He added a personal note about the recent sale of the parent company. Nostalgia twinkled in his eye as he sadly expressed his hope that Heineken would keep the brewery in operation. He quickly rebounded, though, with a demonstration on how to pour a proper pint of Beamish. Then he let the group loose to pour our own pints—as many as we wanted.

"He said I poured the perfect pint," I told Chris. "But I think he said that to everybody."

"He didn't say it to me," Chris replied.

"But he said you could get a job in any pub in Ireland. That's as good as."

Chris downed two and a half pints before the end of the visit was announced. It was 10:30 A.M.

Our main task for the day accomplished, the agenda was now free. The sky looked iffy, but somewhat cooperative, so we decided to take the twenty-five minute train ride out to Cobh, a small seaport town. The site of several poignant moments in history, Cobh (pronounced "cove") was the last port of call for the *Titanic* and the town where survivors of the *Lusitania* sinking were taken. It had also served as the departure point for many Irish people immigrating to America during the Great Famine.

As the train barreled eastward, we watched as the sky darkened. The rain whipped the windows with wet streaks.

While we still hoped it would stop by the time we arrived, it was already clear that we'd lost the gamble to Mother Nature.

The weather had kept the tourists away and the small town was relatively empty. We tried to make the best of it, but in short order the steady wind and rain left us looking like drowned rats. We eventually gave up and retreated to a warm pub on the harbor front to wait for the next train back to Cork.

Later that night, we returned to The Bierhaus just in time for poker night. The Wii-playing Trekkie from the day before prepared the tables as hopeful poker players trickled in. The tension level in the room rose as players put on their game faces. One player arrived friendly enough in his jeans and a t-shirt that read "Poker, she'll like it." He sat down at a carefully chosen table and geared up. First he placed a baseball cap on his head backwards and adjusted it to get the desired fit. The smile he wore when he arrived slowly disappeared. He reached into his pocket for what was presumably his secret weapon: a pair of sunglasses. Lenses polished and frames securely resting on his face, his smile was now completely gone. The influence of one too many episodes of the *World Series of Poker* had clearly taken hold. The wearing of sunglasses just doesn't seem right. As a non-poker player, it shouldn't even matter to me, but in my opinion, it completely negates the meaning of "poker face." Anyone can look menacing and deceptive behind sunglasses.

Dave explained the house rules to us. If a player went bust within the first half hour, he had one chance to buy back into the game. Our *World Series of Poker* friend bought back in first. He may have been losing, but he looked cool doing it.

After two nights in Cork, our schedule had us on the move again, this time toward Carlow, a two-hour drive northeast. Along the way, I enjoyed watching the sheep grazing on the rolling green hills. It was easy to get lost in the idyllic scenery as I daydreamed about what it would be like to live in Ireland. Chris, on the other hand, kept his eyes glued to the road. Our drives between towns were decidedly less romantic and more stressful for Chris.

I had seen on the map an icon indicating a bird watching area. So an hour into the trip, we detoured toward the beach near Dungarvan. As we approached, the signs, which up to this point had been listed in both English and Gaelic, changed to Gaelic only. We had entered An Rinn, a small town with just a few thousand residents and a *Gaeltacht*.

Gaeltachts are officially recognized regions where Gaelic is the primary language. Most are concentrated along the west coast and combined encompass only a fraction of the Irish land mass. We took stabs at translating the signs, but that didn't work. Completely lost and not finding the beach, we turned around and went to breakfast in Dungarvan, where English was again spoken.

After breakfast, we continued on to Carlow for our appointment with the brewer of Carlow Brewing. This brewery visit didn't count on The List because we had visited nine years earlier, when the brewery was just one-year-old.

Another one of the early Irish craft breweries, today Carlow Brewing is going strong. The brewery was originally housed in the Goods Store, a stone building where traders once unloaded their wares, located next to the Carlow train stop. During our first visit to the brewery in 1999, we took the train from Kilkenny. Aware that it was near the railway stop, we were surprised to find that Carlow Brewing was not even 50 yards from the front of the station. We arrived for our second visit by car, which offered a slightly different view of the building. [18]

As we looked for the entrance, two German men found their way into the parking lot and milled around. A few minutes passed and eventually a man with a confident stride emerged from the open brewery door. The Germans inquired about tours and the man politely informed them that tours must be pre-booked. The tall one—apparently not a person to give up easily—decided to ask as many questions as possible while he had the attention of the brewery worker. He compared the Irish craft beer scene to German beer culture, proffered his thoughts on the viability of craft beer in Ireland, and asked for the brewery worker's opinion on the matter.

We stood quietly to the side. Chris deduced that the man at whom the lanky German was throwing a barrage of questions was the brewer, Liam Hanlon. It crossed my mind to invite the walk-ins to join us. After all, it's through kindness and openness that we've met new people. I whispered my idea to Chris, but he suggested waiting and asking Liam because it might not be welcome. Liam turned to us and we informed him of our appointment. It offered him the perfect escape and he ushered us inside.

We followed Liam through the office and into the tasting room. It was small but comfortably sized with large windows to see into the brewery. Turns out, Chris correctly read the situation. In the safety of the tasting room, Liam confessed that the parking lot inquisition drained him. Due to Liam's limited

18 In 2009, Carlow Brewing expanded production and is now located in a business park in nearby Bagenalstown.

time, and with our approval, he skipped the brewery tour and went straight for the beer tasting.

With a strong air and firm voice, Liam presents as serious yet unobtrusive. He offered his thoughts on the growing strength of the Irish craft beer community as he poured us an O'Hara's Stout. Unlike his exchange with the men outside, Liam easily joined us in conversation and his personality shone through. His coy smile turned into broad grins, displaying his adeptness at Irish hospitality. Liam even introduced us to a unique way to enjoy their Curim Gold Wheat Beer: room temperature off the shelf. Not the usual serving style for wheat beers, we had never had a warm wheat beer on purpose. This, of course, segued nicely into a discussion about our plan to drink only Irish craft beer and, in Chris's case, Guinness off the shelf for the duration of our trip. Liam thought it was a "grand" idea and expressed his appreciation for the effort we put forth to see an Ireland beyond Guinness on nitrogen.

In a growing trend, other people were also recognizing the existence of Irish beer, as Liam informed us that he now brewed twice a day in order to keep up with demand. This included exporting to a thirsty American craft beer community. A decade after the start of the Irish craft beer movement, the revolution was established and going international.

An hour later, Liam politely informed us that he needed to get back to work in the brewery. He walked us out to the car, where we packed our purchase—a case of mixed beers—in the trunk. Liam also sent us off with a gift of their 10th Anniversary Stout and a suggestion on where we could watch the European Football Championship soccer match between Germany and Turkey. We planned to make a mellow night of it during our overnight stay in Carlow.

The next morning we traveled an hour north to visit the Wicklow Mountains National Park, a 20,000-hectare nature preserve of bog lands, lakes and woodlands. With all the beer drinking, it was time for a little exercise and a hike in the beautiful Wicklow Mountains seemed perfect. All we needed was for the weather to cooperate.

At the Visitor's Center, we consulted a map and decided upon a trail around Upper Lake. The rain fell lightly, but our determination to continue as planned minimized any concern of getting a little damp. A short distance onto the trail, however, we revised our 9 kilometer hike into a 4 kilometer loop. We finished soaked to the bone.

To cure our rain soaked chill, Chris and I drank a few Guinness at a nearby pub. This particular pub didn't have Guinness in the bottle, so Chris had to settle for a pint on nitrogen.

When we emerged a short time later, the rain had stopped. "Guinness for Strength" the advertisement says, so we decided to give it another go at taking a short hike. As if to mock us, though, the rain started again after a few kilometers. Now depleted of any remaining determination, we packed it in for the day.

The tiny village of Laragh, the location of our B & B, had just one pub, Lynham's. Not only did Lynham's have Guinness in a bottle, it also offered free wireless. The unpredictable weather prevented the primary reason we had come to the area: hiking. Instead, we engaged in the only activity available and in a distinctly modern way (or simply an anti-social one), we enjoyed a pint while engrossed in our respective computers.

A young couple at a nearby table looked at us and whispered. When they finished their drinks and got up to leave, the guy said, “Bye Chris” and held out his hand. Startled, Chris looked up from his computer and reciprocated the handshake. The guy held up a cell phone to show that he had pulled up *thebeergeek.com*. The couple continued out the door before we could ask their names or invite them to share a pint with us. The quick interaction left Chris and I buzzing. Now awake from our computer-induced comas, we tried to figure out how they knew about the website. We chose to believe that we, along with the site, had grown that well known.

Through the window, the couple could be seen as they walked along the road. If they sought another pub, they would be disappointed because there wasn’t one. They eventually wandered out of sight and I returned my attention back to the computer. Still curious, however, I took a sip of my beer and looked out the window again only to see the couple coming back up the street toward Lynham’s. They had just discovered for themselves that there are no other pubs in which to go.

When they came through the front door, Chris and I bickered about who should go talk to them. Since the guy addressed Chris, it seemed perfectly logical that Chris be the one to make contact. They ordered their drinks from the bar and returned to the same table as before. We tried to act nonchalant and unaware of their return. Curiosity soon got the better of me and I turned around and introduced myself.

Two very nice people, Glen and Alissa lived in Dublin. In a blow to my ego, however, Glen confessed that Alissa had noticed that Chris and I both wore *thebeergeek.com* t-shirts. Intrigued as to why, they looked up the site. As they sat and chatted longer, our computers were put away and we laughed with them for the rest of the evening.

On our last day of the trip, we drove back to Dublin and returned the car at the airport. To avoid added stress during the next day's departure, I tried my luck at finding Oliver to give him his bottle of wine. Not in the mood to handle the chaos that is Dublin airport, Chris waited outside.

After twenty minutes and no sign of Oliver, I finally left the bottle at the airline's customer service desk with a note of thanks written on the back of my business card. I didn't know for sure that the bottle would actually get to Oliver, but I had to take the chance. Otherwise I'd be packing it up and bringing it home again.[19]

After re-joining Chris outside, we traveled into downtown Dublin and spent our last hours in Ireland on a pub crawl. We had only one day to visit our favorite Dublin pubs and try a few new ones.

We started at the Stag's Head, an old-school pub that Chris had read about in a travel guide. Directions included walking down the left side of Dame Street, looking for a mosaic on the sidewalk, and turning into a cobblestone alley. It all seemed very secretive and I wondered if a password would be required at the door. As it turned out, the pub was located on Dame Court and could be accessed by routes that did not include the dark, narrow alley. This was just the most convenient way to find it.

Opened in 1780, the pub wore a patina rich in history. The leather-covered bench upon which I sat slanted toward the floor. After sliding forward several times, I finally used my feet to brace myself. Chris pointed out the stag's head presiding over the mahogany bar as he delivered a bottle of Guinness

---

19 We saw Oliver the next day when we checked-in for our flight home. He did, in fact, get the wine and was extremely grateful.

and a glass to the table. Throughout the trip, his experiment in Guinness drinking had been remarkably successful and the Stag's Head added to that success.

Chris returned to the bar to retrieve my pint. Our first beers of the day went down slowly. It was the end of our trip and we were tired. The light coming through the stained glass windows created a twilight effect, making it feel like the end of the night, not the beginning of the day. It only added to the sluggish mood we now found ourselves in. We needed to get into our groove, so we headed towards Christ Church to the Bull & Castle, a gastro-pub and beer hall.

Declan O'Hagan, the Bull & Castle's manager at the time, remembered us from our previous visit. At the bar, we enjoyed our Galway Hooker and listened to Declan explain his take on the Irish craft beer scene. Echoing the sentiments of other people we had met, Declan wanted to do his part to increase the exposure of Irish craft beer and encourage visitors to experience it. He had high hopes that the craft beer community would continue to grow and strengthen.

The clock ticked and we still had several pubs to visit on our pub crawl. Upon leaving, Declan gave us a bottle of Meantime IPA to take home and told us to let him know before our next visit, so he could set aside some special beers for us. Like several others we met on the trip, Declan planned to attend the Great British Beer Festival. We added him to the growing group of people we hoped to see at the festival in August.

From the antique to the modern and back again, we stopped in another Victorian-age pub, the Long Hall. Aptly named, the Long Hall is long and narrow with deep red paint and dark ornate woodwork. The calm, old-fashioned nature of the Long Hall relaxed us after the contemporary bustle of the Bull and Castle. Our minds and bodies tired from our trip, the end felt near. Chris ordered a bottle of Guinness. The thick, rich head on my modern pint looked curiously out of place on the antique bar next to Chris's old-style bottle. I let out a big sigh. The anticipation of tomorrow's travel stirred up my anxiousness to return home. I missed the dogs.

One of our favorite Dublin beer spots, we chose the Porterhouse in Temple Bar for our final pints. Porterhouse is the largest 100% Irish-owned brewery in the country and, along with Franciscan Well and Carlow Brewing, it was one of the first craft breweries we visited in Ireland. On that first visit in 1998 we thoroughly enjoyed the beer and the house band, Sliotar.[20] On every visit since, we have planned activities around Sliotar's performances and it's not unheard of for us to go to the Porterhouse more than once while in Dublin.

By the time we arrived, all three floors of the pub were filled with jubilant beer drinkers. Lucky enough to secure ourselves a pair of seats, we drank our pints of Irish craft beer and enjoyed the sounds of Sliotar's fast-paced whistle playing. It was the perfect way to end another wonderful Year in Beer adventure.

As I lay in bed that last night in Ireland, I thought about the people we had met; people we planned to see again in a few months. It reminded me of something Chris once said. He described the beer media corps as a traveling circus. Not meant to imply that beer journalists are circus freaks, the comparison conveys the idea of people traveling together around the coun-

---

20 Pronounced "slitter," the band is named after the ball used in the Gaelic game of hurling.

try as a group. The same beer journalists attend the same beer events year in and year out.

To refine Chris's analogy, I think carnies at the fair are a more accurate comparison. At the carnival, each person has his or her own unique shtick and a booth to run. With a limited number of festivals to attend, the same general cast of characters shows up to all the major events. People arrive separately, but combine at the venue to create a fun and exciting whole. They all know each other, hope to see certain people, hang out together, and have fun while they work. At the same time, everybody manages their own thing and makes their own living.

With our increased travel during the Year in Beer, we became accustomed to this traveling circus and the sight of the usual troupe of media folk. From the outside, it appeared that Chris and I might now even be considered part of that group. After all, people saw us time and again at beer events. But on the inside, I felt different and out of place; like my focus on beer travel didn't quite measure up to the legitimacy of a focus on beer reviews, industry analyses, or brewing techniques. These feelings aside, the chance to meet up with Irish craft beer people at the Great British Beer Festival in a few months meant that our beer media circus membership had become international. And I took great pride in that.

For many people, travel acts as a means to an end—a method to arrive at the main event. For us, however, travel *is* the main event. Our travel experiences form the basis for our beer stories. It's part of how we experience the world. My realization of that difference said a lot to me about why I felt unlike, and often unequal, to the beer media people with whom we most often associated. We focus on the travel experience and beer is the prize at the end of those journeys.

If our May trip to Germany helped me to discover my purpose in the beer community, our June trip to Ireland helped me realize where I belonged in beer media. When the goal is to drink outside the box, there are no boundaries. With travel as the focus, I belong wherever I want.

JULY

CELEBRATE THE MILESTONES IN LIFE

Chris and I celebrated the fact that we completed the first half of the Year in Beer. We survived six months of frequent beer travel and that, in our minds, constituted an important milestone in our yearlong beer adventure. We persevered despite the high fuel prices that drove up the cost of travel and a weak dollar that made for a poor exchange rate. It shocked me when Chris confessed that we had reached his cost estimates for the whole year already. Our bank account may have groaned, but our motivation stayed strong. The idea to quit this far into it never occurred to us. We simply continued on. At the very beginning of this journey, we agreed that if nothing else, we would have one heck of a year. So far the year had treated us very well.

We launched headlong into the second half of our adventure with a visit to Oregon and the Oregon Brewers Festival. It also set the backdrop for another important milestone in our beer lives: a visit to our 400th brewery.

Upon arrival in Oregon, Chris listed 395 breweries, while I trailed behind him at 394. The disparity has been an ongoing issue in our beer travels. In 1994, Chris stayed in Boston for two weeks on business. He visited several breweries that closed before I had a chance to visit them. I have tried to catch up ever since. Regardless of the difference in count, however, both of us fell just shy of 400. So, before the onslaught of Oregon Brewers Festival events, we drove two hours up the coast to Astoria to add two breweries to The List.

Astoria, with its steep hills and historic homes, sits on the Columbia River a few miles from the Pacific Ocean. A popular movie location, *Kindergarten Cop*, *Goonies*, and *Free Willy* were all filmed in this quaint riverside town. During our January trip to Alaska, we had met Chris Nemlowill, the brewer/proprietor at Fort George Brewing in Astoria. We liked Chris and the barley wine he brought to Alaska. We hoped to see him again on his turf, where his beer would be brewery fresh.

We arrived in town and drove straight to our first brewery of the trip, Astoria Brewing Company, for lunch and a beer. Afterwards, we went out to experience the beaches where the Columbia River meets the Pacific Ocean. The briney smell of salt water filled my nose while the cat-like screams of the Terns and the forceful roar of clashing water rang in my ears. Everything in motion; it all felt so alive, invigorating.

Later that evening, we followed along the tracks of the Astoria riverfront trolley and up toward Fort George Brewing. We missed the brewer, Chris, by just 15 minutes, but that didn't stop us from enjoying a few jars of beer. Fort George Brewing serves beverages in mason jars—wine in small ones, beer in regular-sized ones and large jars for growlers. After dinner, we played a game of Scrabble and then walked back to our hotel located near the Megler Bridge. The sign out front read, "Where sleeping under the bridge is a good thing."

When we returned to Fort George Brewing the next morning to take a picture, we found Chris conducting brewery business. Physically, Chris is an imposing figure, but his gentle demeanor makes him very approachable. Chris's wife and baby daughter arrived as we chatted in the parking lot. We didn't want to interrupt any special family time, though, so we said good-bye shortly after introductions were made. Before we left, Chris, a proud native Astorian, recommended a visit to the Astoria Column. He said it with such admiration that we could hardly ignore the suggestion.

The 125-foot high column, dedicated in 1926, depicts the area's history with a mural. High on a hill, the column offers a spectacular view that emphasizes the steepness of the hills and the town's proximity to the wide Columbia River. With two more breweries added to The List, Chris and I climbed in the car and drove two hours back to Portland for a weekend of festivities. Our first stop was Alameda Brewing Company—brewery number 398 for Chris and 397 for me—in the Beaumont Village neighborhood.

Alameda Brewing's location in a family-oriented neighborhood reminded me of Barclay's, our old hangout in Oakland. Like Barclay's, the location and atmosphere of Alameda Brewing provided a place where locals could gather for any occasion, special or not. I imagined that regulars never found themselves short of friends to laugh with at the bar.

We chatted with the brewery's owner, Matt Schumacher, while enjoying a taster set. Great beer and tasty lemon pepper chicken strips were a great way to start the day, but Chris's chocolate stout milkshake became the highlight of our visit to Alameda Brewing. The unmistakable sweetness of chocolate and the rich taste of the stout overshadowed any other beer-inspired dessert we had ever tasted.

Still on the hunt for #400, Chris and I set out for another new brewery: Amnesia Brewing Company. The corrugated metal siding on Amnesia's front wall made the building look like it should be located on Cannery Row back home in Monterey. The barn-sized doors welcomed us with open arms as we stepped into the large warehouse space. The brewery's accessibility and convenient location, along with its grilled sausages and beer, fit the bill perfectly for what urban sociologist Ray Oldenburg calls a "third place."

In his 1989 book, *The Great Good Place,* Oldenburg defined home as our first place and work as our second. A third place is where a person can relax from the responsibilities and pressures of the first two. Different places for different people, a third place might be a coffee shop, bookstore or a corner grocery. For a beer geek, however, it could be nothing other than a pub or brewery. After 20 years (and no longer living in the neighborhood), we still consider Barclay's our third place.

From our seats at the bar, we watched as regulars rotated in and out, stopping by for a quick beer and a chat with whomever happened to be there. A sizable walk-in refrigerator formed the back of the bar and a sign at the top listed the selection of grilled sausages and beer. Tap handles joined the miscellaneous things stuck to the metal wall: a red and white malt bag affixed with duct tape, a Grateful Dead sticker, and a poster advertising the Oregon Brewers Festival.

Copacetic IPA in one hand and a bratwurst with sauerkraut in the other, Chris looked content. He turned to me and announced that he had something to say on camera.

"So, Amnesia Brewing's heaven. I've got a fresh brilled grat," Chris started, "No that's not right."

Take two. I hit record for the second time.

"So Amnesia Brewing is heaven. I've got a fresh grilled grat," he said. Chris and I laughed. The bartender looked at us funny.

Third time's a charm and Chris finally did it.

"I'm in heaven here at Amnesia Brewing with my fresh grilled brat with kraut and some great beer," he stated proudly.

I explored the outdoor patio while Chris finished his "fresh grilled grat." The picnic tables and grill in the corner created the ultimate neighborhood gathering spot.

"It's like being at someone's backyard barbecue," I commented to the woman behind the grill.

"That's exactly what it is, especially when it's really busy out here," she replied as she extended her arms and motioned in the direction of the patio. "Everyone knows everyone and they all bring their dogs…" Her words trailed off as she focused her attention back on her grilling duties.

It was easy to picture Chris and I seated with beers and sausages on the table and wiener dogs on our laps. "Yes, that would be really nice," I thought, "really nice."

With Chris on the cusp of greatness at 399 breweries visited and me close behind at 398, we pushed off for downtown and the Brewers Guild dinner, our first 2008 Oregon Brewers Festival event. As the annual fundraiser for the Oregon Brewers Guild, the dinner raises money for the Guild's mission of promoting Oregon beer. The dinner started a weekend of "work" for us. Our friends play tiny violins with their thumbs and index fingers when we say that our trips take work, but it's true. Although, I do recognize the loose nature with which we use the term "work."

Alone in the previous days, Chris and I acted as carefree as we wanted. Now it was time to join our cohorts in the traveling circus and get down to business. With a multitude of beer media acquaintances and friends at the upcoming events, we could no longer afford to fool around. We had footage to film and a journalistic image to project. For the rest of the weekend, we would rarely be seen without a beer. It was our job, after all. Tom Dalldorf, editor of the *Celebrator Beer News*, once offered me this sage advice: "Always be seen with a beer, but never be seen drunk." I try to keep that in mind every time I go to "work."

Our hotel was conveniently located across the street from Tom McCall Waterfront Park, the venue for both the Brewers Guild dinner and the festival itself. We knew that a crowd would form before the gates to the dinner opened, so we decided to leave early in order to get our place in line. It was the perfect evening weather for a leisurely stroll through the park along the west bank of the Willamette River to the festival area.

Although the dinner did not start for another 45 minutes, a decent-sized group had already gathered by the time we arrived. Toward the head of the line, we spotted Phil Farrell and his rubber chicken. We had first met Phil in Alaska in January when I was lucky enough to have my picture taken with his famous chicken. I waved hello. Phil lifted the chicken and waved back, but remained focused on maintaining his place in line.

Once the gates opened, the throng of beer geeks migrated en masse to the tables set up to the left of the entrance. We each received our commemorative pint glass and six beer tickets. The main festival included ten semi-trailers of beer plus a food court and a performance stage. For the Brewers Guild dinner, an event limited to 600 people, several tables were set up with 25 beers that would only be served that evening.

We moved through the crowd trying to get a look at our beer choices. Eventually we each picked one—Bridgeport Brewing's 2007 Hop Harvest IPA for Chris and the Red Hills Pils from Golden Valley Brewery for me. We made our way out of the congestion at the beer tables and into an open area. Standing there, we toasted each other and waited. Although our confidence in social situations had greatly improved, we still tended to wait for others to approach us rather than initiate conversation. The event barely open, the fashionably late arrivals had yet to make their appearance.

The dinner presented the first opportunity for the traveling circus to gather. One by one, members of the beer media came round and filled in the unoccupied space around us. Each time I turned around, someone new walked up. In the midst of all the hugs, "hellos," and "how are yous?" I mentally noted how different it felt this time around.

At our first Brewers Guild dinner the year before, we said hello to some familiar faces and made a handful of attempts at journalism by interviewing attendees on camera, but mostly we kept to ourselves. Not really knowing anyone, Chris and I stood at the edge of the gathering. Now we stood among beer journalists and friends happily greeting one another. I considered our inclusion in the traveling circus an important professional milestone, if not a purely emotional one.

Our foray into beer media circles actually happened by accident. One year prior, Chris contacted Oregon Brewers Festival (OBF) organizers to ensure that filming would be allowed at the festival. Organizers not only said it was okay, they offered Chris media credentials. It thrilled us to be considered media because we certainly didn't feel like it. Some of the thrill stemmed from the thought that at any time we would be exposed as crashers and asked to surrender our media badges. Mostly, it excited us to show them off.

The Oregon Brewers Festival is a sentimental favorite of ours. In addition to being our first event where we held media credentials, it also holds other milestone memories. In 1994, we traveled to Portland for the weekend to attend a wedding and stumbled upon the festival grounds by accident as we explored the city. It's funny now to think that two beer geeks like us had no idea that a beer festival occurred in Portland every year on the last full weekend in July. Even then, OBF was a premier beer event on the West Coast, but our ignorance of the festival's existence clearly demonstrated that we didn't know as much about beer as we thought. We managed to visit the festival for a few hours before the wedding ceremony. Awed by the size, Chris and I loved it and wished we'd had more time to stay. We came back annually until 1999 when we decided to take a break, which ended in 2007.

For the Year in Beer, we returned to OBF with a more seasoned attitude and a real purpose. Although, we projected (slightly) more confidence, as a new act in the circus, the task of beer journalism didn't come easily for us. It required a constant, conscious effort to fill our role.

We caught up with our beer media circus friends, mingled with some of Portland's beer legends, and made a few new acquaintances. We sat down to eat with Portland residents J. Mark Angelus, one of the Beerdrinker of the Year finalists we had met in February, and his wife, Jennifer. Since I had been ill during the Beerdrinker of the Year weekend and made a terrible fool of myself trying to interview J. Mark on camera, it was nice talking to him with a clear head. I hoped that he noticed a difference.

After a buffet-style dinner of pork loin, grilled vegetables and a chocolate stout brownie, we walked the length of the tents and took notes on the location of beers we wanted to try. This mellow pre-festival survey of the grounds maximized the actual consumption of beer during the festival because it minimized the directionless searches for beers worthy of a token. This was an important task because in less than 24 hours the three city block-long festival would play host to more than 70,000 frenzied beer drinkers over four days.

Over the course of the evening, we heard people mention the Green Dragon, a Southeast brewpub and bistro. We weren't sure of the exact location, so when the dinner wound down, we followed another group across the bridge in the dark. The Green Dragon was crowded with beer lovers and notables alike. We got in a quick beer before being invited to a gathering at the home of Lisa Morrison, a Portland-based beer writer we'd last seen in March during our press trip to Philadelphia. At first I thought it to be friendly banter, but then she provided us with her cell phone number. This small act helped rid my mind of any lingering insecurities about our inclusion in the traveling circus. We ended our evening at Lisa's house with a dozen others drinking Duchesse de Bourgogne and playing with her dog, Yeti.

Thursday we awoke bright and early to attend the Brewer's Breakfast. We walked the mile to PGE Park[21] and waited outside with the other diehard beer lovers. A few conversations occurred here and there, but mostly the pre-morning coffee crowd milled around in a daze. There we ran into our friend Chadd McNicholas, a homebrewer and beer judge from Sacramento, who introduced us to his friend Daniel. We told them about the plan for Chris to visit his 400th brewery later that evening and invited them to join us. They enthusiastically accepted and we made arrangements to meet back up later in the day.

Once inside, Lisa Morrison greeted people at the reception table wearing the bottle cap crown our friend Matt Venzke had given her during the Beerdrinker of the Year contest where she'd been one of the judges. Lisa is dubbed the "Beer Goddess," but with the crown atop her head of red curly hair, she looked more like a queen. We each received our 12-ounce plastic festival mug and a t-shirt then made our way down to the field level VIP area. Each year a different Portland brewery assumes the responsibility for organizing and sponsoring

21 Now the home pitch of the Portland Timbers soccer team, the park is currently called Jeld-Wen Field.

the breakfast, as well as brewing the beer for the opening ceremony. This year Widmer Brothers Brewery hosted the breakfast and provided the ceremonial first keg of beer.

We found a table in the bright sunshine before joining the buffet line. A Widmer Hefeweizen soon replaced orange juice as my breakfast beverage. Chris opted for the Broken Halo IPA. Waiting for the doors to open, the group was quiet and barely awake, but as the breakfast progressed, the crowd, which had grown to 300 people, livened up and the chatter grew louder.

The party really got started when a life-sized Widmer Hefeweizen and lemon slice arrived. The two people dressed in mascot outfits were quite amusing and I wondered how they decided who got to be what. At my urging, Chris agreed to film the life-size beer and his sidekick, but only if I said "hi" to them. So I shook the beer's hand and patted the lemon. Through my laughter, I thanked them for coming and repeated, "I just had to come up and say hi" about three times before enough time had elapsed for good footage.

Mom always touted breakfast as the most important meal of the day, so with a belly full of bacon, eggs, and beer I had enough energy and giddiness for the parade down to Tom McCall Waterfront Park. I just hoped that I didn't have to pee halfway there; beer tends to have that effect.

Most people put on the t-shirt we received at the door upon arriving. The black Oregon Brewers Festival t-shirts said "Follow me to the Oregon Brewers Festival" on the back. Initially, I put mine on over the shirt I had on. However, once the parade started I decided to show off my pink "Girls are beer-geeks too" shirt instead and took my new one back off.

To the beat of drums, several hundred craft beer lovers followed Portland's then-Mayor Tom Potter as he led the way to the festival grounds. Several guys dressed as masked Mexican wrestlers joined the mayor at the front as they carried the ceremonial keg. It's unclear as to why they dressed like that. Perhaps they thought of themselves as superheroes; "defenders of the keg" who vowed to protect it at all costs. In any case, other people took the opportunity to dress up, as well. Some parade participants dressed in beer costumes, both bottles and cans, while others wore beer glasses and goggles in a variety of styles. One group was clad in monk robes with wigs that made them look bald except for a ring of hair that wrapped around from ear to ear. Although they were probably honoring the monastic tradition of brewing, I liked them because they reminded me of our high school mascot: the Mighty Padres. Just like at our high school football games, the monks jumped around and incited the crowd into a festive frenzy.

Someone initiated a chant: "We brew it. We drink it. We add hops to it." Strong and loud, the mantra echoed off the downtown buildings. Business-attired individuals emerged from doorways high-fiving the marchers as they passed. The enthusiasm eventually quieted down as we all realized that the chant didn't really make sense. The passionate spirit refused to die, however, and whooping and hollering filled the air. The faces of office workers appeared in the windows several stories up. We waved up to them. A few smiled and waved back. All said and done, we formed a boisterous snake that wound through downtown Portland, impeding traffic and disrupting the workday.

Arriving at the festival site, the gates parted for the 300-person parade. We crowded round as former Mayor Potter and the masked wrestlers prepared for the customary tapping of the keg. First proclamations from Oregon's then-Governor Theodore Kulongoski and Mayor Potter were read, declaring July as Oregon Craft Beer Month. Then, fashioned after Oktoberfest's opening ceremony, the keg was tapped and beer flowed. A roar of cheers went up as the mayor sipped the first beer. The festival was now officially open. The crowd broke free of its polite restraint and surged toward the keg. It was the only chance to get a taste of the special brew. Once the keg ran out, that was it.

Chris and I lost track of each other in all the jostling. While Chris aimed to document the moment for the *One Pint at a Time* episode, I struggled to hold my own in the semi-civilized push to get a beer. At one point, the top of Chris's shaved head was visible in the middle of the crowd. Video camera in hand, he extended his arm high for the best angle. The barrel looked out of reach to me. Polite, yet assertive, I lacked the frantic desperation of those around me. But before long, I found myself nudged all the way to the front. When my mug was filled halfway, I turned to make my way out. Mugs with hands attached raced to catch the still flowing beer. The keg ran dry in twenty minutes.

Chris, who had obtained his own mug of ceremonial beer, found me under a nearby tree. With some time before the official media tasting, we went in search of the information tent where we picked up our media passes and festival program.

Entrance into the Oregon Brewers Festival grounds is free, but to partake in the tasting, mugs and tokens must be purchased. We received our mug as part of the Brewers Breakfast, but we still needed tokens, so we picked those up at the information table along with our passes. One token is exchanged for a 4-ounce taste of a beer, while four tokens fills the mug to the top. The difficult part is that over 70 breweries were serving beer, which meant over 70 beers to choose from.

We continued toward the south end of the festival site looking at the signs that hung on each trailer. Eager volunteer servers in bright blue shirts stood behind the tables, ready to accept tokens and pour beers.

"Oh, Hopworks Urban Brewery has a Lager," I said. "I want to try that."

"If all goes right, that will be my 400th," replied Chris.

Hopworks Urban Brewery, referred to as HUB, was one of the newest Portland breweries at the time and we would be happily adding it to The List later in the evening.

I stepped up to the table and skimmed the signs taped on the white plastic tablecloth for the HUB Lager. While the beers are roughly positioned under the large signs on the trailers, it can sometimes be tricky to pinpoint the exact location of the beer you want. Early in the festival, there is plenty of room to look, but once the crowds gather, the scene becomes an unsettled mass of people—some searching for beers, others waiting in what they hope is a real line, and many more standing around oblivious to the fact that they're getting in the way of it all.

I found my beer and looked up at the volunteers. After confirming they were serving the desired beer, the woman took my token and her partner poured the golden brew into my mug.

Further down the trailers, Chris found Resurrection Rye, the Collaborator beer produced in limited quantity. Each year, members of the Oregon Brew Crew homebrewing club compete for the chance to have their beer brewed commercially at Portland's own Widmer Brothers Brewing Company. Four dollars for every barrel of the Collaborator beer sold is donated to the Bob McCracken Scholarship Fund, which supports students at the Oregon State University Fermentation Science program. The fund aids Oregon's future brewers in receiving a comprehensive education in their craft, essentially ensuring that Oregon continues to turn out top-notch brewers. Started in 1998, the joint effort between homebrew creativity and professional expertise had become known as the Collaborator Project.

By now parade participants had dispersed throughout the expansive festival grounds, but the general public had yet to arrive in serious numbers. This made the area fairly empty and quiet. Attendance is the lowest on Thursday, which makes it the most enjoyable. Few locals take Thursday off and most out-of-town visitors don't arrive until Friday. Among the advantages of the Thursday session are no lines for beer, fresh port-a-potties, and minimal whooping, all of which are major plusses in our book.

No line and a dry-floored port-a-potty reeking of sanitizer are something everyone can appreciate, but the spontaneous festival-wide breakout of whooping is a phenomenon unique to beer gatherings. It works like this: Periodically, a festival goer initiates a chorus of "woos" that spreads across the festival like butter on hot toast. The sound crescendos to a deafening level, fades back down and the festival continues on like nothing happened. Amused (and sometimes annoyed) by this collective pronouncement of vitality, Chris and I have our own beer festival rally cry. In a mocking variation of the customary call, ours is the usual "woo" followed by a much higher pitched "woo." Simple in its genius, we crack ourselves up doing it.

We joined twenty other people under a tent for the media tasting. Our table included several friends and acquaintances, including Chris D who had traveled down from Seattle. We felt right at home. Laughter with our tablemates monopolized my attention and I periodically lost focus on our host talking about the beers being served. For the second time in as many days, I was part of a happy beer media gathering.

Completing our 17 beer tasting, the group disbanded and dispersed among the crowd in small cliques. As the Chrisses and I left, Chris recalled how Rowdy Corrick, a friend from my days working at Barclay's in Oakland, had introduced us to the wonderful world of beer industry perks.

"Remember that Rogue Brewing employee party we went to with Rowdy?" he asked.

"Yes. I went a tad overboard with all the free beer," I replied.

Chris nodded his head in agreement. "We were so young back then." We both laughed as a bemused Chris D shook his head. Chris D had met Rowdy in February when he kept us riveted by his animated story telling about the early days of the Bay Area craft beer movement. Now he was getting an even better picture of what it was like to hang out with Rowdy in those days.

"Was it the same year or another year that we went on the river cruise sponsored by Pyramid Brewing?" I asked.

"I'm not sure, but that year Crista came down from Seattle," Chris said.

The memories seemed like a lifetime ago. The festival experiences we sought now were vastly different from what we wanted then. Some might characterize it as a sign of a maturing craft beer palate; I call it getting older.

All these years later, Chris now steadied himself for his 400th brewery visit. We joined up with Chadd and his friend Daniel, who we'd met for the first time earlier that morning, and headed to Hopworks Urban Brewery to help Chris celebrate his biggest beer milestone yet.

Opened just a few months at the time of our visit, HUB was Portland's first "eco-brewpub," serving organic beers and sustainable food in an earth-friendly setting. The brewery cites close to fifty "sustainable points" to demonstrate how green it is, including using the kitchen's fryer oil to fuel the biodiesel-fired brew kettle.

With the broad yellow stripe on the top of the building and the neon sign with HUB's concentric circle logo, there was no way for us to miss the brewpub on the wide Southeast Portland street. Bicycle racks on the right side of the building were filled to capacity, reflecting Portland's bike-friendly nature.

Bright and airy inside, we sat at the copper-topped bar with a base made from old office paneling and a foot rail fashioned out of old boiler pipe. Above, a row of bicycle frames ran the length of the long bar, concealing the small lights that hung in between them. The place was full of festive beer drinkers, which created the perfect setting to enjoy Chris's beer milestone. Although the noise level also made it a little difficult for the five of us to have a conversation that all could hear.

It was everyone's first time at HUB and our bull session at the bar centered on assessments of the beer and atmosphere. Chadd, who sat next to Chris, contributed here and there to the discussion, which wasn't an easy thing to do because both Chris and Chris D were engaged in a buzzed battle of wit and words. Daniel sat at the end saying little. He smiled a lot, though, so I knew he could hear at least parts of what was being said.

Chris sat in the middle basking in the glory of his achievement. I admit that I participated with a tinge of jealousy. Still one brewery behind, my celebration would have to wait until Saturday. I reminded myself that he may have reached the milestone before me, but I was going to have something he didn't. Two of our favorite beer drinking buddies from home, Billy and Kristin, were in Portland on business and would be joining us as I visited my 400th brewery.

At one point, Chris held up his pint of Hopwork's IPA and honored us with an Oscar-worthy acceptance speech.

"I'd like to thank everyone I've ever met in my life, including my parents, my wife, my dogs, my friends..." he began.

Chadd asked Chris how many breweries he thought he might visit in his lifetime. After thinking for a moment, Chris pronounced a lifetime goal of 1,000 breweries. Goals give us the opportunity to honor rites of passage and commemorate milestones throughout our lives. How those goals are defined completely depends on one's worldview. Ours was one seen through the bottom of a pint glass.

We finished up at Bailey's Taproom, a multi-tap establishment located downtown. Bailey's mellow atmosphere that evening was just what we needed to unwind from our busy beer-filled day. The numerous windows in this corner beer café make it feel light and fresh inside, but we decided to sit outside in the mild Pacific Northwest air. Nearing the end of our first full day of festival events, I was barely halfway through my beer when I heard the hotel bed calling my name. Before we left, Chadd and Daniel decided to join us on Saturday for our road trip east of Portland to my 400th brewery.

We started Friday bright and early in nearby Troutdale at one of the McMenamin's Edgefield golf courses. The 4th Annual Sasquatch Brew Am pairs brewers, beer celebrities and beer fans in a suds-filled romp around Edgefield's par-3 course. The day before, Chadd spoke highly of the golf tournament and confessed that every year he looks forward more to playing in the Brew Am than attending the festival itself. It marked our first visit to the golf event where knowledge of the game is not required and is probably best left at home.

A fundraiser for the Glen Hay Falconer Foundation, the event honors the memory of Glen Hay Falconer, the brewer at the now closed Wild Duck Brewing in Eugene, Oregon who passed away in 2002. The foundation provides "opportunities for professional and aspiring brewers to further their knowledge and expertise."

We had only a short amount of time to get our footage of the event because we needed to report for volunteer duty in the afternoon. Lisa Morrison—who each year has her hand in many of the Oregon Brewers Festival events—greeted us at the check-in table before we hit the course.

In uncharacteristic journalistic bravado, we wandered the course asking participants about their strategies for peak performance. Our first foursome was from HUB.

"How did you prepare for the tournament this morning?" I asked.

"With coffee and beer," a woman answered as she held a beer in her golf-gloved hand. "What?" She laughed as she turned to Ben Love, HUB's assistant brewer. "It's true."

"We went by McDonald's on the way," Ben added.

"I saw your shot, though," Chris told him. "So, you might need a few more beers."

"Yeah, I still need to loosen up," Ben laughed.

We watched from above as Jonathon Berry, brewer from New Old Lompoc in Portland, missed a putt that veered several feet to the left. As he climbed the hill towards us to the next hole, I stopped him.

Looking at his orange hop-print shirt and pale yellow polyester pants, I asked, "Is this your lucky golf outfit?"

"This is one of them," he responded. "Usually I wear a kilt."

"Oh, but I like the waffle-textured polyester," I said laughing.

"These are signature Arnie Palmer pants. A vintage store acquisition."

The group moved on, dishing out a fair amount of good-natured ribbing about how much luck Jonathon's "warm and snug" pants brought him on his last putt.

Further along the course, we found Shaun O'Sullivan, the founder and brewer at 21st Amendment Brewing in San Francisco, who we'd last seen in February at the *Celebrator* anniversary party. Among others in Shaun's entourage was Bay Area beer writer Jay Brooks. Standing at what we thought was a safe distance, Shaun hit a shot that headed straight for us. Chris actually had to skip to the side to avoid getting a golf ball in the shin. Shaun pointed his club directly at Chris and smiled knowingly. Jay sank his putt for a birdie, which prompted cries of being a ringer. Chris was asked to putt a ball. Unfortunately, he missed his opportunity to be a hero and the ball rolled to the right of the hole.

We even saw Chadd on the course wearing his signature Utilikilt, a non-traditional canvas kilt made for everyday wear. He noticed us as he waited to tee off. With a club in one hand, Chadd hoisted the beer he had in the other as a way to say hello.

Our volunteer shift at the festival started at noon and after a short two hours at the golf course, we needed to get back into Portland. At the volunteer tent we received our bright blue shirts and instructions about choosing which beer we wanted to pour. We looked at the numerous sheets of paper with beer names on them. Because we reported early for our shift, we had our pick of beers. It had been recommended to us that we pour a beer located in the shade, but after scanning the beer list, we had no idea which ones would be shielded from the sun. Earlier at the golf course Shaun O'Sullivan had suggested that we pour 21st Amendment's Hell or High Watermelon Wheat.

Fifteen minutes later, organizers gathered the 100 volunteers for our final instructions before letting us loose.

"No wristband, no beer," the man emphasized. "Only serve beer in this year's mugs and if a customer gets out of hand, call your supervisor. Now go out and have some fun!"

We excitedly went in search of Watermelon Wheat and found it located in the shade. The volunteer supervisor assigned to our area helped us to get settled and reminded us what to do. "Remember, only fill it to here," he said as he pointed a third of the way up the mug.

During the slow start at the opening of the festival we chatted with an older couple stationed next to us. They were volunteer veterans and looked remarkably relaxed. We, on the other hand, were bubbling with excitement.

Within a few minutes, our first customer came up and gave me his token. I deposited it into the plastic bucket and Chris poured his beer. We had two pitchers of beer that we filled from the tap in the trailer behind us. That way, at least one person was pouring beer at all times. However, in no time at all, we could barely keep up with demand. A line thirty people deep stood in front of us. The volunteer supervisor offered his assistance by filling a third pitcher, which allowed us to concentrate on pouring. The older couple barely had customers, so they watched as we scrambled to collect tokens and fill mugs.

I took my role seriously and followed every instruction of our supervisor to the letter. He warned us of random non-festival tokens mixed in with the real ones and directed us to not accept them. We were instructed to tell the person to return to the token table for a valid token. Chris accidentally accepted a wooden token for a free coffee, but had already put it in the bucket when he realized it.

In an embarrassing confession, I confused a non-English speaking Japanese visitor by refusing his non-OBF beer token. The poor guy had no idea why I wouldn't serve him and lacked complete understanding of my directions to obtain another one. Looking back on it, I should have relaxed, given the guy a beer, and made his day a little easier.

Our supervisor had also instructed us to only fill the current year's festival mugs. A girl with the previous year's mug came up for a beer. I politely informed her of my supervisor's direction to only accept 2008 mugs. She protested, stating that the website indicated that other mugs could be used. She also mumbled something about recycling and being eco-friendly. Unfazed, I stood steadfast in my fervent adherence to my instructions. She walked away annoyed. Undoubtedly, she used the mug the rest of the day without incident, but I followed the rules and that, to me at the time, was all that mattered.

While making his rounds, the supervisor asked the veteran couple how we fared. She respectfully reframed my rigid observance of the rules. "They're taking their responsibilities very seriously," she said.

I served my customers as I like to be served at large festivals: fast, no chit chat, just hand over the beer. With an aim to keeping the line moving, I did one thing that annoys me at beer festivals, filled the mug to the exact pour line. No more, no less. Well, that is until we got really busy. A repeat customer suggested that I pour slower because the last round his mug was filled with foam, shorting him on his pour. I brushed him off saying, "Sorry, a little busy here. Trying to get beers out as quickly as I can."

At the height of our shift, we were so swamped we didn't have time to think. Rather than look people in the eye, I concentrated on their mugs as I filled them up. My focus was broken for just a moment, though, as a woman appeared in front of us wearing a shirt from the Dublin brewery Porterhouse. "We were hoping we'd see you guys," she said.

"Hey, I love the Porterhouse!" I yelled as she walked away with a full mug.

Completely engrossed in my task at hand, it didn't immediately register that she followed our website and knew we visited the Porterhouse whenever we traveled to Dublin. While pouring another beer for yet another customer, my heart began to race with excitement.

I nudged Chris, who had been too occupied to fully notice the interaction. "That woman had a Porterhouse shirt on."

"I know, I saw her," Chris said as he pushed a token into the bucket.

I poured another beer as I continued. "Yeah, but she recognized us and said that they hoped they would see us."

Chris, focused on the line in front of him, barely looked at me. "That's cool."

Tokens continued to come in and beers continued to go out as I thought about the fact that she actually hoped to run into us. It thrilled me to see that we had fans out there. It reminded me that people really visited our website and watched *One Pint at a Time* episodes. It would have been nice to talk with her, at least get her name, but she was out of sight before I had a chance to tell her when we finished our shift. The exchange felt incomplete, yet very satisfying nonetheless.

Four and a half hours later, a new group of volunteers came to relieve us. Just like that, I put down my pitcher, stepped back, and someone else took over. The supervisor thanked us and I let out a sigh. During our shift, I barely had time to think, let alone breathe.

Beyond my physical aches and pains came a bit of soul searching. After that volunteer experience, I examined my rigidity and deeply embedded need to follow rules. My fellow volunteer's remark about me taking my role seriously rang in my ears. I appreciated her diplomatic description of my strict loyalty to the rules, but the subtext was loud and clear. I decided that next time a more flexible attitude might serve me better. So would a massage.

A full day of festival activities wore us out. Chris D planned to return to Seattle the next day, so we met back up with him and sought a quiet way to round out our visit together. Our last chance to spend time with him, we crossed the river to Belmont Station, a bottle shop and beer café in Southeast Portland.

We walked into the corner shop and passed through a doorway into the café side. It looked and felt like an old bar, complete with funky tables and chairs, and the walls were covered in beer memorabilia. The bartender handed us a beer list, which included 17 beers on tap. It took us a few minutes to decide, but we eventually ordered a round of beers and the "Everyday Cheese Plate," a portion of Pepperjack, Swiss, and Cheddar with Ritz crackers.

The chaotic atmosphere of the beer festival had left the three of us exhausted. Chris and I were beat due to our volunteer efforts while Chris D, who can be quite snarky and animated after an extended stint of beer drinking, had advanced into a more aloof, non-confrontational mood. With few other customers in the pub, the laid-back atmosphere felt almost homey.

Conversation was easy going and mostly consisted of commentary on beer-related issues. I did, however, manage to give Chris D a hard time for not joining me on my 400th brewery visit. He felt bad for missing such an important milestone, but said he had other obligations. After seeing him several times over the last seven months, Chris D had become part of our Year in Beer journey. We'd seen others, mostly members of the beer media circus, as frequently, but it was different with Chris D because we'd spent whole days with him. His active role in our adventures had made them his own and the shared experiences deepened our friendship. A slight sadness filled the air as we all realized this was the last time we'd be getting together for a while.

We wrapped up our visit with a bit of beer shopping in the bottle shop. With coolers along the walls, a rack full of magazines, and packaged snacks and bottle openers at the counter, it looked like a typical corner liquor store. Upon closer examination, however, the shelves and coolers were filled with over 1,000 different bottles of craft beer.

The shopkeeper noticed us wandering the aisles and asked if she could assist. She was extremely knowledgeable and very helpful as she helped us pick out Oregon beers to take home. During checkout, we discovered that our friendly helper was none other than Teri Fahrendorf, founder of the Pink Boots Society. I don't know how it came up, but something Chris D said prompted Teri to introduce herself.

Teri, who at the time was employed at Belmont Station as a beer clerk, had previously worked as a professional brewer. In 2007, she started the Pink Boots Society as a list of female brewers she met or heard about during a 13,000-mile road trip around the United States. Today, the Society defines itself as an "international charitable trade organization created to inspire, encourage, and empower women to become professionals in the beer industry."

An original promoter of women in the beer industry, Teri's name was well known in beer circles. It embarrassed me to not recognize her by face, but she didn't seem to mind the lack of immediate recognition. Teri's perseverance in the male-dominated world of brewing inspired me. She paved the way for the acceptance of women in all aspects of the beer industry, including journalism.

So we made our purchases from the famous Teri Fahrendorf and stepped outside. Chris D had become a regular Year in Beer participant. Now we were saying goodbye to him without knowing when we'd see him next. The bottles of beer clinked in his backpack as we hugged goodbye.

On Saturday, I pursued my own quest in the beer world with a Teri-inspired perseverance. It was the day I would visit my 400th brewery. The minivan came in handy, as a few friends planned to join us on our driving tour out to Parkdale and Hood River, towns east of Portland. After meeting up with Chadd and Daniel, we picked up our friends Billy and Kristin at their hotel.

One of the things we could say about most of the people in our lives is that beer brought us together. Billy and Kristin are prime examples. While at one of the few places in our area that served craft beer one evening, Chris observed a man order a Green Flash West Coast IPA. Thinking that might be someone we'd like to know, he started up a conversation with the man who turned out to be Billy. We have been friends with Billy and his wife Kristin ever since.

Lovers of craft beer, Billy and Kristin frequently travel to Portland for business. This time, they coordinated their trip to coincide with the Oregon Brewers Festival. Lucky for me, they also wanted to join us on my visit to brewery #400.

Chadd, who was feeling the effects of the previous day's beer drinking, graciously agreed to be our driver. An hour and a half outside of Portland, we arrived at Elliot Glacier Public House in Parkdale. With a round of beers (and a glass of water for Chadd), we headed out the backdoor to the outdoor seating area. I thought we'd stepped into the backyard of a friend's house. Mismatched outdoor furniture was scattered around. Tables and chairs remained where the last occupants left them. A large open meadow with an unimpeded view of snow-capped Mt. Hood extended before us. The view was absolutely stunning, a wonderfully peaceful way to celebrate my very special milestone.

Billy is an inquisitive individual who truly enjoys getting to know people by engaging them in conversation. Kristin, on the other hand, is relatively quiet and observant. While she can often be seen rolling her eyes at something Billy says, she is also very adept at chiming into conversations at just the right time.

Immediately upon sitting down outside, Billy asked me what it was like to visit my 400th brewery. To be perfectly honest, I didn't know. I answered something about not remembering all the breweries I had been, which didn't address the question. Different from his usual barrage of probing questions, though, Billy let me off the hook with that response.

This was *my* day to celebrate, but it was a goal Chris and I had achieved together and could both revel in. I drank my Parkdale Pale Ale in the sunshine, as Chris and I reminisced about some of the travels and adventures that got us to this point. Before we left Elliot Glacier, I attempted my own Oscar-worthy thank you speech. However, mine wasn't nearly as eloquent and witty as Chris's had been. Our friends were kind enough to clap anyway.

Our next stop took us to Hood River at the hub of the Columbia River Gorge. Created by Ice Age floods, the natural beauty of the Gorge and the surrounding Hood River area prompted its inclusion in the book *1,000 Places to See (in the U.S. and Canada) Before you Die* by travel journalist Patricia Schultz. The small town is popular with windsurfers and is home to three breweries.

Chris and I had tried two other times to visit our first stop in Hood River: the Big Horse Brewpub. On previous trips to the area, we either found the pub closed or not yet open for the day. Fortunately, it was open on this day and we climbed the stairs to the door. Set high on the hill, the pub overlooked the town, as well as Columbia River Gorge, one of the world's best spots for windsurfing and kite boarding. The view was beautiful, but this stop was a quick one and we left after finishing our taster set. We still had two more breweries to go before leaving Hood River.

Our group walked down the street to Double Mountain Brewery. Billy and Kristin had been there before and spoke very highly of the beer. They confidently told us that we'd all love it. Every table in the small taproom was full, so we followed Billy through the door on the right into an expansive garage area that doubled as a lounge. The door into the taproom closed behind us and the garage felt dark and isolating. We were the only customers out there. Billy assured me that a waitress would find us out there. Much to my relief, he was right.

The brewery is better known for their IPAs Hot Lava and Molten Lava, but our friends indulged me in a pitcher of Kölsch. When the beer arrived, Chris demonstrated a pouring motion and complained about having a sore wrist from our volunteer shift the day before. We all gave him a hard time for being a big baby and in the end I poured the round of beers myself. Even Chadd decided to have a small taste, as this was his first time at Double Mountain and he wanted to see what all the fuss was about.

Soon after we settled into the garage, the large doors rolled up with a clamor that startled us. The light came in and I no longer felt like a teenager hiding a party from her parents. A band, preparing for a show later that night, lugged their instruments and stage equipment in through the garage door and past us as we ate pizza and drank beer.

Then it was on to Full Sail, our last brewery stop in Hood River. Chris and I had visited Full Sail several times before, but some in our party had never been there. From the outside it looked just as it always had but inside, we barely recognized the place. Thanks to our friend Rowdy, our first visit to Full Sail in 1993 was an industry party. At that time, the tasting room was much less glamorous. Besides a tasting bar and large round rack of merchandise, the room was bare. I remember that party because each person was allowed to choose one t-shirt off the rack. Rowdy told us later that people had helped themselves to as many shirts as they wanted and nearly wiped out the whole inventory. Even back then, Chris and I were ardent rule followers and took only our allotted one shirt each. I chose a long-sleeved turquoise green one with "Full Sail" written down the sleeve.

Now, the tasting room was a busy restaurant decorated with rich oak wooden features. While Chris and I were impressed with the interior changes, we had the outside deck in mind. Many other people had the same idea we did, but we still managed to find a few seats where we could enjoy our beer and the view in the warmth of the sun.

The deck, perched high on a bluff and sandwiched in between two taller buildings, is rectangular in shape, reminding me of a movie theater. The multi-level deck provides the perfect view of the gorge for everyone, no matter where they're sitting. In this case, the movie was always a captivating one with nonstop action. Our group sat mostly quiet, as we stared at the tumultuous river dotted with color from the sails of the windsurfers as they crisscrossed the white-capped water.

We ended our day at the Walking Man Brewery in Stevenson, Washington, a half-hour drive across the Columbia River from Hood River. Walking Man was another brewery that Billy and Kristin had raved about. We parked across the street and easily identified the brewery by the bright yellow pedestrian crossing sign on the building. Not to be mistaken for the real thing, though, on this sign the pedestrian was holding a mug of beer.

To get to the brewery's beer garden, we walked along a balcony, passing what seemed to be someone's house. Down below, we could see a casual grass area with tables and chairs, and patio umbrellas for shade.

Walking Man brews excellent beer in a quaint setting, but more importantly, they have hilarious names that all derive from a celebration of man's evolution to walking upright. This includes Knuckle Dragger Strong Pale Ale, Biped Red, and Homo Erectus Imperial IPA, to name a few.

The air outside was still warm in the late afternoon. A bagpipe could be heard on the other side of the shrubbery that created a natural boundary of the beer garden. It provided the perfect backdrop for the *One Pint at a Time* episode opening, so in front of all our friends, I filmed the introduction.

"But there's a lot more to experience, so welcome to 'OBF and Beyond,'" I finished.

If you listen carefully, an "Oh yeah," courtesy of Daniel, can be heard. He had barely said two words the whole day, but when he did, his timing was impeccable. The laid back way in which he said it perfectly encapsulated the tone set by Owner/Brewmaster Bob Craig. He resembles an aged hippie with his long salt and pepper hair pulled into a ponytail and bushy gray facial hair. A friendly man, Bob made the rounds chatting with each of the tables outside. He even brought his mellow, carefree attitude to our table as he joined us for just a moment. We were able to tell him how much we enjoyed Walking Man before he moved on to the next table. It was a great way to finish out not only our day's beer excursion, but also our trip to Portland.

Sunday ended our five-day stint of Pacific Northwest hoopla. We had traveled to Oregon to drink world-class beer and to attain a milestone only a beer geek could appreciate—visiting our 400th respective breweries. The goal gave July's trip a special meaning beyond being part of the Year in Beer.

In the aftermath of our accomplishment, though, the feat somehow lacked solidity and definition. We captured it on film, but I longed for an object to hold and admire. A medal, for example, to wear around my neck as a symbol of the commitment and determination it took to achieve this milestone. A certificate of achievement to bring home to my mother would be equally gratifying, perhaps something that read:

"Let this certificate verify that
Merideth Canham-Nelson demonstrated her
commitment to drinking quality beer and a
determination to spend her entire
bank account in pursuit of her 400th brewery.
An achievement accomplished on
July 26, 2008"

However, I knew there wasn't time to rest on our laurels. In one of our quickest turnarounds of the year, we had just five nights at home before our upcoming August trip to England. In less than a week, we would begin the drive toward brewery #500.

The milestone I achieved on this trip was simply the latest of what I planned to be a lifetime of beer achievements. I anticipated many more beer milestones in the future, including reaching the end of the Year in Beer.

Once home, Chris confessed that the lack of fanfare and fireworks upon reaching our historic milestone proved anti-climatic for him, as well. Still longing for that tangible object, we decided upon t-shirts: "I've been to 400 breweries. Ask me how."

AUGUST

BETTER LATE THAN NEVER

Four days after returning home from Portland, we hit the skies again for London. For most people, a trip overseas requires weeks of packing and preparing. At this point, all I needed was quality time with the dogs and a moment for my checklist: meds, money, passport. Check.

London, with its iconic red phone booths and bowler-capped Bobbies, generally represented a travel intermission to us. Often, it served as a stopover on the way to or from somewhere else in Western Europe. The most consecutive time we'd spent in London, or even England for that matter, was two days. Our August trip to the Great British Beer Festival (GBBF) aimed to change all that as we finally focused on everything English. First, though, we had to get there.

A one and a half-hour delay to London caused us to make a mad dash out of Heathrow toward our first destination, Wadworth Brewery in the town of Devizes. For us, the delay was not only inconvenient, it meant the potential loss of a new addition to The List because the brewery's public tasting hours would be over by the time we arrived. Luckily, we got there twenty minutes prior to closing; just in the nick of time. A sympathetic tasting room staff allowed us entry and beer tasting, so we promised to drink fast. Better late than never, we added Wadworth to The List.

In England, the beer to drink is "real ale." A term coined by the Campaign for Real Ale (CAMRA) in the early 1970s, it refers to a top fermented beer that undergoes a secondary fermentation in the container (cask) from which it will be dispensed. When ready, the beer is served at cellar temperature (55°F) without the addition of carbon dioxide, resulting in a light, natural carbonation.

American macro-brewed beers, derived from German beer traditions, contrast with real ale conditions. Real ale's warmer serving temperature and lack of added carbonation give rise to the myth that English beer is served warm and flat.

German beer styles are my favorite and prior to our trip I fretted over how to survive a week in England.

"What am I going to do? Not drink beer for a whole week?" I whined.

"You'll probably like it," Chris responded.

I tried to look on the bright side and added, "Well, I probably won't drink as much, so that means no hangovers."

The underlying philosophy of our travel is to experience a beer style within its own context. When in England, one drinks real ale. Besides, with several friends who work as cellarmen at real ale pubs, I would never hear the end of it if I drank anything other than the real deal.

The job of a cellarman is to tenderly care for the beer every step of the way. Real ale is their life and they take pride in serving a good and proper pint.

"English beers are some of the best beers in the world, so long as they're looked after properly," our cellarman friend Paul Daly once told us. "It's all down to ten or fifteen minutes every day. A little bit of care, a little bit of attention, and a little bit of love, that's the way you get a good English beer."

At Wadworth, we got a taste of the tender loving care that Paul talked about. Over samples of Wadworth's JcB and 6X, we groused about the delayed flight. Our hostess marveled at our dedication to beer. She found it remarkable that we drove straight from the airport to the brewery. Despite missing the refreshing tingle of carbonation, I managed to finish my samples of real ale. I started to think that maybe I worried too much about my survival in England.

Our hostess apologized for not allowing us to stay longer and directed us to a pub that served Wadworth beer in the traditional style—out of a wooden cask. She told us that the brewery's cooper, a maker of wooden barrels, frequented the pub. We thanked her for all her hospitality and walked down the street.

At Three Crowns, a crowded table of blue-collar lads enjoyed pints after work. They looked in our direction as we walked in the door, but quickly returned to their pints when they didn't recognize us. When we ordered, the bartender pulled our pints from below the bar. Presumably, the cask was down there somewhere. We both had romantic visions of watching beer stream out of a brass spigot in a wooden barrel. Disappointed, we were forced to use our imagination instead.

In a way unparalleled in America, the English pub is the center of village life. Children with their soda and crisps sit quietly next to parents or dart in and around the tables. A ten year-old girl walked up to her father who sat on the stool next to me.

"Dad, can we go home now?" she asked.

Chris and I chuckled. Some things are universal, no matter what country you're in.

A woman with a cast on her arm and a 13-year old daughter at her side ordered a round of drinks. The daughter, trying to be helpful, picked up a pint of beer in one hand and a glass of wine in the other. The mother immediately admonished her daughter and instructed her to put them down. Under the legal drinking age, it was okay for her to be in the pub, but she couldn't be in possession of any alcoholic drinks. The daughter protested that she only tried to help since her mother obviously couldn't carry them all with one hand. We sat at the short-ranged bar and smiled.

"She just can't wait to get a drink of her own," the mother said.

"Yeah, you better watch out for her," replied the father with the impatient daughter.

"Here, I'll help you," I offered.

I picked up the pint of beer and glass of wine just as the girl had done and followed the woman outside to her table. Her friends looked surprised to see me, but offered thanks before resuming their conversation.

The full pint at Three Crowns went down much slower than my sample-sized beers at Wadworth. Our flight delay had put us behind schedule and according to Chris's agenda we had little time to spare. That meant there wasn't enough time for me to be nursing my beer. Chris, who drinks much faster drinker than me, kept up with his time schedule better than I managed to. My unfinished beer remained on the bar as we walked back to the car.

Another two-hour drive to the Somerset village of Nether Stowey and the Old Cider House Bed & Breakfast lay ahead of us. While I had the luxury of being a passenger, the jet-lagged Chris needed a high degree of concentration to drive on the wrong side of the car and the wrong side of the road. Chris corrects me when I say it that way, since it's the *right* side of the road to drive on in England, but from my perspective, it is absolutely true.

We arrived at the Old Cider House Bed and Breakfast just forty-five minutes before dinner. The Old Cider House is also the home of Real Ale Walks and Stowey Brewery. Chris found it during an Internet search. Combining two of our favorite travel activities, hiking and beer, he booked it right away.

Chris, unsure of where to put the car, parked it haphazardly along the narrow lane. We walked to the front door where proprietor Ian Pearson greeted us warmly and guided us to the private car park hidden behind a large set of carriage house doors. We had just enough time to shower and freshen up before dinner.

Ian introduced us to his wife Lynne before leading us upstairs. He opened the door to our room and said, "Here you go. If you need anything just ask."

We stared at the two twin beds. In Europe double occupancy rooms are generally two separate twin beds or two twin beds pushed together to look like a double. Almost to our breaking point from first day jetlag, we had hoped for comfortable beds. For us, sleeping apart wasn't our idea of comfort, but neither was squeezing into one twin bed. We dropped our bags on the limited floor space and explored the compact room.

After refreshing showers, we went downstairs for dinner where we joined two other couples in the sitting room for our before dinner beers. The cozy room made personal conversation not so personal. Yet none of us were extraverted enough to get a group discussion going. Each couple spoke in hushed voices and eavesdropped on the conversations of the others. One couple traveled with their dog, a spaniel that sprawled on the floor at their feet. With thoughts of Porter and Stout in my head, I turned to Chris, who spoke first.

"I know. I miss them, too," he said. "Don't you wish we could bring them with us?"

"No. Don't even go there," I replied.

"Come on, wouldn't it be great?" he implored.

Chris's vision of traveling to Europe with the dogs was pure fantasy. He pictured Porter and Stout sitting on our laps as we played Scrabble in an Irish pub or lying at our feet on the graveled ground of a Munich beer garden. The reality is that our dogs would never lie quietly like the spaniel or any other dog we saw in the pubs and beer halls of Europe. Porter and Stout would be scouring under the table with noses pressed to the floor sampling whatever leftover bit of food they could find.

They would bark at anyone that came near us and go ballistic when they sensed another dog.

"No. It wouldn't be great," I said.

A short while later, Lynne invited us all into the dining room for dinner.

Ian and Lynne, who knew we traveled for beer, had created a four-course beer-inspired dinner. Ian presented the first course with a Stowey Brewery beer brewed with wild nettles, a botanical relative of hops, for bitterness. The three sets of guests each sat at their own table. We happened to sit at the table closest to our hosts. Ian eyed us closely as we tasted his beer for the first time. The pressure was on. What if we didn't like it?

"Wow! Very tasty," I commented and set my glass back down. Despite my general lack of enthusiasm for real ale, Ian's beer was solid and tasted good.

Chris offered a reassuring nod of agreement and we all relaxed at successfully managing the moment of truth. Polite conversation continued throughout dinner. An evening of meeting new people, drinking craft beer, and eating good food helped Chris and I truly enjoy ourselves.

After dinner, Ian suggested a half-block walk to the Rose and Crown for a nightcap. Ian and Lynne's local pub, it was one of only two in the village. The Rose and Crown lived up to our idealized vision of an English village pub. The bartender pulled real ale and the atmosphere encouraged friendly conversation. The crowd was sparse, but a few villagers sat at the bar. They addressed Ian and Lynne by name and extended a warm welcome to Chris and me. We watched as Ian negotiated with, and eventually hired, a man at the end of the bar to wallpaper the Old Cider House.

It only took one sip of my beer to remind me of why it's important to drink beer within its own context. In that moment, I actually appreciated (and enjoyed) the slight carbonation and malty flavor unrestrained by a cold serving temperature. It was a long first day in England, but the first of eight real ale-filled days was over and I had survived.

The next day, after a traditional English breakfast of fried egg, bacon, and baked beans, Ian and Lynne led us on a guided Real Ale Walk. The four of us, joined by a pair of Labradors named Buster and Ozzy, set out for the Quantock Hills. I was grateful for their guidance on the four-mile trip to the town of Crowcombe. Barely visible pathways traversed private pastures, which would have caused us pause on our own. Cutting through heather-covered hills, the beautiful 360° view included the sight of Wales across the bay.

Up and over a hill, we encountered a corral full of sheep. We climbed the fence while the dogs flattened themselves to the ground and slid underneath. A symphony of "baas" greeted us. With every step forward, the sheep parted like the Red Sea. I felt like Charleton Heston in *The Ten Commandments*.

We soon arrived at the Carew Arms, a real ale pub that has served as the center of Crowcombe village life for 400 years. I sat down at the table with Lynne as Ian and Chris explored the rooms and nooks of the well-worn pub.

The traditional appearance of the front bar looked as though it had changed little over the centuries. The same could be said of the two older gentlemen who sat at the bar. Their cap covered heads drooped over pints. Hunched tweeded backs faced me and the men scarcely looked in my direction as I approached.

Over lunch, we explained *thebeergeek.com* and the Year in Beer to Ian and Lynne. They talked about how Real Ale Walks and Stowey Brewery developed. Afterwards, Ian—proud of English beer traditions—led us on a tour of the pub.

"Come this way. I want to show you my favorite part of this pub," he said.

We stepped into a room with a mini bowling alley.

"Have you ever seen this game?" Ian asked.

"Bowling?" I said in a highly uncertain tone.

"It's skittles," Chris replied.

Skittles, a classic Somerset game similar to bowling, is played mainly in the winter. Ian explained that the real purpose of skittles is to go to the pub for a beer. The non-bowling team disappears into the bar for pints while they wait their turn. Each team trusts the other to be honest in their play. Still popular, the local area supports over a dozen leagues.

Each pub's skittles lane possesses unique quirks, shapes, and grooves. This gives a distinct home advantage and leaves the visiting team scrambling to adjust. At the Carew Arms, the old stable now housed the skittles lane. Designation as an historic building required that the interior remain intact when they created it, so old horse stalls were converted into cozy booths on the side. With a beer in one hand, and an irregularly shaped wooden ball in the other, Ian helped us learn the game's lingo.

"There's lots of words that have sort of grown up in relation to playing skittles," he began. "The person that puts up the skittles is known as the 'sticker upper' and if you knock all the skittles down, it's called a 'flobber,' we think." He turned to Lynne who nodded her head in agreement. "If you knock all the skittles down twice, it's known as a 'double flobber,' " he finished.

I released the ball down the lane. It echoed loudly as it bounced toward the end. I knocked down only two of the nine wooden skittles. No flobbers for me. I needed a lot more practice before joining a local team.

The return to Nether Stowey turned into more of a hike than a walk. Now traveling uphill, our jet lag caused it to be even more of a challenge. Chris and I were relieved when we saw the car up ahead as we came to the end of the journey.

The other guests had all departed, so when we got back to the house, Ian and Lynne generously invited us to join them for a beer tasting in the brewery followed by a simple pasta dinner. We happily accepted.

At the appointed hour, we let ourselves out the kitchen door into the large garden in the backyard. We wandered in and around flower patches and vegetable beds until Ian and Lynne emerged from the main house. They welcomed us into a nearby shed.

The brewery provided the perfect escape. With beer posters on the walls and a bar inside, most people would call it a man-cave. I liked the idea of having a backyard getaway and would have enjoyed it for my own. A closet-sized area on one end housed the brewing set-up.

Ian presented us with a representative sample of English beers, helping to familiarize us with the breweries we could anticipate seeing at the Great British Beer Festival in a few days. They waited patiently as we tasted over a dozen bottles. Once again, I felt the pressure to offer a beer geek's assessment of the brews. Chris enthusiastically embraced each of the samples. I, on the other hand, was still adjusting to the time change and real ale, so I held back with timid sips and polite comments about the beer being good. My hope was that Chris would finish the collection of open bottles that had quickly piled up on the table because I couldn't drink much more of them. When it was time for dinner, we brought the remaining beer in the house to have with our meal.

For the second night in a row, the after dinner activity included a walk down to the Rose and Crown. A few people dotted the pub, with several more sitting at the bar. After a few beers, the man at the other end of the bar agreed to entertain us "Yanks" with a traditional last call. The stout gentleman in a blue oxford shirt looked right at home as he stepped behind the bar and grabbed the large brass bell. With each flick of his wrist, the bell cracked.

"Time, gentlemen, please," he bellowed.

With a thwack and dull clank, the bell landed back on the bar. After a brief pause he took up the bell one more time.

"On second time. Time, gentlemen, please," he bellowed again.

Satisfied, he set the bell down and came out from behind the bar. Staged or not, Chris and I thought he performed brilliantly.

The next morning—armed with instructions provided by Ian—we ventured out on a self-guided walk to the town of Holford and the Plough Inn. We were a little nervous about our ability to follow the seemingly vague directions.

"Turn right just after a grassy clearing with a solitary tree," I read aloud to Chris.

"Back there looked liked a grassy clearing," I turned around and pointed in the direction from which we just came. "Did you see a solitary tree?"

"I'm not sure," Chris replied. "Let's go a little bit further and see if we find anything else."

A few minutes ahead, we came upon a distinct clearing and dutifully turned to the right-hand trail.

The walk took us through fields and woodland, and finally alongside a meandering brook straight into the town of Holford. After a little over four miles, we arrived at the Plough Inn ready for some pints and food. The pub served three real ales and Chris chose the Tawny Bitter from Cotleigh, a Somerset brewery. Pubs usually serve a "proper" cider along side their real ale selection and, since Somerset is home to English cider, I decided to give one a try. The color of my crisp Cheddar Valley Cider closely resembled an orange soda or, more fittingly, a slice of cheddar cheese.

The friendly publican watched Chris take a picture of the tap handles.

"I've got something to give you to better remember your visit," he said.

He pulled a plastic grocery bag from below and plopped it on the bar. The room filled with the crinkling sound of plastic as he rifled through the contents. Finally finding what he was looking for, he pulled out a Cotleigh bar towel and handed it to Chris. We find most publicans friendly, but usually they don't often offer up such special mementos. The man correctly predicted that the gift would help us better remember our visit to the Plough Inn.

The pints and ploughman's lunch provided the necessary energy for the walk back to Nether Stowey. Our return journey took us through moorland similar to what we'd hiked the previous day. In no time we found our way back to the Old Cider House. Our last evening in Somerset, we once again stopped in to the Rose and Crown for a pint and a game of Scrabble. The following day, a train delivered us to London.

With connections from a friend, Chris and I had garnered tickets to the Great British Beer Festival's trade session. When we arrived, the doors had yet to open, so we joined the back of the line. Chris turned on the video camera in the hopes of capturing my spontaneous excitement of being at GBBF. Over the last eight months, Chris proved much better at expressing child-like wonderment at the events we attended. I, however, liked to avoid the appearance of overexcitement and more frequently opted for cool and reserved. God forbid I should publicly embarrass myself with a show of geeky eagerness. Actually, in moments of self-reflection, I have contemplated my unwillingness to be goofy and considered making a concerted effort to be more carefree. Admittedly, the effort has resulted in little change.

I snickered into the camera and held up my ticket. Restrained enthusiasm rarely makes good footage. Chris turned off the camera, disappointed with my failure to oblige him with an outward expression of excitement. He ended up using the footage in the *One Pint at a Time* episode anyway.

We stepped inside and the vast array of beer tables, brewery bars, and food stalls left me awestruck. That might have made good footage, but Chris stood equally stunned. Our awe quickly turned to confusion; we really had no idea what to do. No one offered us a primer on attending GBBF, so we improvised. The woman at the front table offered us 33 ml, half and full pint glasses. She also informed us that it was acceptable to bring our own drinking container, as long as the units of measurement were properly marked.

We purchased two pint glasses. At the end of the festival we had the option to keep our glass or return it for our money back. All we had done so far was obtain our glasses and already GBBF was very different from any other beer festival we'd ever attended. And that was only the beginning.

We randomly chose to walk to the right. The "U.S. and the Rest of the World Bar" seemed as good a place as any to start. Before we reached the bar, a voice with a distinct Irish accent called out, "It's the Beer Geeks."

My heart fluttered with excitement that, not yet ten minutes into the festival, someone recognized us!

Chris walked up to a short, shaven-head man who wore a black t-shirt with *Irishcraftbrewer.com* on the front. "John," he confidently stated, "The Beer Nut."

"Chris, the Beer Geek," John replied.

John Duffy, aka "the Beer Nut," is one of the administrators for the website *Beoir.org* (formerly known as *Irishcraftbrewer.com).* Established on St. Patrick's Day 2007, the site created an online community that aims to increase an awareness of quality beer and brewing in Ireland. They also campaign for a wider beer choice in the country's pubs and restaurants. During a random Internet beer search one day, Chris stumbled upon the site. He joined and had been actively participating in the discussion groups ever since.

Irish craft brewers are few in number and close in relationship. Together with John, they gathered near the International

Bar. We talked with Aidan from Galway Hooker and Liam from Carlow Brewing, both of whom we'd visited in June. John introduced us to Cuilan Loughnane from Mssrs. Maguire in Dublin.[22] A conversation with a group of Irish people is truly an experience. Frequently with pint in hand, the Irish converse with an animated emotion that embraces and comforts. Their warm welcome rid us of our shyness. It no longer mattered that we had never before visited GBBF or that we had no idea what to do.

In that moment I once again recognized the expansion of our beer world. Just as I had felt after our June trip to Ireland, standing with the Irish brewers highlighted for me the travel part of our beer adventures. From our travels we had friends in other countries and from that my world became free of borders and boundaries.

I looked over at the bar and realized we were standing in front of the American beers. More than an esoteric musing, my revelation applied to real life. After all, I didn't come all the way to England to confine myself within the boundaries of American beer. A convention center filled with beers I'd never heard of lay before me waiting to be explored. Our confident exploration, however, often looked more like aimless wandering. Unfamiliar with the breweries, we picked beers based on the name. For my first beer I chose Hebridean's Berserker Export Pale Ale.

In hindsight, I really should have thought my beer choice out more thoroughly. Berserker is the name of an ancient Norse warrior who fought with frenzied rage, possibly due to the ingestion of hallucinogenic mushrooms. The GBBF program

22 Cuilan has since founded the White Gypsy brewery in County Tipperary, but continues to brew for Mssrs. McGuire as well.

described Berserker as "matured to develop a smooth intricate flavor." Far from smooth, my mouth experienced a bad trip. I took one sip and unceremoniously poured the rest into the nearest rubbish bin. At many American beer festivals, the entrance fee is all-inclusive, so there is little guilt associated with dumping a beer. This event was more like one huge pub. I actually paid for that half-pint I just dumped. Chris fared better with his first choice, Hogs Back Hop Garden Gold.

For my next trick, I pulled a real rookie traveler move. The beer cost £1.70 for a half-pint and I gave the volunteer a handful of change, which I thought equaled the exact amount. He walked away, but promptly came back and handed me the coin marked with the number 50.

"I can't take this," he informed me.

Completely lost as to why, I stared at the coin in my palm. He tried to explain the reason more clearly.

"A cent is not the same as a pence," he said.

He repeated it more than once, but it still didn't register with me why he refused to accept it. I put the coin back in my pocket and handed him some more. When I returned to Chris and explained what occurred, I looked more closely at my money. Chris looked in my hand. At the same time, we both realized the error.

"That's a 50 Euro cent piece, you eejit," Chris eloquently pointed out.

We moved along with no particular plan except to absorb the festival vibe. Forty-yard-long bars grouped beers by geographical region: North West England, Central Southern England, and Mid-East England. Knowing nothing of English geography, the designations held no meaning for us.

Some individual breweries set up their own bars. Greene King created a pub, complete with shelves, bottles of beer, and decorations behind the bar. Shepherd Neame lined up picnic benches with large umbrellas to shade patrons from the blinding lights of the convention hall. Parked nearby, the famous red and white double-decker bus from Wells Bombardier proclaimed their beer as the "Drink of England."

A large man with long curly fake eyelashes, an ill-fitting gaudy dress and a pink foot-high beehive wig walked passed us with dramatic flair. A woman trailed closely behind him in her blue Jackie O-style wig. She flung her feather boa about while behind her a dress the color of grape Kool Aid flowed. As Chris chased after them to get video, I watched and wondered if I could ever be as outlandishly bold. Individual expression like that is extraversion to the hilt. As much social growth as I had made up to this point in the Year in Beer, the answer was no, I really couldn't ever be that bold. In that moment I wished I could, though, because those two looked like they were having fun.

A troop of beer drinkers came dressed in matching red polo shirts, proudly representing their local brewery. Another group wore blue t-shirts with the name of their favorite pub. We especially loved the contingent from the Cornish brewery, Skinner's. Thirty-odd people strong, they spent the session near the Skinner's taps drinking beer and singing songs. One man in the group dressed in drag as Betty Stogs, the namesake of their bitter. Any man who agreed to wear bright blue eye shadow and large fake breasts got a nod in my book. Once it was announced that Skinner's Betty Stogs Bitter won champion best bitter, the revelry went through the roof.

"We're bound for South Australia
Haul away, you rolling king
Heave away, haul away
All the way you'll hear me sing
We're bound for South Australia."

I sang along with the chorus. Jolly beer drinkers belting out traditional songs in unison elevated the simple act of drinking to an experience to remember. Together with others who sang along, we each contributed to the fond festival memories of those around us. Rather than passively attend, we added to the festivities. After all these years of beer travel, I finally understood the difference. Chris's participation in the festival extended beyond singing when he decided to try his hand at skee ball.

He rolled hand-sized wooden barrels, one by one, down the ramp. They popped up in the air before falling through holes marked with differing point values. Chris's total score wasn't high enough to earn a prize, but he scored points on each barrel, which earned him a consolation gift. The man running the game gave Chris a ticket to redeem at the prize booth. Chris passed on the desk calendar and bottle opener and instead chose CAMRA's *National Inventory of Pubs* booklet.

After several hours, the trade session wound down. Now open to the general public, the festival became crowded. The time had come for us to move on. We looked forward to another session in a few days, especially since we were now familiar with how the festival worked.

We returned to the hotel to rest and gear up for the second part of our day, a visit to (what was then) our local pub in London, the Old Fountain, to meet up with our friend Paul Daly. An excellent example of a place serving real ale at its finest, the Old Fountain marked its fourth consecutive appearance in CAMRA's *Good Beer Guide* in 2010. Only establishments that serve proper well-cellared ale are chosen for inclusion and it's a badge of honor that is worn proudly by those who earn it.

Exiting the Old Street Underground stop, we walked a few minutes north on City Road and turned left onto a quiet side street. The pub's bright blue exterior made it easy to find. We entered and waited patiently for the bartender to notice us. A broad grin filled his face when he finally looked up from washing glasses. Our friend Paul put down his towel and excitedly came around the bar. Paul has a bounce in his step, a bushy red beard (depending on the season), and the unmistakable lilt of the Irish accent. He welcomed us with a big hug and offered us a pint, the perfect beer lover's reception. Pub patrons looked on with curiosity as an Irishman living in London welcomed a couple of Americans.

Our meeting of Paul and his wife Eilís illustrates beer's power to break down borders and bring people of different cultures together. In May 2006, we spent the night in London on our way back from Ireland. Prior to our trip, Chris learned about a highly rated pub in Belgravia called The Star Tavern. Once off The Underground, we walked around in circles for an hour trying to find this elusive little pub. Tucked down Belgrave Mews, we must have passed the Portuguese and Syrian embassies a hundred times before we found it.

In any case, we eventually stumbled upon it and joined another couple sitting at the bar. We intended to make a short night of it because we were flying home the next morning. In between swigs of beer, Chris picked up one of the pocket-sized

World Cup schedules scattered around the bar. I know nothing about soccer, so my eyes glazed over when Chris commented on the groups and the U.S. team's chance in the tournament. I smiled and agreed with him to give the illusion of an actual conversation. Our pints got low and Chris's one-sided conversation tapered off. We agreed to leave when we finished our beers. From the other side of me, a redheaded man with thick eyeglasses and an Irish accent scoffed at one of Chris's soccer comments. That sparked a two-hour conversation, several more pints, and a lasting friendship with Paul and Eilís.

Seven months later, we again passed through London during a Christmas trip to Germany. Paul invited us to meet him after his shift at the Old Fountain. Fast forward to 2008 and once again we found ourselves enjoying pints and conversation in the Old Fountain. A half hour later, the arrival of Paul's wife Eilís inspired another lively round of hugs, smiles, and exuberant voices. Paul finished his shift and, like his own patrons, wanted an after-work pint at *his* local pub. The four of us set out on foot for the nearby Wenlock Arms, our second local in London. The Wenlock, listed in the *Good Beer Guide* every year since 1995, has won the North London Pub of the Year award four times.

We walked into the Wenlock Arms to familiar faces, including "John the Ticker." John keeps a list of every beer he drinks, a hobby known as "ticking" or "scooping." When we first met John at the Old Fountain in December 2007, he fit the stereotypical appearance of a CAMRA member—long, scraggly hair with a beard to match and Birkenstocks on his feet. His list at that time included 9,400 beers.

"Wow, that's a lot of beers," I had marveled.

"Yes, well, my doctor told me I have to cut down on my pints. I'm allowed only five per day," he paused, "and I'm having trouble limiting myself to five."

Seeing John now, we almost didn't recognize him. His hair was cut close and neat and his beard was gone. He no longer looked like an aged hippie and appeared younger and more like he belonged in the current decade. Paul informed us that John had donated his hair to a program that makes wigs for people with cancer. I never realized that beard hair could serve such a useful purpose.

We left John at his corner table and the four of us gathered at the end of the bar. I sat on a stool and stared at the list of beers on the blackboard in the corner. No part of any of the names looked even remotely familiar. Chris stood next to me just as disoriented. We were out of our element with English beers. I looked at Paul who started at the top and described each of the beers to us.

"There's not one beer over 5.5%," Chris laughed.

"I know. Look, the second one down is only 3.2," I replied.

Paul shook his head at us. "This isn't America, kids. We sport drinkable alcohol levels."

At Paul's recommendation, I chose one made with honey. The ordeal of ordering a beer over, I noticed that hunger had crept in. I ordered one of the Wenlock's famous "sandwedges." Two slices of white bread, each measuring about two inches thick, with a few slices of ham and spicy mustard in between. Simply delicious.

Not the only chance we would have to spend with Paul and Eilís, we called it an evening after just a few hours. They walked us to The Underground and sent us on our way.

"You two okay getting back? You know where you're going?" Paul asked.

"Yeah, no problem," Chris assured him.

We felt confident in our public transportation skills, even after a night of beer drinking. Perhaps a little too confident, though, because it took a few stops for Chris and me to realize that we boarded the wrong train. We stared at the map above the door. It took us another few stops to gain some bearings on our whereabouts, but it still wasn't altogether clear. We cut our losses and got off at the next station. With some help from the front desk person at the Euston Square station Travel Lodge, we caught a cab back to the hotel. Our adventure wasn't over, though.

Construction detoured the cabbie from his usual route and he became turned around. First, he consulted his GPS. Chris and I sighed. Then he called another cab driver on his cell phone. Meanwhile he continued to drive the streets in attempt to find his way. I closed my eyes and tilted my head back, praying he would find his way sooner than later. Sleepiness came on fast and we just wanted to get back to the hotel. We eventually did. It was one in the morning.

I woke up the next day feeling bright-eyed and bushy tailed. Drinking most of the previous day, I fully expected to wake up with a headache and maybe a little nauseous. Maybe there was an upside to real ale after all, I thought.

With more time to spend in London than we'd ever had, Chris and I planned to act like normal tourists for the day with a river cruise down the River Thames to Greenwich.

The captain drove slowly and provided commentary in a thick cockney accent. "Over to the left is the Old Billingsgate fish market. A fish market had been at that location for over 900 years until a few years ago when it moved to the West India Docks." All heads turned to the left, cameras raised to get the perfect shot.

The boat continued down the river as its passengers looked from side to side depending on the instructions of the captain.

"And over to the left," the captain continued, "you can see the pier pilings where convicted pirates were chained after hanging. It was customary for the body to remain chained for three tides."

The trip to Greenwich took an hour and a half, more time than we expected. This, combined with our late start to the day, meant we had little time in Greenwich before the last boat departed back to our starting point in the shadow of Big Ben.

We arrived on dry land and immediately reverted to our natural, and more comfortable, state as beer travelers. Paul recommended a pair of respectable real ale pubs up the street away from the crowds at the pier.

The Greenwich Union pub served as our first stop. In November 2001, the pub became Meantime Brewery's original tied house, a pub owned by the brewery where products from no other brewery are sold. A "free house," in contrast, is a pub that is not associated with one particular brewery and serves beer from whichever breweries it chooses.

Today, Greenwich Union is the brewery's official tap. Unfortunately, no brewing is done at the pub so we couldn't count it on The List. We enjoyed a taster set with a savory dish of potato cake, salt pork, and poached egg.

Conveniently located right next door, Richard I, a pub tied to Young's Brewery, offered us a second opportunity to enjoy beer at a top-rated drinking establishment. I ordered a Waggle

Dance. The bartender's biceps flexed as she pulled down the handle. A gurgle echoed in the empty glass. A few pulls later, a thin head of loose bubbles topped the golden-colored drink—the vision of properly poured real ale.

After our pints, we wandered further up the hill to the Royal Observatory in Greenwich Royal Park. As we arrived, a stream of older Russians passed by on their way back to their tour bus. We swam against the tide of people and climbed to top of the hill.

As we came up the hill a large clock set into a brick wall caught my eye. Black Roman numerals on the white face cluttered the perimeter of the clock with lines.

"Oh, I get it. Greenwich Mean Time," I thumped the heel of my hand on my forehead and laughed.

"You just got that?" Chris laughed.

The smell of bacon wafted passed us and we both looked to see where it was coming from. We tracked the smell further up the hill and soon heard sizzling emanating from a food truck selling "Bacon Butties." We didn't know what they were exactly, but anything with bacon is good. A butty, it turns out, is a sandwich served on a small, buttered roll. In our case, the roll held a hot hissing piece of back bacon. The taste of our butty made the walk down through the park like a stroll in heaven.

We wandered through the grounds of the Royal Naval College on the way back to the boat. While the trip back seemed to take twice as long as the ride there, we eventually made it back to our starting point.

Back on the other side of the Thames, the quest for Thai food began. It may seem like an odd combination, but Thai food in pubs is not so uncommon. Generally operated separately, the restaurant is located within the pub. The Churchill Arms came highly recommended.

As it was slightly humid out, the long trek from the boat dock created sweat on my brow and heat under my clothes. Throughout the walk, I looked forward sitting down to a good meal.

A block away, gold lettering clearly stood out against the shiny black exterior of The Churchill Arms. The beautiful colorful baskets of flowers hanging from high above were eye catching. So was the large crowd milling about the front door.

Chattering groups of people parted to allow us in the door. The inside of the pub was just as crowded and every table was occupied. At a tiny table near the door, two people looked almost finished with their meals. While Chris went to the bar to order beer, I hovered around the prospective table, ready to pounce the moment it became free.

After what seemed like forever, the occupants finally departed and we quickly moved in on it. The low, child-sized table was practically in the doorway and was barely big enough to hold our beers and plates of Rad Na and Pad Thai. Our knees loomed over the top as we sat on padded step stools for seats, but it didn't matter. We had a seat to enjoy our beer and food. Drinking real ale was still a struggle, but my Fuller's Golden Ale, a refreshing cold blond ale, offered a nice reprieve.

Towards the end of our meal, we noticed that the crowd had started to thin. The kitchen was closing soon, but table space continued to be a hot commodity. Another couple scooped up our table as quickly as we had.

We awoke on Thursday with a mix of excitement and anxiety. It was our big day to volunteer at the Great British Beer Festival.

Pulling pints at the festival thrilled us, but the idea of making change in foreign money was terrifying. We got the lay of the land a few days before, so we knew what to expect as far as the festival went. Still, it had been a long time since I had worked in a job where money was exchanged. For Chris, it had been even longer.

We circled around the outside of Earl's Court in search of the volunteer check-in. After a bit of wandering, a security guard finally directed us to an employee entrance. We rode the escalator up to the next floor to the volunteer check-in/lounge area. The woman at the desk asked our preference for job assignments. The words "pouring beer" quickly left our mouths. Clearly, we knew exactly what job we wanted to perform.

"Okay, here are your badges. You've been assigned to B5, Mid-West England," she told us. Mid-West England meant nothing to us. She might as well have told us "A8, the dark side of the moon."

"Here's a map of the festival," she said as she circled B5. "Go downstairs and ask for Zippy. He's your bar manager."

We donned bright yellow vests before riding another escalator down to the convention floor. Forklifts zigzagged across our path on the way to B5. A few mistaken identities later, we found Zippy. We joined several other volunteers as Zippy explained the evacuation route to us. He then went down the line and offered a brief description of the twenty-plus beers in our area: milds, bitters, best bitters, porters, and stouts. Zippy's words swam around in my head. If I thought twenty-eight semi-familiar beers at Barclay's had been tough, this was going to be darn near impossible. I fretted to Chris, who was straining to remember the information himself. The most important point Zippy wanted us all to remember was to have fun.

Our bar's location in the back of the hall created a lag in customers after the doors opened at noon. Festival goers gradually made their way to us and I appreciated the slow start. Chris pulled his first pint, Slater's Top Totty, about 12:15 P.M. I nervously pulled my first pint a short time later. Handing the beer over to the customer, my hands shook so much that the glass tipped from side to side, spilling beer on the bar. Lucky for me, he handed me the exact change.

There is definitely a trick to pulling beer from a hand pump. With a tap that uses CO_2, you pull the tap forward and beer comes out. You push the tap handle back and it stops. But with a hand pump, you pull a long handle all the way down toward you to force a spray of beer out the end of a nozzle placed deep inside the glass. This type of serving was new to me and it was hard to know how many pulls each serving size required. Requests for pints resulted in waterfalls of beer flowing down the sides of the glasses. Requests for half-pints turned into three-quarter pints or more. Chris told me later that he experienced the same problem.

The crowd waxed and waned over the afternoon, sometimes being several deep at the bar. Unfortunately, I correctly anticipated the money to be a problem. The first few times I stood staring down at the cash drawer for minutes calculating the change. The method of making change that I learned as a teenager in my first job didn't work in England because the denomination of money was different. I soon adopted a system of determining how much change I owed my customer, and then collected the coins that added up to that amount. It was smooth sailing after I figured that out.

Chris didn't devise any method and continued to have some difficulty. An older gentleman handed over a large bill. Chris returned change to the man, who informed Chris that the amount was incorrect. After several attempts, they both gave up. It didn't really matter, though, because everyone was having fun and that was the point.

Halfway through our shift, Chris and I took a break. We boarded the escalator back upstairs to the volunteer lounge where the pints were free at the staff bar.

"How's it going so far?" Chris asked.

I plopped down in a chair and said, "This is hard work. You would have thought I would know that since we volunteered last month at OBF."

We picked at a cheese plate. "The biggest problem is the accents," I said. "I can't understand people and I don't know the names of the beers well enough to make an educated guess." Our fellow Area B5 volunteer, Les, who sat at the table with us, chuckled.

"I think I've asked every single person to repeat their order. Can't these people speak real English?" I said as Les chuckled harder.

Break time over, we returned to Mid-West England to finish the last few hours of our shift. Volunteers for the next shift started arriving and it became full behind the bar. With plenty of people to serve customers, Chris and I took the time to film each other pulling pints. Before we knew it, it was 5 o'clock—the end of our volunteer efforts at the Great British Beer Festival.

We headed straight to the Wenlock Arms for our after work beer and quiz night. There, Paul and Eilís were waiting for us to complete their quiz team. We had played quiz at the

Wenlock Arms once before and thoroughly enjoyed the quizmaster. His deep tone and deliberate deadpan delivery made it more fun to listen to him than actually attempt to answer the questions. Besides, our knowledge of British pop culture was scant and we hardly knew any of the answers anyway. Our Irish teammates had an equally difficult time and we placed sixth out of thirteen teams. At least we didn't finish last.

Paul and Eilís again left us to our own devices on The Underground. This time, we boarded the correct train and returned to the hotel without delay. The soft bed perfectly cradled my sore back and throbbing feet. We fell right to sleep.

For all we did and saw on this trip, the pace was actually leisurely, which meant that Chris didn't make me get out of bed at the crack of dawn each day. With the help of Paul, Chris created a real ale pub crawl for us on Friday. Unfortunately, Paul had to work and wouldn't be able to join us. We were on our own.

Chris and I arrived at our first stop, the Market Porter, during the lunch hour. Near Borough Market, the place bustled with activity. It shocked us to see how many business people imbibed at lunch. I hadn't realized the level of social acceptance this activity maintained in this day and age. With 3%-4% ABV beers, however, one could have a pint or two and still manage to function in the afternoon. Perhaps these English people were onto something. Instead of a dip into the chocolate drawer to cure the post-lunch lethargy, they went to the pub.

At the bar, I closed my eyes and pointed to a tap. The brewery names had become more familiar, but knowledge about the individual beers still eluded me. Unfortunately I made a poor choice; even Chris thought so. In spite of that, though, I finished my pint and we crossed the street to the famous Borough Market.

London's oldest food market, the Borough Market has existed for hundreds of years in various locations around the city. It has become a trendy place to buy food, as well as a tourist attraction

We dodged business people in suits and drifting tourists to enter the crowded maze of food stalls. Pushed about with the mass of other rambling individuals, I quickly found myself in the center of the fray. When I spotted a bakery, we moved like salmon during spawning season to make our way to the counter. In the same gauntlet-running fashion, we purchased ham, cornichons, and drinks for our picnic lunch. For cheese, the last item on our list, we braved the nearby Neal's Yard Dairy.

Rounded wheels covered in mustard-colored wax and circles of gray, moldy rinds filled the shelves and cases. Handwritten cards with names like Westcombe Cheddar, Seator's Orkney, and Stinking Bishop dumfounded us. Cow's milk, sheep's milk, goat's milk. Hard cheese, soft cheese, bleu cheese, and cheese with washed rinds. Despite being completely overwhelmed, we managed to make a purchase. I haven't the slightest notion of what it was, but it was good.

After lunch, we walked down Fleet Street to Wine Office Court and turned down the narrow alley. A large round sign, "Ye Olde Cheshire Cheese rebuilt in 1667" loomed high above the door. A board on the wall read, "Under 15 Sovereigns," below which listed the name of every monarch since the rebuilding during the reign of Charles II. Elizabeth II, 1952 completed the list.

I opened the door and stepped inside. Reminiscent of a Charles Dickens novel, a historic gloom permeated the air of the dark and creaky building. A plaque above the threshold of the front bar to our right proclaimed, "Gentlemen only served in this bar." Hmph, I thought indignantly as I passed underneath. An open antique fireplace dominated the cozy den.

The lack of available seats at the front bar forced us to explore the numerous rooms and alcoves in the cavernous pub. It would have been a shame to stop right inside the door anyway. Much more remained undiscovered toward the back and on the floors above. Narrow stairways led upwards and dark nooks were tucked around every corner. I tiptoed down the hallway in a state of hyper-vigilance, ready to defend myself against Jack the Ripper. Actually, in all fairness, it really didn't exude so much a haunted house feel as it projected a charming sort of melancholy. We found a bench built into the wall toward the back. Chris fetched us pints of Samuel Smith's Best Bitter as I considered my surroundings.

The extensive histories of European countries amaze me. As a Californian, my idea of history is rather short in comparison to the thousand-plus years of English lineage. Here I sat in the shadow drinking a pint in a London pub almost four-and-a-half centuries old. Chris tried to film so we could share this remarkable ambiance of antiquity, but it was just too dark.

We emerged from Ye Olde Cheshire Cheese like vampires, shielding our eyes from the daylight with our forearms. Even with sunglasses on, it took several more minutes before my eyes adjusted. A sharp eye was definitely needed to make it across Holborn Circus to our next stop, Ye Olde Mitre Tavern.

We approached the roundabout and stood as double-decker busses, cabs, motorcycles, and the occasional bicycle whizzed around the circle. Getting across was not going to be an easy feat. Without running shoes and a reflective jacket, we pretty much took our lives into our own hands. Chris gave the signal and we dashed across.

"This pub better be worth it," I yelled as a rally cry.

We found Ye Olde Mitre down the very narrow Ely Alley. The original tavern, built in 1547, served as the pub for the servants of the Palace of Bishops of Ely and is technically on land controlled by the Diocese of Ely, Cambridgeshire. Despite its reputation for being difficult to locate, we came upon it right away.

We squeezed through the narrow doorway. Deep-colored wood paneling adorned the walls and the floor was covered in dark, patterned carpet. Sconces and light fixtures on the low ceiling tried to compensate for the lack of natural light, an effort not entirely successful. The pub was pleasantly populated and we waited briefly for an available table. Chris and I sat down in armed, wood chairs lined against the wall to drink our pints. Soon enough, however, the low ceiling got the best of us and we ventured out into the front courtyard. In the light of day, we stood at a barrel that doubled as a table and finished our pints.

"Where are we off to next?" I asked.

"The Princess Louise," Chris answered. "They have cool bathrooms."

On the move again, we set out down High Holborn to the Princess Louise, a 136-year-old pub named for Queen Victoria's fourth daughter. Chris and I stood across the street to film the introduction to the pub.

"Across the street here is the Princess Louise and it's known for one unique feature," Chris teased. "So, I want to show it to you."

The interiors of historic London pubs, like the Princess Louise, say a lot about the psyches of the early patrons. In this case, discretion and privacy must have been the order of the day.

Dark wood features and beautiful etched glass partitions created private booths along the bar. We walked into the pub and peered into each cubicle as we passed. It felt intrusive and voyeuristic, but I wasn't sure how else to find an open seat. We found a pair of empty stools and stepped up to the bar. Large hutches in the middle of the U-shaped bar prevented us from seeing patrons on the other side. The size of the space closed in on us with its numerous partitions and hutches, but it was beautiful.

No one joined us in our cubicle, so we decided to venture to the back where the bar was open and spacious. In order to get there, though, we walked through yet another partition, a closed door with decorative glass features.

The area on the other side of the door was arranged in a more modern pub style with shin-high tables scattered about. Chris left me on my own at the end of the stand-up bar as he filmed inside the famed men's room. I sipped at my pint and longed to be in Munich drinking a Helles. Knowing that Germany was the following month's trip comforted me. In the meantime, another tiny sip of real ale passed through my lips as I waited for Chris.

On the video, a shaky image sweeps back and forth across the bathroom showing the stalls and a brief glimpse of the urinals. In each stall a pattern of teal, tan, and brick red tiles is edged with sculpted ceramic moldings. In the background, dripping water and the din of a crowded pub can be heard.

"One of the more noteworthy things about the Princess Louise is the ornate decorations in the men's room," Chris whispers.

He turned off the camera and asked, "What do you think? Pretty cool, huh."

I laughed, "Nice camerawork."

"Hey, I had to hurry before anyone came in," Chris explained.

Since the bathrooms were the real reason we visited this Samuel Smith's pub, we finished our pints and concluded our historic London real ale pub crawl. However, we had one more visit before calling it a night. We hopped on The Underground and headed back to the Old Fountain.

My real ale breaking point had finally been reached. I walked in, apologized to Paul, and ordered a bottle of Schneider Weisse, a German wheat beer. A thick, dense head topped the tall glass. I cupped my hands around the glass and let the cold chill my palms. The cool, sparkly goodness of the beer created happiness from the inside out.

Paul finished his shift and Eilís soon joined us. Paul introduced us to a bleach blonde spiky-haired man named Spizz. He was the frontman of the late 1970s punk band Spizzenergi, which we had never heard of. We had also never heard of their hit song "Where's Captain Kirk?" (I've since seen video of various live performances of the song and find it rather entertaining.) Thirty years on, his spastic, rapid-fire personality showed little sign of aging. He was a hoot to have a beer with!

A tray full of shot glasses made its way to our table. In general, we don't drink hard alcohol, but when a generous tablemate offers, it's hard to refuse, at least for me. I drank my shot of Sambuca, as well as Chris's. The video camera soon emerged, which sent Spizz through the roof. His spinning energy was enough to induce vertigo. Attempts to get Eilís to chug her shot failed and she interrupted me to get serious.

"No, no, Meridet listen," she said, dropping the 'th' sound at the end of my name. "Here's to friendship, Transatlantic. And I'll swim all night to America, if I ever go there."

Her beautiful Dublin accent made the sentiment all the more endearing. She was right. It was important to appreciate the friendship that beer helped to create.

"Here's to ya," I replied.

With no intention of slowing the evening down, I started to order another beer. Chris gently suggested that I re-think that idea. The suggestion was a definite buzz kill, but I listened anyway. We wrapped up our night and headed back to the hotel. I would thank Chris in the morning.

Saturday morning we met Paul, who had arranged a mini brewery tour for us, at the King's Cross Station to travel to the North London suburbs. Harry Potter fans will know that the train for Hogwarts leaves from platform 9 3/4 King's Cross. I read the first few books in the series, but didn't think of it at all when Paul suggested we meet there. Our train departed from platform 10, so we would be passing right by the famed, imaginary platform.

Not so imaginary anymore, I waited in line behind a group of pre-teens for a photo op. Ten minutes later I stepped up to the luggage trolley and attempted to transport myself onto the magical train bound for wizard school. Unsuccessful, it meant no Hogwarts for me. I'd have to settle for a visit to Red Squirrel Brewery instead.

On a previous trip to London, Chris tried Red Squirrel's Colorado IPA and thought it was brilliant. Paul was nice enough to set up a brewery visit for us.

We got off the train at the Hertford North rail station and went in search of the brewery. Located in an industrial park, Red Squirrel brews close to 20 different beers. The owner Gary Hayward is an amazing one-man operation. During our visit, Gary explained that he handles every task of the business: brewing, washing casks, distribution, sales, accounts receivable, and accounts payable. He offered us each a beer and went back to work. Due to the 2008 "hop crisis," the Colorado IPA was no longer brewed. In its place, Chris, Paul and I tasted the Springfield IPA. While not as hoppy as the brewery's American West Coast-style IPA, Springfield satisfied Chris's inner hophead. We explored the brewery as we drank our beer and tried to stay out of Gary's way. When our beers we empty, we thanked him for his hospitality and left him to continue his work.

We explored the town of Hertford, including adding another brewery to The List, before it was time to return to London. When we arrived at the King's Cross Station, we said our goodbyes to Paul, who went off to catch his train back home. We caught another train to Earl's Court for our final appearance at the Great British Beer Festival.

During our third session of GBBF, we continued our manner of drifting from bar to bar. Occasionally something exciting sidetracked us and we veered off in that direction, only to be sidetracked again a few minutes later.

With an empty glass, I needed another beer to wash down my authentic Cornish pasty. I held out my money to pay for my pint and, in a random act of beer kindness, the man behind the bar waved it away.

"Girls are beer geeks, too. That's a great shirt that surely deserves a free pint," he said. His good-natured comment lifted my spirit and renewed my faith in the bumper sticker religion mantra "Practice random acts of kindness and senseless acts of beauty."

Chris attempted to order the festival's Champion Beer, Triple fff Brewery's Alton's Pride, but it was gone. I offered my condolences on his poor planning. You just don't wait until the last day to try the winning beer.

By 6:00 P.M., the festival began to wind down. Chris planned to stay until the bitter end in order to film people streaming out of the building at closing time. However, as more and more casks ran dry, people started leaving on their own. At closing time an hour later, the convention hall was almost empty. Not quite the dramatic finish Chris had envisioned.

Our exit from GBBF that evening marked the end of our trip. Another successful Year in Beer adventure completed. I crawled into bed and Chris turned to me.

"Well, we finally made a real visit to England," he said.

"Better late than never," I replied and turned out the light.

SEPTEMBER

IT PAYS TO PERSEVERE

The destination for September's Year in Beer adventure was a no-brainer: Oktoberfest in Munich, Germany. Most people incorrectly guessed that the granddaddy of all beer festivals would be our October trip, which seems like a logical assumption. However, while the Oktoberfest celebration ends the first weekend in October, it actually begins two weeks earlier in September. We planned to be in Munich for the opening weekend of the biggest beer gathering in the world. We also had something special planned: a tour of the Hallertau hop region north of Munich.

We landed in Frankfurt on Tuesday morning and planned to take a few days to get acclimated before facing the Oktoberfest insanity on Saturday. Our pre-Oktoberfest adventure included a trip to Berchtesgaden, near the Austrian border. Not ones to pass up valuable List opportunities, we planned to stop at breweries along the 340-mile journey southeast. Thirty minutes from Frankfurt, we added our first brewery of the trip: Woinemer Brauerei in Weinheim.

A large round sign hanging above a wide brick archway guided us through the beer garden to the restaurant. Inside, only a few diners sat at the pine wood tables. We had our pick of places to sit, so we chose a table against the wall. The waitress handed us our menus and Chris immediately placed our beer order.

We ate our meal and drank our beer with the calm satisfaction of familiar surroundings. Adjustment to the German culture is never hard for us. The food, the atmosphere, and, of course the beer all feels comfortable and almost second nature; except the language. Despite numerous visits to Germany, I've only picked up a few nouns and an ability to pronounce words. Chris took German in high school and understands more than I do. Even so, we're both far from proficient.

When it was time to leave, Chris pulled out his credit card to pay. The waitress waved her hand and shook her head. They didn't accept credit cards. Too anxious to get beer, we didn't even bother to stop and get money. Chris left me as collateral and walked out the door in search of an ATM.

Twenty minutes later, he returned sweaty and winded.

"What happened to you?" I asked. "I got worried."

"The ATM right down the street wasn't working, so I had to walk further down the street and then up," Chris explained.

The woman came over and with a heavy thud, plopped a large wallet on the table. The *kellnergeldbörse* (literally "waiter money purse") is attached by a chain to the belt of most servers in Germany. The sound of clinking metal filled our ears as she dug through the coins collecting Chris's change. A few "dankes" later, we were out the door.

Our stop for the evening was Murnau, which we located easily. However, the narrow streets and pedestrian-only zones of this cute little village made the search for our hotel a frustrating experience. After circling the area three times, we gave up and parked the car in a back-alley parking lot. I crossed my arms and shoved my hands into my armpits as we set out to find the hotel. Exploring the town on foot gave us a chance to perk up from our jetlag and the four-plus hours in the car.

Braueri Karg, our second addition to The List, was located in the pedestrian zone. We stepped inside and looked around. All the tables were full, not even enough room to ask people to share.[23] The warm smell of grilled bratwurst put me in a trance. Without any room inside, we opted for one of the empty tables outside.

Chris caught the attention of the waitress and ordered beers. He motioned that we planned to sit outside. She looked down at Chris's shorts and gave a little snort. With the flick of her wrists, she gave the pan-cultural hand signal for "I'll bring them out to you." Seated patrons throughout the *bräustüberl* (brewery tavern) observed our exchange near the door. They,

23 A common practice in Germany, sharing a table is uncomfortable for many Americans and took us a bit of getting used to.

too, looked at Chris's exposed legs before turning to whisper amongst themselves. It was around 55ºF out; not exactly warm, but still shorts weather as far as Chris was concerned.

Six weeks earlier in England, I longed to ditch the pints of real ale for a helles, one of my favorite styles of beer. Now, here in Germany with a helles on the way, everything was right in my world. The feeling of pure contentment even insulated my rear end against the cold metal chair outside.

Within a short half hour, however, my fingers were nearly frozen around my glass. My happiness no longer protected me against the ice cube upon which I sat. In the interest of survival, we drank our next beers indoors.

Across the pedestrian mall, we passed through the doorway of the bräustüberl at our hotel, the Braurei Gastehaus Griesbrau. The smorgasbord on our right created a cloud of wonderful smells, which weakened as we delved deeper into the long hall. Large wooden tables lined in a row guided us to the bar.

"Go see what they have for food," Chris said. "Get some *Käsespätzle*."

Made by running batter through a colander into boiling water, spätzle can be thought of as a kind of German pasta. Käsespätzle is made with cheese and is often described as "macaroni and cheese" on English-language menus. It's our German comfort food. I especially like it topped with crispy fried onions and accompanied by a beer.

Standing in front of the smorgasbord, I realized that the logistics of ordering were a bit more complicated than anticipated. I'd like to think that my German pronunciation isn't so bad that people can't understand me at all, but the value of pointing at words on a menu as a back-up plan couldn't be overlooked. The woman behind the counter watched impatiently as I paced back and forth. The pressure of her stare almost made me break into a sweat and blurt out, "*Bratwurst mit Kartoffelsalat*" (Bratwurst with potato salad), my go-to order when under stress. Käsespätzle was listed on a blackboard behind the counter, but I didn't see any. I gathered my courage and made my move.

"Käsespätzle, bitte," I said.

"Keine Spätzle," the woman said gruffly as she shook her head.

"Uh, okay," I stammered.

I rejoined Chris and gave him a report. "I think she told me they don't have any Käsespätzle. She used the word *keine*."

After Chris confirmed that "keine" meant no, I returned to make a second attempt. This time I successfully ordered a few items, including *Schweinshaxe* (pork knuckle) to share.

In between bites of crispy pork skin, Chris and I reminisced about the first time we saw pig knuckle many years ago while visiting the Andechs Monastery, southwest of Munich. A large hunk of meat with a knife sticking out of it, the dish looked nothing short of barbaric. The image didn't improve when the man we were watching picked it up in his hands to gnaw the last bits of meat off the bone. Given how much we thoroughly enjoy schweinshaxe now, it's hard to believe our initial reaction was to be grossed out.

After our meal, Chris went back toward the entrance to look at the brewery. A few minutes later, the lights dimmed. The theme to James Bond blasted out of the loud speakers. Chris emerged from behind a pillar and motioned me urgently with his arms. I shrugged my shoulders unable to understand what he wanted. It was clear that something monumental was about to happen, but what that was continued to be a mystery. Then I saw it: the *Spanferkelspektakel.* Aside from sounding like a faux-German word in a Chevy Chase movie, it means "suckling pig spectacular."

A cook who earlier had been behind the counter at the smorgasbord was now slowly pushing a cart along tracks embedded in the brick floor. A small roasted pig wearing sunglasses lay flat on its stomach on top of a chopping board. The James Bond music reached its infamous horn crescendo with dramatic effect as the cart continued down the beer hall. Two crackling sparklers stuck out from the pig's back, shooting out bits of light. I got out the video camera and followed the path of the suckling pig spectacular as it passed. Everyone in the beer hall, patrons and workers alike, stopped what they were doing to catch a glimpse of the sparkling piglet. A large table at the end of the hall broke the stunned silence as they clapped and laughed with delight. Their meal had arrived and boy did it look tasty. Our diet when in Germany is one continuous serving of beer and pork and we make no apologies for it. We hoped the table would invite us to join them, but knew it was an unlikely prospect.

"I think we better call it a night," Chris eventually said. "Nothing more exciting than that is going happen tonight."

On Wednesday morning we hit the Deutches Alpenstrasse for Berchtesgaden, an idyllic Bavarian town that sits under the watchful eye of the Eagle's Nest, Hitler's mountain top retreat. I gazed out the window as Chris sped down the road in our rental car. Chris always drives when we're in Europe because I'm too afraid to do it. Instead, I get to enjoy the scenery. At autobahn speeds, however, the trees and scenery along the road became one long green blur.

After two failed attempts to visit breweries (they were both closed) and a stop for lunch, we arrived in Berchtesgaden in the late afternoon. The sky was partly cloudy, blocking our view of the Eagle's Nest, to which we planned to hike the next day. We had last visited Berchtesgaden the previous December when we practically had the town to ourselves. But now, the town was still full of tourists and the restaurants packed, including the Hofbräuhaus Berchtesgaden. With every table in the main area filled, a waiter led us to a room in the back.

Our hearts sank as we entered a small, completely empty dining room. The waiter slapped two menus down on a table and motioned for us to sit. We managed to order *zwei Helles* (two helles) before he dashed back out the door. The faint sound of happy chitter chatter could be heard coming from the main part of the bräustüberl. We sighed.

The waiter returned a short time later with our beers, but he walked back out before we had a chance to order food. We sipped our beer and watched as several more groups of people were seated near us. Soon enough, our room was full and the waiter made his rounds to collect food orders. We may not have been isolated anymore, but it still wasn't quite the beer hall atmosphere we had envisioned. On this trip, however, there would be no shortage of chances to drink in a beer hall, so we just had to keep trying.

Our third day in Germany dawned sunny and clear. The clouds that had obscured our view of the Eagle's Nest the day before were now gone. Our rented silver Opel groaned around the curves of the narrow road as we climbed higher up the mountain to Obersalzberg. We parked in a large lot at the Dokumentation Obersalzberg, a permanent exhibition of the area's history and its role during the Nazi era. This was as far up the hill as we got during our visit in December. At that time, snow covered the ground and the road up to the Eagle's Nest was closed for the season. While visiting that first time, Chris had overheard several people discussing a hiking path up the mountain. He decided then that we'd have to return some day for a hike to the Eagle's Nest.

On this visit, the same parking lot that had been nearly empty now teemed with cars, tour buses, and tourists. No private cars are allowed on the road up to the Eagle's Nest, so whether buying tickets for the bus or going by foot, everyone starts at the same place. While most people waited in line to board the buses, we prepared for our own adventure up the mountain.

A few people with hiking poles headed up the hill. We walked alongside the road behind them while tour buses lumbered by. A half hour later we came to a crossroads. The couple we followed up the hill was also at a standstill. The four of us stared at a map posted near some restrooms. The man spoke to us in broken German.

I shook my head and said, "I'm sorry. I don't speak German."

"Oh, you speak English," he said with a beautiful upper crust accent, "We're from Britain."

Together, our English-speaking foursome determined that the trail was up the road on the left. Each couple wished the other good luck and we went on our way.

The uphill climb already had us breathing heavy. Stops for photo opportunities of breathtaking panoramas across the valley offered a chance to rest. The path soon turned into a series of short, arduous switchbacks and the air turned chilly.

The snow that had seemed so far away down in Berchtesgaden now rested along the trail in the safety of the mountain shadows. This wasn't the longest hike we'd ever undertaken, but we'd climbed over 2,500 feet in elevation on our way to the top.

A middle-aged couple came up the hill and passed us as we rested.

"The Germans sure know how to hike," I said.

"Oh, I don't know about that," Chris replied.

On the move again a short time later, we passed the same couple as they took a smoke break. Ironic. If their smoker's lungs could get them up the mountain, so could my relatively fit ones.

From various points on the trail, the observation deck (the destination of the buses that had chugged past us earlier) appeared close, filling me with both a sense of accomplishment and relief. At other times, however, it appeared far out of reach as I stared straight up a sheer cliff. Eventually, we made it and joined the busloads of elderly tourists in witnessing the splendor of the valley below.

After purchasing tickets to the Eagle's Nest, we walked 400 feet down a wide tunnel to the elevator where a group of people waited. As we continued deeper into the mountain, the walls felt like they were closing in and the entrance became a speck of light in the distance. We had previously visited places where Hitler was purported to have been. Here, however, he had most certainly stepped upon the very same stretch of Earth that we now walked. Eeriness filled the air and no one dared speak above a whisper.

When the elevator arrived and the doors opened, a dozen of us shuffled in and packed ourselves as tightly as reasonably possible. Pulled upwards over 400 feet in just forty-one seconds, the ride was quick.

We emerged from the solemn innards of the mountain into the bright sunshine. We joined hordes of others as they snapped photographs, looked for the bathroom, and admired the view from over 6,000 feet. It was a bit of a shock to the system after the quietude of the tunnel and elevator ride.

"Let's find a beer," Chris said. He had read my mind.

The man who worked at the snack stand handed me two bottles of Hofbräuhaus Berchtesgaden Helles and two plastic cups. Chris looked at me and shrugged his shoulders at the idea of drinking a fine German beer out of a plastic cup. Away from the stand, we took in the beauty of the mountains, valley, and the Konigsee down below. A large lake dotted with tourist towns, we first visited the Konigsee in 2001. It was the first time we'd discovered "huts" while hiking.

Along the hiking trails in the Alps there is an organized system of *hütten* (huts), substantial buildings that serve as outposts for hikers. They range from providing overnight accommodations to serving beer and simple snack foods and are usually staffed by Alpine hiking organizations. We had no idea they existed until we accidentally came across one.

I don't recall what that first hut looked like, but I do remember how it felt. Completely exhausted from a long, challenging hike, we could hardly believe our eyes, a small cabin with a car out front seemed to appear out of nowhere. Being so high up in the mountains, we were far from civilization and hadn't seen any other people for hours. But here was what looked like someone's personal mountain retreat. It wasn't until a woman came out to offer us beer and cheese that we realized it wasn't a dream.

Now at the top of the Eagle's Nest, we once again rewarded ourselves for our hiking efforts by ordering bratwurst, potato salad, chocolate cake, and beer. This wasn't a hut, however. The Eagle's Nest, which was originally built as a residence, was now a large restaurant and tourist destination, complete with a souvenir shop and snack shack. The place was teeming with tourists who had traveled up the mountain to enjoy the extraordinary views.

In between bites, I closed my eyes and raised my face up toward to the sun. The warmth felt good on my eyelids and cheeks. Thoughts of happiness in the moment drowned out the cackling and banter of those around me.

"This is all so weird," Chris said. "Don't people realize that this was a birthday present from the Nazi party to Hitler?"

I opened one eye to look at Chris and stammered, "Um."

"Even though he was only here a few times, everyone seems to forget its history," he continued.

"Well, it's easy to forget in this beautiful setting," I replied.

I closed my eyes again and tilted my head back. This time, however, my heart felt a little heavier.

Mindful of the time, we decided to head back down. Descending the mountain was much easier than going up, but it seemed to take longer. After what felt like hours we finally made it to the car and drove back to Berchtesgaden to explore the village.

During a quick stop at an internet café, I checked my email. It turned out to mostly be junk, including a chain letter forwarded to me by a friend and a request for financial assistance from someone in Zimbabwe, but one message caught my eye as different from the rest.

"Hey, my article was accepted by the *Monterey County Weekly*," I said.

"Congratulations, hon," Chris replied. "That deserves a beer."

As my first paid writing assignment, the article titled "Fantasy Drafts" earned me $78.

Friday, we made our way to Rosenheim, a market town southeast of Munich. It was the day before the start of Oktoberfest and the thought of driving into the city with the rental car sent Chris into a panic. We chose to drop it off in Rosenheim because it was an easy train ride into Munich and they had a brewery.

After exploring the town and visiting a beer garden or two, we ended the evening with dinner at Gasthof Flötzinger. While Chris went in, a shop a few doors down sidetracked me. When I joined him a few minutes later, Chris was sitting alone at a rather large table in the back right corner.

"Chris, you're sitting at the stammtisch," I said.

"I sat over there," he said pointing to another table, "but the waiter moved me here."

As a visitor, you don't seat yourself at the S*tammtisch*, the table reserved for regulars. Occasionally the stammtisch is difficult to identify, but usually it's elaborately adorned with metal work or carved signs and clumps of hops are almost always hanging from the ceiling above. Most often, it's the table closest to the beer taps. If you choose wrong and accidentally sit at the stammtisch, the staff will ask you to move. We know this first hand and all I can say is that it's embarrassing.

We had no idea why Chris had been chosen to sit at the stammtisch, but it was a great accomplishment. Once the proof of Chris's historic moment was documented in a photograph, I drank my beer and ordered a plate of käsespätzle. The light fixture above the table was a prime example of stammtisch decorations. A large wood disk, beautifully carved with flowers and the brewery name, rested on top of a polished horizontal tree branch. Two animal skin shades and an arched wooden sign with the word "Stammtisch" dangled below.

Everyone who walked in the door glanced our way with a look of confusion followed by the stink eye. No one else was invited to sit with us and they must have wondered how two American tourists had the nerve to sit in such a hallowed spot. Even though it felt estranged, like we had been set apart from other patrons, it was still one of our proudest moments.

On Saturday, we traveled by train to Munich and immediately launched headlong into Oktoberfest festivities.

"You ready?" Chris asked. "Today starts a big weekend."

"Yep, let's go," I said confidently.

On our way to the Grand Entry of the Oktoberfest Landlords and Breweries parade, the official prelude to the opening of Oktoberfest, we walked through the Englischer Garten (English Garden). A large public park in the center of Munich, it includes two beer gardens, a Chinese pagoda, and a Japanese teahouse. Wooded pathways follow alongside rushing streams and open into expansive grass fields where individuals sat reading, couples got cozy and groups played frisbee. Several times on our walk, a "ching ching" sound chimed in our ears moments before people rode by on their bicycles. Joggers ran towards us and whooshes of brisk air hit our faces as they passed.

Within a half hour, we found ourselves in the city center along the parade route. Bystanders watched as the landlords from each of the Munich breweries and their families rolled by in colorfully adorned horse-drawn wagons. The beer tent bands followed behind, all making their way to Theresienwiese, the site of Oktoberfest. Literally translated, "Theresienwiese" means "Therese's Meadow." Today, however, it's a large concrete open space that is used for a variety of large festivals, not only Oktoberfest.

We walked along the sidewalk, pausing every so often to peek through spectators at the parade. Eventually a break in the wall of people gave us a good place to watch. We enjoyed a mostly unimpeded view, save for the occasional *polizei* (police) standing in our way.

A band of men in matching lederhosen, red vests, and brown collarless jackets beat on drums as they marched along. Young girls dressed in pastel-colored dirndls looked adorable, yet somewhat bored as they carried baskets of flowers.

Around us, older women in dressy black taffeta dirndls hooked arms with proud men in knee-high cable knit socks and lederhosen. Girls, from the very young to pre-adolescent, wore thick wool sweaters with decorative buttons and braids in their hair. Most people think of Oktoberfest as large beers and oversized pretzels, young women in low-cut dresses and men in drunken states. It is all those things, but it's also about tradition and pride, something that gets lost in all the hoopla.

Back in the parade, a tall wagon full of buxom women in black dirndls and white low cut blouses rolled by. They danced and hoisted liters of beer toward the crowd. Their boisterous laughter and cheers drowned out the dull clank of their prosting mugs.

Four Appaloosa horses with solid flanks pulled a cart loaded with two-dozen full-sized beer barrels. The lone driver, roosted high above his team, pulled on the reins with the force needed to control the thick, heavily bridled horses. The animals jerked their heads up and down in defiance as their metal breastplates jingled and their manes flowed in the breeze. Beautifully decorated with sprays of yellow and blue flowers, this wagon, along with those of the five other Munich breweries, celebrated the integral nature of brewing and Bavarian identity.

We continued to watch as robust women led tan oxen pulling hop-laden carts. Groups of men performed carefully choreographed routines with whips, the sound of which snapped sharply in our ears. Bands of men, women, and children marched down Sonnen Strasse as they blew into their horns.

The opening time of Oktoberfest approached and we decided to make our way to the Theresienweise. At noon on the first day of Oktoberfest, the mayor of Munich taps a keg in the Schottenhammel Festhalle and proclaims, "*O'zapft is!*" ("It's tapped.") Oktoberfest is then officially open and beer can be served.

Oktoberfest originated during the wedding celebration of Crown Prince Ludwig (who would later become King Ludwig I) to Princess Therese of Saxe-Hildburghausen on October 12, 1810. The citizens of Munich were all invited to attend the festivities held in the fields in front of the city gates, now named the Theresienweise in honor of Ludwig's bride. People had so much fun that the festivities continued to grow each year and Oktoberfest was born.

Leaving before the end of the parade, I assumed we would be in the first wave of attendees. How wrong I was. We arrived to find the site in full festival swing. A friend later told us that people start entering the tents at 9:00 A.M. to stake out their seats. The term "tent" is a gross misnomer. Not the two-man pup tents of my Girl Scout days, these are semi-permanent structures that seat thousands of people, as well as house beer dispensaries, kitchens, and bandstands. The early birds won't get served beer until noon when the festival officially starts. So they bring their own, plus picnics and playing cards, to entertain themselves for the next few hours before they hear the opening signal. Given the numbers of people already there, the 9 o'clock opening time was no secret.

We entered the 104-acre festival site from the side on Strasse 3. People of all types and ages promenaded down the wide lane. Old couples in fancy traditional dress slowly walked arm in arm as groups of rowdy young men pushed past them on the way to a tent. Whole tourist families wandered nervously, overwhelmed by all the commotion, but still trying to absorb the Oktoberfest experience.

We attempted some filming, but my first take was interrupted by cannon fire. The crowd whooped and hollered. Several small puffs of smoke drifted upward into the sky.

"O'zapft is!" Chris proclaimed.

"O'zapft is!" I repeated.

Oktoberfest was now officially underway.

I was prepared for the challenge of finding a seat and determined to overcome the only obstacle standing in the way of a beer and me. At Oktoberfest, you must have a seat to be served one of the famous liters of frothing golden brew.

We walked toward the center of the action to the main street. Once on Wirtsbudenstrasse the festival exploded into densely crowded pandemonium. We looked to our left: the Schottenhammel Festhalle, a Spaten tent and location of the official opening of Oktoberfest. Chris and I looked at each other and didn't even bother. With the guarantee of a full house, it wasn't worth trying to navigate through the crowd to get there. Across the way, the Pschorrbräu tent looked as good as any, so we cut across the flow of people to the tent door. A line was formed to get inside.

"Forget that," said Chris.

Instead, we slowly wandered the narrow aisles of the outside seating area focused on locating bare spots on benches. Row after row, long picnic tables were packed with people and beer. Quick paced wait staff with arms full of sloshing mugs buzzed by, cursing at us under their breaths as we sauntered along. Boisterous conversation waxed and waned as we walked passed the different tables, but the deep clank of mugs clashing together and slamming on tables remained constant. My hopes were not yet dashed because I knew that finding a seat on the first try was unlikely.

We left that tent and crisscrossed our way down the street in continued pursuit of a place to sit. When the tent entrances were free of lines, we went inside to look. Hackerbräu Festhalle on the left: no available seats. Augustinerbräu Festhalle on the right: the same story. With Hackerbräu seating 9,300 people and Augustinerbräu another 8,500, it was amazing that not one open seat could be found. Now my determination was beginning to wane.

"Maybe we should just give up and call it a day. We'll get some footage tomorrow," I said.

"No. We can do this. You just have to have perseverance," Chris encouraged.

"Well, this is frustrating and not very fun," I replied.

In the Hofbräuhaus Festhalle, a one-in-a-million encounter would re-energize my dwindling spirit. Chris and I poked around the outside beer garden, scanning for even the slightest hint of enough room at a table. Table after table, people shook their heads "no" when we asked if the seats were free. A young man tapped Chris on the back of the shoulder.

"Excuse me," he said. "I think I saw you at the Berg in May."

"Oh, yeah! Wow, what are the chances of seeing you again?" Chris said.

It was the guy Chris had spoken to while I was off standing in line for the bathroom. Before we had the opportunity to ask if he had a seat, or even just to chat more, he walked away. It was a brief and random encounter that left Chris and I thinking about what a small world it is.

Further down the center street, we turned left into the Hippodrom. A Spaten tent, it was the last one before turning around to make a second go around the festival. The sight of almost a thousand people broke up the brightness of the red paint on the walls and tables in the beer garden. One area looked conspicuously clear; a half-empty table with four men. We asked about the seats and were told they were, in fact, available.

"That didn't take very long," Chris said.

"What? Are you kidding?" I exclaimed. "It took an hour and a half!"

"Well, I meant once we walked in here," he clarified.

Despite the ridiculous numbers of people in attendance, once you sit down, getting a beer at Oktoberfest is easy and surprisingly quick. With only one size and one kind, you simply indicate how many you want.

Once we had the famous super-sized beers in front of us, we were ready to go. Chris offered a toast to our Italian tablemates. Shortly thereafter, a German couple came by and asked if there was room for two. We all scooted over and they sat down. Now seated thigh-to-thigh with the person next to us, the table was officially full.

Such coziness builds camaraderie. Strangers at first, it doesn't take long before you discover a common language, which luckily for us is usually English. Discussions about the culture and politics of your respective countries start and the first of many prosts gets going. Tables are placed closely together, with barely enough room between benches to get out. This tends to create multi-table grouping, and sometimes groping, that is loud and obnoxious if you're not included, but fun if you are.

On this day, Chris and I, our four Italian and two German tablemates joined forces with eight young German men at the table next to us to create a stream of endless prosting.

Chris pulled out the video camera, which incited the group more. It was hard to tell if any of us were actually having conversation. Take a swig of beer, sing a verse of "Qué Será, Será," prost, whoop, holler and repeat. One of the young Germans mugged for the camera and started a chant. The others soon joined him. "Oo, ess, ah. Oo, ess, ah." Apparently they liked the good old U.S. of A.

The constant clanking of beer mugs, or perhaps the especially loud impersonations of our state's then-governor Arnold Schwarzenegger, caught the attention of a woman in charge. Keeping a keen eye on our tables, she finally came over and told the group that we were five hours too early to be behaving in such a manner. If the aim was to settle us down, it didn't work. The manager's attention was soon elsewhere anyway as a waiter briskly walked past our table with several mugs of sawdust.

"You know what that means, don't you?" I said. "Gross."

"That's Oktoberfest for ya," said Chris.

Three hours, four liters, twelve rounds of "Ein Prosit," and too many toasts to count later, Chris and I finally said goodbye to our Oktoberfest friends. The time we spent with them created another entry in our "friends for a day" beer travel mental diary. Oktoberfest: it might be hard work and it might be frustrating, but the payoff is worth it.

Later that evening, we returned to people watch and experience Oktoberfest at night. The bright lights of souvenir stands, food stalls, and carnival rides set the dark night ablaze. The large number of people out on the festival grounds made strolling a shoulder-to-shoulder affair. Long lines formed outside each tent, which meant they were all at full capacity. Chris and I stopped to watch the giant animated lion atop the Lowenbräu tent. Sitting on his haunches the lion slowly raised a mug of beer to his mouth. "Low-in-brow," he roared long and deep. Continuing on, the displeasing smell of the fish stand made me pinch my nose. So did the guy walking by with vomit down the front of his shirt. This is the scene eight hours into the Oktoberfest celebration, a far cry from the pageantry earlier in the day.

We approached more food stands and the pleasing smell of bratwurst reminded us that it was time for dinner. We left Oktoberfest for the city center.

The further away the festival got, the quieter things became. I hadn't noticed before, but my ears were ringing. A long line of cabs waited along the road. As we approached one, a guy stumbled towards us mumbling incoherently. We're pretty sure he was speaking English and we think he wanted to share a cab. The closest cabbie motioned for us to quickly get in and close the door. We were a safe fare, meaning we weren't going to throw up in his car.

"Marienplatz, bitte," Chris said.

I laughed and asked the cabbie, "How do you choose who you'll take in your cab?"

"I watch as they walk up and I lock the door if I don't want them," he answered.

Despite his German accent, the cabbie was much easier to understand than the man we left swaying on the sidewalk.

The cabbie dropped us off and we walked arm in arm up the street to our favorite Munich restaurant, the Wirtshaus Ayingers. Located across the *platz* (plaza) from the Hofbräuhaus, we enjoy sitting outside watching the tourists go in and out of the famous beer hall. It's fun to watch the timid, somewhat quiet people go in through the large wooden doors to exchange places with the wobbling loudmouths that leave. As the Hofbräuhaus came up on our right, we were surprised to see a large crowd. With the option of the real Oktoberfest, we assumed the place would be practically empty.

We sat outside in the cool air and watched large tour groups herd into the Hofbräuhaus. Tourists passed by, some venturing inside, others simply observing the madness with chuckles and wonderment. A silver-painted street performer who was set up nearby entertained those who stopped to watch his robotic pantomime act. Between the activity in the platz and the beagle at the next table, we were kept occupied until our meal came. The dog was friendly and cute. He soothed the familiar pains of missing Porter and Stout. It was a quiet way to wind down a rambunctious afternoon and evening. The next day it would start all over.

We had big plans for Sunday's Oktoberfest visit. First, I wore my dirndl, a two-piece linen ensemble with a short skirt. Purchased in Germany several years before, I have only two occasions to wear it each year: Halloween and Oktoberfest. Chris finished zipping the top up for me, as I stared in the mirror and turned from side to side. My confidence in my ability to pull off the short-skirted outfit was limited. I tugged at the skirt and sucked in my stomach.

I put on a light coat over my puffy off-the-shoulder sleeves and we left the hotel. I felt ridiculous. How could I possibly compete with the skinny teens and twenty-something girls with heaving, half-exposed bosoms? The reality was that I couldn't. So I sucked it up (and in) and dealt with it.

Everyone on the train seemed to get off at the Hackerbrücke station. Even if we didn't know the way to Oktoberfest, all we had to do was follow the crowd.

The story of our second day at Oktoberfest could have easily been called "Beergeeks and the Three Tents." The first tent we went to had no action. The outside crowd was reserved and boring. We shared a liter and left to try again someplace else.

The rowdiness of the next attempt, a Lowenbräu tent, proved too much to handle. Only after we ordered beers did we realize that the beer garden was filled with hundreds of twenty-something Aussies. Their loud drunkenness and frequent attempts to engage the whole crowd were over the top. One especially enthusiastic lad with a bright yellow sweatband around his head walked the length of the beer garden trying to initiate the "Mexican Wave." It wasn't until later that someone told us about the tent's reputation for being the place to party.

Despite the second tent being too hot, I actually became cold. Before we finished our liters and bratwurst with sauerkraut, I changed out of my skirt and into a pair of jeans and put my coat on over the large puffy sleeves of my top. We were now ready to find the tent that was just right.

Third time's a charm and the Hofbräuhaus tent fit the bill. Prior to settling in the beer garden (we prefer the fresh air outside), we went inside the tent to check out the action. A middle-aged woman rushed by, leaning back to counterbalance the weight of a dozen beer-filled mugs. A security person motioned for us to keep walking, no loitering allowed. Although indoor smoking was already banned in Germany, the futility of enforcement convinced Oktoberfest organizers to allow it. The further we delved into the thick of the party, the more the combination of smoke and no ventilation stifled the air.

Curiously, a section of people moved in unison, pumping their arms in the air with invisible dumbbells. In the distance, a blonde spiky-haired child of about six with a blue bandana around his neck stood on the railing. His loose-fitting lederhosen moved up and down as he led the crowd to the beat of the Oompah band.

In hindsight, the presence of a six year-old at Oktoberfest is a bit odd. I don't know why he was there or what his parents were thinking when they brought him, but at the time, we didn't even question it. He just seemed to fit in with the celebration. I know it wasn't a figment of my imagination, though, because we have the video to prove it.

The inside of the Hofbräuhaus tent offered great scenery for filming and the perfect level of revelry. However, the smoky air made it hard to breath and left our clothes smelling like ashtrays. The beer garden outside suited our taste much better. We quickly found seats at a table with two young German couples.

Chris had previously come up with the idea to film a German language primer for the *One Pint at a Time* episode and our table had a sound level conducive to filming.

"Even though most of your wait staff will speak English, it's always nice to know a little German," I said. "So, '*Ein Bier, bitte.*' A beer please."

Our tablemates chuckled. I continued.

"*Oder, 'Zwei Bier, bitte.*' Two beers, please."

That's all it took. We had made the connection with our friends of the day. The discussion eventually came around to the appropriateness of carnival rides at beer festivals. One of the women, who turned out to be a real daredevil, became very excited and immediately agreed to go on a ride with me. Together, we convinced the other young woman to do it too. The three of us, plus Chris as our cameraman, left in search of the best ride we could find.

As we waited for the chosen ride, I started to sober up and actually get scared. Courage drained from my body with each passing second, but I was now in the middle of a very long line. Twenty minutes and the equivalent of $7 later, I sat down in a row of seats. With my seat belt on, the operator pushed down the harness, which clicked as it locked. I grabbed the harness and held on tight.

Back and forth it rocked, going higher and higher until we swung around in a complete circle. The car spun around as well. It was a good thing I had changed into my jeans or else my skirt would have been up over my head. Several stories up, I slid forward against the harness and faced the ground. Not even the several liters of beer I drank before the ride could guard me against a crisis of faith in the protective mechanism. I thought for sure I would plunge to my death at any moment. While I simultaneously screamed and prayed for the whole thing to come to an end, it continued. I eventually survived the ordeal with vocal cords intact, which is more than I can say for the eardrums of the guy next to me.

I ran toward Chris and screamed (incoherently), "Shites-ah!" into the camera. Anyone who ever took German in high school, which I didn't, knows the correct swear word to be "*Scheiße*," pronounced "shies-ah" without the 't' sound. It's okay, though, because one of my new friends looked straight into the camera and stated, "I'm so scary."

We reunited with the spouses of my fellow Cyber Space riders to have one more beer inside. Chris suggested that I "take it easy," as we had our appointment to tour the Hallertau hop region in the morning. But by this time of the evening, the tent was in full party mode and I wanted to be part of it all—the dancing, the laughing, the drinking. However, I soon realized I'd had one liter too many. Luckily, the first cab driver we approached allowed me in his cab.

Needless to just say, the next morning wasn't a good one for me. Especially because sleeping in was not an option. We had a 9:00 A.M. appointment with Willy Buholzer, Director of European Hop Purchasing for Anheuser-Busch and General Manager of the Busch Farm Hüll.

Earlier in the year, we'd received an unexpected invitation to tour Anheuser-Busch's hop farm in the Hallertau region of Germany. We wanted to do it, but wondered if accepting an offer from a macro-brew corporation would compromise our integrity and credibility in the craft beer community. We asked a few veteran beer journalists, many of whom, it turned out, had been on the tour. No one thought our reputation would be tarnished and several said that Willy's personality and warmth far outweighed the fact that he worked for one of the "big guys."

I opened my eyes and straightened up in my chair. A blonde man with a confident stride and the physique of Clint Eastwood walked through the front doors of the hotel lobby.

"I think this might be him," Chris said.

Willy picked us out before we had the chance to fully stand and greet him. His broad smile softened his commanding stature as he introduced himself.

During the forty-minute drive through the Hallertau, we passed field after field with rows of eighteen-foot tall poles. They were connected to one another by wires strung across the top and descending wires were anchored to the ground. At the height of the growing season, long masses of hops would have grown up the rigging to the top of the poles. At the time of our tour, however, most of the farms in the area, including Busch Farm Hüll, had already completed their yearly harvest. All that remained were straggly bits of green and brown clinging to the wires. Gone were the long, lush tangles of vines.

A traditional Bavarian maypole, complete with the Anheuser-Busch insignia, marked our arrival at the farm. With the harvest complete, the fields stood bare and the hop processing facility was silent. After a quick demonstration of how the machinery worked, we followed Willy into a room that looked half office-half lab. He reached inside a burlap sack and pulled out a handful of hops. He inhaled, examined, and picked apart a small soft pinecone-shaped flower while he described the process of choosing the perfect hop. We copied him, rubbing hops in between our palms and opening them up to take a look. Tiny green leaves stuck to the insides of my now yellowish palms. Chris cupped his hands to his face like an air mask and inhaled deeply. I did the same, smelling the aromatic resin that had been released and nodded my head with approval.

Our friends were spot-on about Willy. His enthusiasm for hops made it easy to forget that he worked for Anheuser-Busch. An extremely gracious everyman, Willy repeatedly thanked us for coming out to the farm. The attention felt awkward yet flattering, but more importantly, it spoke volumes about Willy's character.

Busch Farm Hüll not only grows hops for the production of Budweiser, it's also a place where newly developed hop varieties are field-tested. For the next part of our tour we went across the street to the Hop Research Institute Hüll.

The institute is a private/Bavarian state collaboration working independently to develop new varieties of hops that are heartier, more resistant to pests and diseases, and able to produce higher yields. Willy introduced us to important-looking researchers, including a man who called himself a "breeder" and people whose jobs it was to develop ways to combat bugs and other things that harm the hop plants.

After a trip out to the green house to observe experimental hops, we thanked the breeder for his time and followed Willy back to the farm's reception house. He left us alone for a minute as he went to fetch some beer samples.

Willy returned with several bottles of beer that he had recently used in a presentation to a group of food writers and critics; people who didn't necessarily know about the importance of hops in the brewing process. To demonstrate what hops adds to beer, Willy offered us a comparison of four beers: Budweiser brewed with no hops, only local Hallertau hops, only Willamette hops from the Pacific Northwest, and finally the Budweiser we find on convenience store shelves, which uses both Hallertau and Willamette hops.

I managed polite sips of the samples. However, my memory of the tasting primarily consists of my efforts to not throw up on the table. Chris, being of sound mind and stomach, fully experienced the event. He recalls liking the Hallertau and Willamette-only beers the best.

Chris and I thought the tasting would be the end of our tour, but Willy had other plans. We hopped (pun intended) back into his car and drove to a nearby farm that was still harvesting. Willy explained that this farm had not yet completed its harvest due to its large size and the late-maturing variety of hops it produced.

As we got out of the car, green flakes drifted down like snow leaving a layer of hop cone petals on the car. Willy led us towards the sound of heavy equipment inside the barn, passing a man on the back of a tractor-trailer filled with thickly tangled bunches. The man heaved the masses of hop vines up and hooked them on a machine that lifted them high off the trailer. The bunches swung as they lurched forward one after another toward the next machine.

The farmer saw us and extended a warm greeting. Willy's unassuming personality overshadows his high importance and influence in the region. If I didn't know his lofty position, I might have thought he took us to the farm of an old friend. For all I know, he did. After all, Willy replaced his father, who had purchased hops for Anheuser-Busch for forty years.

As a child, Willy went to the farms with his father. Not knowing that he would someday manage it, as a young man Willy worked at the privately owned hop farm that became the Busch Farm Hüll in 1989. With a personal history like that, it wasn't farfetched that he had known this farmer for years.

Before Willy returned us to the hotel, he treated us to a lunch of käsespätzle and helles at a local Augustiner bräustüberl. Four hours after he had picked us up, Willy was dropping us back off at the hotel. We thanked him for his generous hospitality and exchanged contact information. What started as a beer business contact ended in a friendship. Now, whenever we're in Munich we try to hook up with Willy.

As Willy drove away, I turned to Chris. "He was a Willy nice guy." I slapped my thigh and laughed at my own joke.

"Hey, that was pretty good," Chris said.

After a short rest, we returned to Oktoberfest to gather some final footage. The small crowd in the early weekday afternoon created a great opportunity to observe the elaborate decorations of the tents. The scant groups of mellow locals seated inside made an acceptable noise level for my still aching head. It was hard to imagine that within hours every seat in the now near empty tent would be filled to capacity. The only clue we had was the group of twenty people whooping it up right beneath the bandstand. They danced to the music and enjoyed their own party, seemingly unaware that they were the only ones in the tent.

Drapes of bright yellow cloth stretched across the ceiling, something that is unimportant and practically invisible when you're busy downing a liter of beer. When it's crowded, security guards ask loitering individuals to keep moving, so murals depicting various stages of the brewing process are left unexamined and unappreciated. The thick cigarette smoke of the nighttime scene obscures the clumps of hops and ribbons strung from above. We got to see all that on this Monday afternoon.

In the previous days, Chris had started toward a goal of drinking a liter at a tent from each of the six breweries at the festival, a feat he would have to finish on his own. The very thought of drinking a beer stirred up my settling stomach. It must be really boring to drink alone at Oktoberfest, but Chris made the best of it.

For our last night in Munich, we chose to have dinner at the Weisses Bräuhaus. Early visits plagued by intimidation from snarky waitresses had been replaced with more recent pleasant experiences, including our May visit with Ute and Wolfgang. Strengthened confidence and increased knowledge of the beer hall culture helped a lot, too. We found our own two seats and placed our orders.

A manager-looking type in a collarless Tyrolean jacket moved through the room assisting new arrivals with finding seats. This new attitude towards customer service made reticent tourists wandering the aisles afraid to ask people to share a table a thing of the past. It took me several years of practice to gain the confidence to successfully manage Weisses Bräuhaus. Now people have it way too easy.

Our last full day in Germany, Chris and I took the train from Munich to Mannheim, just south of Frankfurt. We found our compartment and settled into our seats next to three men already seated.

An hour-and-a-half later, when the conductor asked for our tickets, Chris showed them the online printout, his ID and the credit card used. However, the credit card did not match the printout, which listed the last four digits of a credit card we no longer had. Our tickets were not valid. Our card-playing compartment mates stopped to watch. I was embarrassed. Chris was angry and confused. One of the card players asked about the problem and offered us a fourth ticket that they had purchased, but not used. In the end, we only paid for one other ticket. That's one reason why traveling is such an amazing experience. It's a chance to see how kind people can be to one another.[24]

At the Mannheim station, we struggled down the aisle with our bags. Chris helped me onto the bustling platform. In between couples saying good-bye, business people rushing on and off the trains, and travelers like us wrestling with their bags, we saw Ute and Wolfgang heading in our direction. Only a few months had passed since we last saw them, but there were still big hugs all around.

"To Murphy's Law?" Wolfgang said.

"Of course," Chris and I said in unison.

A short distance from the station, Murphy's Law is Ute and Wolfgang's local Irish bar. We found ourselves a corner table where we could put our bags out of the way. It's never hard to pick out the non-locals at an Irish pub in Germany. While Ute and Wolfgang each ordered a Guinness, we ordered the local beer.

"Ah, Eichbaum," Ute laughed. "The cemetery beer."

---

24 Chris later explained to our credit card company that a glitch in the DeutcheBahn online ticketing system reverted to an old card we once used to buy tickets. They credited our account.

Eichbaum, a local Mannheim brewery, uses a water source that runs under the cemetery. Locals call it "*Leichen Wasser*" ("corpse water").

"I didn't come all the way to Germany to drink Guinness," Chris said.

Ute arranged for us to leave our bags at the pub for a few hours while we headed to the nearby town of Frankenthal. By this time in our friendship, Ute and Wolfgang were well aware of our quest to visit breweries and frequently helped out. Unfortunately, our 20-minute train ride was fruitless. The brewery they had planned on taking us to was closed for a private party. We got back on the train and went to dinner in Mannheim.

All of us were tired and by 8:30 P.M., they sent us on our way via train to Moerfelden, a town close to the airport. We had barely arrived at the station when a train pulled up. After a quick check, Wolfie put us on and said, "This is your train." We barely had time to hug good-bye and in a matter of minutes, the train pulled away from the station.

The train car was dim and old, not fancy and modern, as we had come to expect from German rail service. There were no maps on the walls indicating what train we were on or where it went. No advertisements for learning English. Not even signs forbidding passengers to smoke. The uncertainty of it all was unnerving.

At the next station, a guy with a messenger bag slung across his back lifted a bicycle to his shoulder and stepped off the train. Now only one other passenger remained on the train with us—a stern-faced middle-aged woman who stared straight ahead. The name of the stop didn't sound familiar, but I was too afraid to ask our fellow passenger about the train's destination. The heavy doors banged closed, the thick metal latches snapped together and the train started moving again.

Chris finally pulled out his driving map of Germany and confirmed we were traveling in the right direction. As comforting as this new information was, we still had no idea how far it was to our stop. The trained stopped without announcing the stations first, so we sat poised each time the train slowed. At the stations, we looked carefully at the name, ready to jump off at a moment's notice. Every station appeared dark and deserted. Eventually, we arrived at Moerfelden, our stop.

The hotel instructed us to take a cab from the station to the hotel, so we expected a line of cabs to be waiting out front. However, as the train departed, we found ourselves almost completely alone. The sound of a drum circle cut through the air, the only sign of life at the station. We walked around the building and peered inside. A dozen women pounded rhythmically on the large wooden drums between their legs. Eyes closed and heads down, they were completely absorbed in their drumming. The door was locked.

We looked down the street, which appeared as dark and lifeless as the station. Chris telephoned the hotel on his cell phone and the woman at the front desk agreed to call us a cab. Within a few short minutes, one arrived.

After barely enough time to settle into the backseat, we arrived at the hotel. Even though it was much closer to the train station than we thought, it was still too far to walk in the dark. The cabbie let out an "ugh" as he lifted Chris's bag out of the trunk.

"Beer," I said. The cabbie smiled and nodded his head.

While Chris paid, I dragged my heavy bag toward the entrance. The automatic doors opened with a *swoosh*. After an exchange of "dankes" and "guten abends," Chris joined me as I stepped into the lobby.

I had survived our fourth overseas trip of the year and probably the most challenging of all beer events: Oktoberfest. The next morning, we were flying home, where we would have two weeks to rest before going to Denver for the Great American Beer Festival. One final challenge of the trip awaited me, however—a good night's sleep.

OCTOBER

EVERY GEEK HAS HER DAY

The two of us returned home from Germany with a bit of a cold. However, after surviving such a colossal beer gathering, I thought a stuffy head and one broken beer bottle in our luggage were small prices to pay. We had two weeks to rest up and get well before flying to Denver for the Great American Beer Festival (GABF).

Going to GABF completed what Chris called a "Beer Geek's Dream": attending four of the world's greatest beer festivals in the same year.[25] "What some people hope to do in a lifetime," he told me, "we did in four consecutive months."

Every year, GABF is the most talked about event on the American beer social calendar. One might even say it's the Senior Prom for beer geeks. While people may not care about who's wearing what or who came with who, they definitely want to know who was there and what breweries won awards.

Oddly enough, we had never attended GABF. Like many others on our same level of beer geekism, we had just never gotten around to attending. The Year in Beer provided the perfect timing for our first visit. We were moving our way up the ranks of the beer media circles and while we didn't know everyone, we already had many contacts in the beer community. By joining in GABF festivities we were guaranteed to rendezvous with friends, unexpectedly run into people we know, and have the chance to network. All that sounded great to us. Attending GABF in October marked our second visit to Denver during the Year in Beer.

While we had never been to GABF, over the years we had traveled to Denver on several occasions. On our previous trips, we had visited most of the breweries in the city plus several nearby areas, including Boulder and Fort Collins to the north. In order to add breweries to The List on this trip, Chris planned a one-night excursion visiting several towns on the western slope of the Rocky Mountains, virgin territory for us. This was followed by a night in Colorado Springs to visit several new breweries and see a few friends before heading to Denver for the main event.

---

25 Oregon Brewers Festival, Great British Beer Festival, Oktoberfest and Great American Beer Festival

We arrived at Denver International Airport on Tuesday and headed directly to Idaho Springs. Well, that was the plan anyway. Forty-five minutes into the trip, we were sidetracked by a visit to Buffalo Bill's grave. The detour was brief, however, and in no time we had reached the quaint mountain town.

Our earlier than expected arrival in Idaho Springs meant we had an hour to kill before Tommyknocker Brewery & Pub, our first brewery of the trip, opened. We explored the small town before parking ourselves on a nearby bench to wait.

The first customers of the day, we went in right after the "open" sign was put out. The bartender was finishing up his bar set-up and several brewers in clunky black rubber boots were milling around the pub when we walked in. Wasting no time, we ordered a taster set.

One by one the bartender placed small glasses of beer on a laminated place mat.

"Okay. The names are on the mat. I would try them in order of lightest to darkest," the bartender suggested.

He left us on our own and we started in on the nine different beers. I grabbed the glass of straw-colored beer with a lemon on the rim. The name on the mat read "Jack Whacker Wheat, an American Style Wheat" and the label depicted a bent-over miner getting kicked in the rear by a mule. Chris picked up the Pick Axe Pale Ale and took a sip. "Check out the bar," he said.

I stood on the rungs of my stool and leaned over to get a better look. The lower cabinet on the back wall was painted like tracks leading into a mine. The tracks stopped at the back of the bar, where a set of mining cart wheels rested. Behind the tap handles, wood affixed to the wall looked like a cart. Clever artistry had created the illusion of a mining cart going down the tracks.

"Wow! That's really cool," I said.

From an information sheet left on the bar, I learned that the brewery was named in honor of the superstitions and legends of the immigrant English and Cornish miners that arrived in the area around 1860. Tommyknockers are mythical elf-like beings that lived in the cracks and crevices of the mines. Mischievous Tommyknockers blew out the miners' lamps and hid their picks and shovels. Friendly Tommyknockers, on the other hand, knocked on the walls, alerting miners to more bountiful ore veins. Superstitious men would leave bits of their lunch for the pint-sized people to encourage good fortune and safety. We had lunch plans elsewhere, though, so we just left a tip.

According to Chris's trip agenda, we planned to eat lunch at Dillon Dam Brewing, a forty-minute drive from Idaho Springs. Unfortunately, even the best plans experience wrinkles. We pulled into the brewery's empty parking lot.

"I have a bad feeling about this," Chris said.

He went to the entrance of the darkened pub and turned right back around.

"They're closed for two days for cleaning and repairs," he reported.

"Cleaning and repairs?" I asked.

"I can't believe it. Why would you be closed for 'cleaning and repairs' the week of GABF?" Chris ranted.

He went on for another few minutes before he pulled himself together and got out the map. Our next destination was only a short distance away, but didn't open for another four hours. It was time to use an element key to successful beer travel: the ability to improvise. A new plan in hand, we drove to nearby Frisco for lunch at Backcountry Brewery, a place we weren't planning to visit until later in the evening.

Fifteen minutes and 1,500 feet higher in elevation later, the thermostat on the rental car registered a cool 50°F in Frisco. We stepped out of the car and it was hard to believe that the temperature was accurate. It felt more like 80°F.

We settled outside on the deck of the second story restaurant. When the waitress came by to drop off menus, we ordered a taster set. Chris and I both looked up toward the mountains dusted with snow.

"It says here on the menu that the brewery is at 9,097 ft." Chris informed me. "I think that officially makes it the highest brewery we've ever been to."

While we lunched on our turkey wrap and buffalo chicken sandwich, two crane engineers from Salt Lake City at a nearby table struck up conversation with us. Among other things, they regretted to inform us that they had heard that Dillon Dam Brewing brewed excellent beer. "Even better than this place, I hear," one of them said.

There wasn't much we could do about Dillon Dam being closed, though, so we didn't let our disappointment get in the way of a good time. With the sweet smell of brewing in the air, blindingly bright sunshine in the sky, and a beautiful mountain view, nothing could make the scene more blissful.

From Backcountry Brewing, we went to our hotel to check in. The front desk clerk told us about a paved recreation path accessible a few blocks away that followed along the Dillon Reservoir all the way to Dillon. A walk seemed like a great way to get ourselves to Pug Ryan's, our last brewery of the day.

After negotiating our way through the nearby condominium complex, we found the path. We strolled underneath canopies of golden leaves fluttering in the breeze and observed birds preening themselves as they sat on the water. Cyclists zoomed past us but other than that, we encountered few people.

The journey took longer than we expected and along the way we joked about the possibility of the brewery being closed.

"Wouldn't that be funny if it wasn't even open?" Chris said.

"No, it wouldn't," I replied. "And if it is closed, Dillon, Colorado will be off my list forever. They don't get a second chance."

"But I thought everything deserved a second chance," Chris commented.

"Hmmph. Not this time," I said firmly.

After two hours, we finally made it to Dillon and an open Pug Ryan's Steak House and Brewery.

We chose a table out on the sunny deck to recover from our long haul from Frisco. No longer responsible for driving, Chris relaxed. We enjoyed ourselves playing Scrabble, drinking beer, and having a bite to eat. Eventually, the evening came to a close, which meant paying the check and asking them to call us a cab.

The waiter intercepted me on my way out of the bathroom. Somewhat sheepishly he informed me that they did not have cabs.

I laughed, not only because he had to be joking with me, but also because just a few minutes before, Chris had mused about whether the small town had cabs.

"What do you mean you don't have cabs?" I said. "You're a bar, what do you do with your drunk people?"

"Well, there's a free bus, but I don't know when it comes. Where are you going?" he asked.

"Just over to Frisco."

The waiter stared at me and said nothing more.

Completely perplexed and still in shock, I returned to the table and told Chris the news.

"What do you mean they don't have cabs?" he asked in disbelief.

"I mean the waiter told me they don't have cabs, but we can take a free bus and we have to transfer in order to get to Frisco. He had no idea how long it would take for us to get back."

Uncharacteristically resigned to the fact that we'd probably have to walk, I didn't bother to complain about it. Chris signed the credit card slip and looked across the table at me. I hoped he had a solution in mind because I drew a blank. The owner came over to introduce himself and offer his assistance.

"I just assumed that there would be cabs," I said.

"Well, we did have one in town, but the guy couldn't make it work," he explained. "I could call your hotel and see if there's a shuttle, but I'm pretty sure there isn't."

Without saying a word, we stood up and followed the owner through the restaurant toward the bar. I requested a phone book, although I had no idea what I was going to do with it. If the town had no cab companies, then none would be listed.

"There's a cab service in Breckenridge," the owner said, "but that's twenty miles away. It will probably take a while to get here and it'll be expensive."

He stepped away and left me to leaf through the phone book. When he returned, he said, "I have my car and we're not that busy, so I'm going to have my bartender, Chris, drive you."

No time for polite protestations, the offer was accepted without hesitation. Once in the car, we offered bartender Chris money for gas, but he declined.

"Eh," he said. "It's not my car anyway. It's the boss's gas."

Ten minutes later, we were back in our hotel room. And shortly after that, Chris started the next day's blog. It included a plug for Pug Ryan's exceptional customer service.

We awoke on our second day in Colorado ready to drive the three hours to Colorado Springs. After recovering from my accidental use of Chris's toothbrush, we headed south through Park County on State Highway 9. We traveled through the snow-covered mountains—where at one point the car indicated the temperature outside to be 31°F—to the wide, open valley at an elevation of 10,000 feet. In the west-central portion of the county known as South Park, we passed through Fairplay, a town named by gold prospectors who settled there in 1859. Despite the South Park area's famous namesake, there was almost no mention of the adult-oriented cartoon anywhere.

"I'm surprised they haven't embraced the *South Park* phenomenon," I said. "You'd think they could really capitalize on the merchandising opportunities."

"I guess these little towns want to remain true to their historic Gold Rush roots and not go all pop culture-ish," Chris said.

"Or maybe it's just hard to embrace a politically incorrect, wrong-on-so-many-levels cartoon," I laughed then broke into song. "I'm goin' down to *South Park* gonna have myself a time."

"Friendly faces everywhere, humble folks without temptation," Chris joined in.

I was happy about going to Colorado Springs because we had plans to connect with several friends who lived in the area, including a beer friend, a high school classmate and my best friend from elementary school. We were also planning to visit several breweries, which is always a good thing. However, my enthusiasm was slightly dulled by the fact that two of the breweries wouldn't count for me.

As a side excursion during a work trip to Denver several years before, I had visited my childhood friend, Diane. Without Chris, Diane took me to Bristol Brewing Company and Phantom Canyon Brewing Company. On our Year in Beer trip to Colorado Springs, Chris and I planned to visit both of those, in addition to four other breweries that would be new for both of us. With this plan, Chris would pull further ahead of me on The List count. He insists that The List is not a competition, but that's easy for the one who's ahead to say. In my mind, I was running to keep up, not to pull ahead. So until we were evenly matched, it most definitely was a competition.

I pouted on the way to our first destination. As my second visit, Bristol Brewing Company didn't count on my list. After several wrong turns we found it. Despite what Chris thought, my poor navigation was completely unintentional and not related in any way to my feelings about Bristol already being on my list.

Bristol Brewing didn't look familiar to me from the outside. We opened the door to the modern-looking brewery and vague recollections of being there before started to surface. The evening-time crowd during my first visit had created a very different feel from the empty brightly lit pub in which we now stood. On the right, a wall of glass blocks separated the brewery from the large curved sheet metal bar.

We drank our pints and snacked on pretzels from a shiny metal dog bowl on the bar. An off-duty employee sat near us with a thick open textbook and a scattering of notebook paper in front of him. Looking for any excuse to avoid his college chemistry homework, the employee watched as Chris filmed my whiney rant about not counting the brewery. Of course our barmate asked what we were doing. I explained The List and told him about the Year in Beer. Like many others we'd met over the past nine months, our new friend wholeheartedly approved of our yearlong beer adventure.

We left Bristol Brewing for our downtown hotel. Chris was eager to park the car because only then would he be relieved of his driving duties and really be able to enjoy the beer tasting. Our hotel was conveniently located across the street from Phantom Canyon Brewing Company, the next stop on our Colorado Springs beer tour and where we planned to meet our friend Eli.

Phantom Canyon is located on the corner of Pikes Peak and Cascade, the first corner in Colorado Springs. All addresses and street plans originated from this spot, although today, the brown three-story brick structure is dwarfed by several bank buildings nearby.

Walking through Phantom Canyon's double set of doors is like walking into a bit of history. The antique wooden bar has Tiffany-style stained glass accents and old-time style fans hang above, wobbling as they spin.

Our friend Eli Shayotovich, whom we had first met during the Beerdrinker of the Year contest in February, was waiting for us inside. Sitting at a table near the bar, he waved us over as we entered.

In Denver, Eli, a man of imposing size, was loud and boisterous. Now, he was calm as he happily chatted away in a much more reserved manner than I had anticipated. Unbeknownst to us, Eli had kindly arranged a visit to Arctic Craft Brewery[26] a short distance away. As a Colorado Springs-based beer writer, this was Eli's territory and we were happy to follow his lead around the area.

Our visit to Arctic was an unexpected addition to The List because while Chris was aware of the brewery, their public tasting hours did not coordinate with our time in Colorado Springs. With Eli's help, however, they agreed to open their doors and taps to us.

We pulled up to what looked like an oversized shed. A large sign with bright blue lettering hung against the white corrugated siding. "Arctic Craft Brewery: Adventures in Taste."

We opened the hollow metal door to find two men frantically sorting keg labels that were spread out on the stainless steel tasting bar. Although we couldn't see the brewery from the where we stood, the sounds were unmistakable, including the frequent metal clank of full kegs on the cement floor. Brewery workers darted back and forth at the back of the warehouse building. Outside of the public tasting hours, the brewery wasn't fully prepared to host visitors.

I looked to Chris and whispered, "They look a little busy."

"They're preparing not only for GABF, but the pre-GABF party at Trinity tonight," Eli said.

The man behind the bar looked up and greeted us.

---

26 Unfortunately, Arctic closed seven months later in May 2009.

"I see you're busy, but we were hoping to taste some beer," Chris said.

"Uh, yeah. Sure," he said.

The man pushed the items cluttering the bar aside with his forearm like a bulldozer. The other man looked up as the pile encroached upon his workspace. A sampler set was quickly poured and we all chatted briefly. Obviously anxious to return to his work, the man finally said, "Sorry, we're running a little behind, so if you want any more samples, go ahead and help yourself. I need to go in the back for a sec."

The man rushed off and Chris wasted no time positioning himself behind the bar. He turned his back to us and faced the row of a dozen identical long, flat tap handles. His hand followed along the top of the handles as he decided which one to try. Having found what he wanted, Chris pulled down a handle and a dark brew flowed out the tap and into his small glass. He looked quite satisfied with himself as he turned around to face us again.

"What would you like to try, sir?" he said to Eli, who laughed.

"What did you pour for yourself there," I asked.

"The milk stout," Chris answered.

In less than a half hour, we tasted several beers, including a vanilla porter and a peach lager, purchased a six-pack of their On-On Pale Ale, and left. After a short and sweet visit, Arctic was added to The List.

With Eli behind the wheel, we arrived at our next destination a short time later. The Trinity Brewing pre-GABF party didn't start for another hour, but fearing it would be crowded, Eli thought we should arrive early to get a table. It sounded like a good plan to us.

The Trinity Brewing Company sign, with its red triskelion, added some pizzazz to the otherwise dull brown-tiled building. Following Eli into the "newest kid on the Colorado Springs beer block," I noticed a colorful array of twenty-five tap handles that extended along the left side of the long narrow pub. A high bistro table near the door was available, so we staked out our territory for the evening.

Now at our last stop on our Colorado Springs beer tour, Chris placed a call to a high school classmate who lived in the area and I called my childhood friend, Diane. They each planned to join us at the brewery for a beer. Plans set, Chris ordered Trinity's Flo IPA, which Eli explained was served using a device they called the "Randler." We all chuckled.

"I guess Sam doesn't have a trademark on Randall," Chris said.

He was referring to Sam Calagione and the device invented at Dogfish Head Craft Brewed Ales in Delaware. Described by the brewery as "an organoleptic hop transducer module," Randall is a three-foot tall clear cylinder, filled with whole leaf hops, that is attached to the line between the keg and the tap faucet. The beer flows through Randall, creating an aromatic, flavorsome hop explosion.

Trinity's Randler worked in much the same way and courtesy of Eli's connection with the head brewer, Jason Yester we went in the back to see it firsthand. Jason explained how the IPA traveled from the keg through the blue PVC pipe filled with fresh hops and herbs, then through a second filter to trap any leafy bits. He pointed to the tube connected to the second filter and traced it to the wall with his finger.

"From here it goes to the tap on the other side of the wall and into your glass," the brewer said.

Our Randler explanation complete, we left the chilly cooler and stepped back into the warm pub, which had filled up in our short absence. Chris, Eli and I weaved our way through the crowd back to our table, which was just as we had left it.

My friend Diane who was accompanied by her husband and young daughter, as well as Chris's high school classmate Kim and her husband Ralph, arrived a short while later. Chris and I now had all the people we knew in Colorado Springs at one table, which made it difficult to focus on one person long enough to properly catch up. The energy in the pub combined with my beer consumption turned me into a chatterbox. My voice became hoarse as the evening wore on, and in an effort to avoid completely straining my vocal chords, we thought it might be time to pack it in. A few hours after arriving, we said our good-byes and accepted a generous offer from Kim and Ralph to drive us back to our hotel. That ended our pre-festival excursion. The next day we would make our maiden visit to the biggest beer gathering in the United States: the Great American Beer Festival.

"Are you nervous about going to GABF for the first time?" Chris asked me the next morning.

"No. I don't think so. Why? Are you?"

"I don't think so," he replied.

We arrived in Denver around noon. The first session of the festival didn't start until 5:30 P.M., but media check-in was available. After making a quick stop at our hotel, we walked to the Colorado Convention Center to pick up our media passes.

During the planning stages of the trip, Chris had contacted GABF organizers to inquire about filming inside the festival. In order to film, they told him he'd have to apply for a media pass. Obtaining full media privileges was not our intention. In fact, Chris had already purchased our tickets to the first session and the Brewer's Association members-only session. The idea that we had to "apply" made me nervous. Would they find us to be legitimate beer media? A few weeks later they granted us our passes, so the answer must have been yes.

I held the hot pink laminated badge up by its lanyard. A smile spread across my face. More so than any other media badge we had received before, this one filled me with pride. For that moment at least, I thought perhaps we had really made it into the center ring of the beer media circus.

Chris and I floated up Blake Street away from the liveliness of the 16th Street Mall, the one-mile pedestrian and transit mall that runs through downtown. The mood along the street became more calm and quiet. The first session was still a few hours away, but the air buzzed with GABF excitement. The thrill of going to Falling Rock caused our hearts to beat quickly and our pace to be brisk. Set back from the street, we couldn't see Falling Rock as we approached but we could most certainly hear it. The jumbled crowd noise grew louder the closer we got.

Falling Rock is *the* place for any self-respecting beer geek to be while in Denver. When the Great American Beer Festival rolls around, it becomes the absolute epicenter of the beer social scene. If you're not there to stalk brewers, chat up beer journalists, or take photos with beer celebrities, you go there to be seen. Every beer-focused website in the blog-o-sphere mentions being at Falling Rock and lists who was spotted drinking what. During GABF, special events and limited-release beers ensure large, thirsty and boisterous crowds at Falling Rock.

We turned to our left to see the deck out front packed with a herd of happy beer drinkers. Individuals streamed back and forth down the long sloping ramp talking on their cell phones. "Where are you? What? No, I'm already here. We have a table."

A few stragglers rested up against the railing and I could see the exasperation in the security guy's face as he told them to keep the ramp clear. It must have been the hundredth time he'd told someone that. We got to the top of the ramp and I wondered how we would ever maneuver through the crowd to the bar. Just as I reminded myself that it was more about being seen than actually getting a beer, I heard a yell in our direction.

"Merideth! Chris!"

We looked over to see Jessica Jones (JJ), a friend from the Bay Area. At one time, JJ wrote a beer blog under the name "The Thirsty Hopster." A pretty young woman with a slight build, JJ is smart, opinionated and not afraid to speak her mind. We had often teased her for her lengthy blog posts. "I just have a lot to say," she'd tell us.

Hearing our name called out the minute we stepped into Falling Rock during GABF, I felt the sensation of having arrived in beer's highest social circle.

With JJ's table positioned fairly close to the entrance, it took relatively little nudging and squeezing to get to her. JJ, her sister Allie and Allie's partner Melissa, made room for us by scooting chairs closer together. It was an unexpected meeting and a very pleasant surprise. They offered us sips of their beer while we patiently waited for our server to come by.

Falling Rock at that moment reminded me of Oktoberfest—very crowded with little room to spare. The aisles were a gauntlet of sloshing beers and animated conversationalists. People stood in any available spot and did their best to stay out of the way of the servers and others trying to get to and from their tables. Servers weaved through the crowd, turning sideways to slip by with full beers in their hands. "Excuse me. Excuse me! Beer coming through," I heard one cry out. Oblivious individuals engrossed in buzzed banter hardly noticed them until the server yelled at them to move.

"A little crowded, huh?" I said to JJ.

"Yeah, we were lucky to get this table as some people were leaving," she answered.

"We've been here for a few hours now," added Allie.

"Well, it's good for us, I guess," Chris said. "Thanks for letting us join your table."

With so much activity it was hard to focus and I frequently turned away from the conversation at our table to scan the crowd. Falling Rock's owner, Chris Black, took to the PA system. "Breckenridge 471 IPA is now on tap!" A roar of cheers rang throughout the pub—inside, outside, and even downstairs on the basement level.

Tom Dalldorf with the *Celebrator Beer News* handed out promotional postcards for the inaugural San Francisco Beer Week happening in a few months. A small bar set up on the deck offered a selection of Bay Area beers and served as the official kick-off headquarters for the redefined and expanded version of what we had previously known as Beerapalooza. It was a reunion of sorts, as other Bay Area beer notables joined Tom in the campaign. Shaun O'Sullivan from 21st Amendment Brewing, beer writer Jay Brooks, and Bruce "The Beer Chef" Paton all did their part to spread the word about the event. We saw these guys frequently, but GABF spirit had put everyone in an enthusiastic mood, making the encounter especially fun.

"Oh, and Port's Hop 15 won Alpha King," JJ informed us as she motioned toward the inside of the pub.

We looked over to see a hop-wreathed head moving through the crowd. It belonged to Tomme Arthur, Director of Brewery Operations for Port Brewing Company from San Marcos, California. Chris nodded with approval and vowed to get one.

Each year, lovers of hoppy beer pack into Falling Rock's basement to bear witness to the crowning of the Alpha King. Although it's a contest to find the hoppiest beer in America, a balance of flavor is also important. The event occurs each year during GABF week and attracts hop bomb brewers from all over the country. On this day, Port Brewing's Hop 15, an Imperial IPA, beat out over seventy competitors to capture the coveted title.

After a few beers, we returned to the hotel to freshen up before the first session of our first ever visit to the Great American Beer Festival.

Held over three days, including three evening sessions (Thursday, Friday, Saturday), and one Brewer's Association members-only afternoon session (Saturday), the festival is the current Guinness World Record Holder for the most beers tapped in one location. With more than 1,900 brews on tap, festival organizers expected to serve approximately 18,000 gallons of beer. The competition included seventy-five categories of beer styles and the winners would be announced at the members-only session on Saturday.

Over 46,000 people were expected to attend the 27th annual festival and like any other sold-out event, GABF attracted the scalpers. Along the way to the Convention Center for the first session, half a dozen people asked if we needed tickets. We shook our heads no and kept walking. Prior to learning we had been granted media passes we purchased tickets to two sessions. Now having media passes in our pockets, we were hoping to sell our extra tickets at face value to a beer lover not fortunate enough to have gotten one. However, the only people buying were those who planned to capitalize on the sold-out status of the event. In the end, we chose to keep our tickets rather than sell them to a scalper.

"Sheesh. Check out that line," Chris said.

I stared in disbelief at the line snaking around the building and underneath the pedestrian sky bridge linking the Convention Center with the Denver Performing Arts Complex. Standing in a haphazard row, some people looked bored and annoyed, while others could barely contain their excitement. In front of the entrance, festival goers on cells phones looked every which way trying to locate their friends. Vendors with hand trucks and armloads of merchandise marched deliberately toward the VIP entrance, dodging brewers with their entourages, who sauntered along.

We flashed our hot pink media badges to the volunteers working the door and entered through the VIP entrance. As we queued for our wristbands, the echo of a large gathering could be heard inside the convention hall. The festival hadn't even opened yet. While a volunteer wrapped a band around my wrist, I attempted to catch a glimpse inside, but couldn't see much. That was okay, though, because we had just jumped through the last hoop to getting inside.

The sheer size of the event stopped us in our tracks and bewilderment engulfed us, a replay of the Great British Beer Festival.

Hundreds of banquet tables lined up in rows with red-curtained partitions behind them. The resulting wide lanes could have passed for village streets. Signs with the names of over 400 breweries from all over the country indicated which beers were poured where. A look at the floor plan in the festival program showed how the beers were conveniently arranged by region. Banners advertising breweries, beer magazines, and brewing supplies hung on the walls and waved gently from the ceiling. Near the entrance, a merchandise store was set up. A thirty-foot-long collage of brewery shirts covered the wall behind a row of cash registers. Temporary barriers zigzagged back and forth, an indicator of how long the line might become. For now, however, it remained empty.

We wandered further inside and discussed our festival strategy. For the *beergeek.TV* episode, we decided to ask people to give first time attendees like us advice on how to tackle this thing.

We started down our first aisle and it didn't take long to find someone who looked like he knew what he was doing. I approached a burly man with unkempt shoulder length hair and a beard. Taking his dark sunglasses and bathrobe into consideration, he looked like a Harley rider who just got out of bed.

"Do you mind if I ask you some questions on camera?" I asked.

"That's fine," he replied.

"Okay, so how many times have you been here?"

"This is my third time," he said proudly.

"And what is your strategy for this craziness called GABF?"

He tilted his head to get the hair out of his eyes. "The Dude says this: I would recommend going to the area you are not from to try beers you haven't heard of or can't get in your area."

His deep voice and dramatic hand gestures punctuated his points as he outlined a different plan for each session. "The last session drink anything you can that ain't spilled on the floor," he finished.

We laughed and thanked him for his words of wisdom before continuing down the aisle taking in the sights. We encountered the usual beer festival outfits: a man dressed as a monk, buxom women in short dirndls, kilts of all tartans, beer mug hats, and beer goggles in a variety of styles.

I stopped to try Walter Payton's Roundhouse Oompah Loompah Chocolate Beer. The volunteer dutifully poured the beer right up to the line on my glass—one ounce exactly.

"What's with the pretzels people have around their necks?" I asked.

"I wondered what Eli was talking about last night," Chris said. "Now I know."

The night before, Eli spoke of needing to get home to make "pretzel necklaces." I pictured assembling pretzel dough into a chain and baking it. In fact, pretzel necklaces are regular store-bought pretzels looped together on a string and worn around the neck. It's a portable bar snack that leaves both hands free for beer. This was the first time we'd ever seen pretzel necklaces and they seemed to be all the rage at GABF.

We stared at the brewery names as we walked along. I occasionally bumped into someone because I wasn't watching where I was going. Bumps came at me as much as I gave them, but it didn't matter. With only one ounce of beer in the glass, there was virtually no chance of beer spilling on me or anyone else.

"Blue Point Brewing. Patchogue, New York," Chris said out loud. "I think I'll try their Hoptical Illusion."

"I'll meet you back here," I said. "I see a Kölsch over here."

We went our separate ways and met back up—each of us with a splash of beer at the bottom of our glass.

"How is it?" Chris asked.

I held up my glass and tilted it so Chris could see the scant amount. "It's good, but I don't know about these one ounce pours. By the time I decide I like it, it's gone."

"Oh, hey. There's JJ, Allie, and Melissa." Chris pointed further down.

"As thorough and organized as JJ is, she's bound to have some sort of strategy for trying the beers. Let's go get her on film," I said.

Everyone manages the overwhelming selection at GABF differently. While some develop more organized plans than others, few attendees approach the festival without any sort of system at all. JJ's plan was one of thoughtful common sense.

With all three of them on camera, JJ took the lead in describing their approach. "We looked at the list and then marked the ones we wanted to go to on the map," she explained. "Then just went up and down the aisles hitting those."

"We're starting with the beers we think will run out first," Melissa added.

"If you want organized," JJ told us, "we talked to these guys in cow print hats—Tim, Ted, and Steve. You need to find them."

We wandered down a new aisle and ran into our friend and Bay Area-based beer writer Jay Brooks, who I found out was a big peanut butter fan.

"You've got to try Blue Moon's peanut butter beer," he said.

Chris and I both scrunched up our faces in disgust.

"No, really," he insisted. "If you love peanut butter like I do then you'll like it. I mean, I don't think I could drink a whole lot of it, but poured over chocolate ice cream, it would be great."

We went in search of the peanut butter beer. Not surprising, only a few other people were around to try it, so I was able to walk right up to the table for my taste. It was just as Jay described it. Interesting is the best I can say.

Chris and I developed the strategy of going to tables without lines. It wasn't so much a time saver as it was a way to dodge one of Chris's biggest annoyances. Lines for breweries like Russian River and Lost Abbey snaked down the aisles. My beer crush, Sam Calagione, poured beer at the Dogfish Head table, so of course the line was very long. (Okay, I admit that I stood in that line for the chance to be served by Sam, but that was the only time.)

Chris waited patiently for me. I don't even know what beer I tasted from Dogfish, but it didn't really matter. It was Sam's. We resumed our exploration of GABF.

"There are those guys JJ was talking about," Chris said.

We approached a trio of men in pointy cow print hats and I asked my standard initial question: "Do you mind being on camera?"

Of course they didn't mind. One thing I had started to understand was that the people who dressed to be noticed at beer festivals got noticed. That's the way they wanted it. Crazy outfits, funny hats, and groups with matching t-shirts—those were the people who got interviewed by every media crew crawling around GABF. The girls in the sexy outfits had their pictures taken by not only news people, but also by every guy bold enough to approach them.

"How many times have you been to GABF?" I asked.

"This is our 11th year," Tim spoke for the three of them.

"We go for the Gold Medal Run," he started. "You take last year's GABF and World Beer Cup winners and put them in a list."

He held up curled pieces of paper that had been rolled up in his pocket. A large spreadsheet with tiny font covered the whole of each page.

"Then you print out the GABF floor plan," he continued. "This year there's 360 beers, so we divided it up for Thursday night and Friday night. We plan on 180 beers each night."

His plan left me speechless. I'm one of the most organized people I know, but that was a little much even for me.

"Do you realize that 180 beers is the equivalent of nine imperial pints?" Chris said later.

If I previously wondered how people managed to get drunk on one-ounce pours, I now had my answer. They drink a hell of a lot of beer.

We came across the *Beer Magazine* table where our friend Brad Ruppert, an editor-at-large for the magazine, and Rich Durkin, a contributing writer, were working. When we last saw Brad in Boston on St. Patrick's Day, he had worn a kilt commando style. For GABF, he donned lederhosen. I don't know if it was sans underpants, but when it comes to Brad, I've learned it's best not to ask. I knew he would have no problem being on camera.

"So you guys may remember Brad from our March episode," I said. "He's joined by Rich, who's also with *Beer Magazine*. They're both first-timers like us, so let's hear their strategy." That's all I needed to say. Brad was off.

"The way to pop the cherry is that you start off trying to find the most remote beer you can," he explained.

I tried to keep a straight face on camera, but inside I was hitting the heel of my hand against my forehead. The whole time Brad spoke I wondered what he might say next and questioned why we ever opened that can of worms in the first place. It would have taken great effort to close it again, so I didn't even try. Besides, that's Brad.

"Rich here likes to go for the softer, sweeter lemony-type beers," Brad goaded. "Whereas I like the more robust and hoppy beers."

With Brad's arm around his shoulders, Rich quietly stood there taking jabs at his manhood. It's hard to compete with Brad's boisterous voice, frequent laughter, and hyperactivity and any companion of Brad's is effectively rendered his straight man. Rich didn't seem to mind, though.

The night wore on and the pandemonium increased. The trio of guys using the "Gold Medal Run" strategy totaling 180 different beers were somewhere near 100 by then and the effects were showing. We were on beer festival overload and needed a break.

Chris and I emerged into the crisp evening air and I leaned into him for warmth. People in varying stages of drunkenness also made their way outside. Even so, the reduction in decibel level made me realize how loud it had been inside.

"Well, what'd ya think?" Chris asked.

"Overwhelming," I said. "And my ears are ringing."

"You know, GABF is like the beer geek annual convention," Chris said.

I nodded in agreement as he explained his comment. "Trekkies have their gatherings. Comic book people have theirs. Even computer geeks have techie conventions. GABF is ours. It's a way for us to see our beer friends from all over the country in one place."

Chris's summation of GABF rolled around my head as we walked across the downtown streets of Denver toward our hotel. GABF as a beer geek's annual convention made a lot of sense to me. There were the perennial festival attendees that we knew with certainty we'd cross paths with at some point. Then there were the friends with whom we'd made specific plans to meet. Much of the time, however, we ran into people we knew by chance; some we simply exchanged greetings, others we drank multiple rounds of beer with. Throughout GABF there is no shortage of festivities to attend and there is always a good chance of finding some other beer geek to hang out with.

As far as beer fanatics go, we eclipse even the most ardent craft beer drinkers in our immediate circle of friends. We travel for beer. We keep a list of breweries. We named our dogs after beer. With their good-natured teasing and gentle mocking, our friends sometimes inadvertently made me feel like I was the crazy one; like our love of beer was somehow over the top.

At GABF, I was just one of many in a sea of beer geeks. That could probably be said of any beer festival, but it's the size of GABF that makes the difference. The Oregon Brewers Festival, for example, brings together thousands of beer geeks. However, OBF is smaller and primarily a regional event focusing on west coast beer. The Great British Beer Festival is another large beer event, but it focuses on real ale, the traditional brewing style of England. Perhaps it was the accents, but

I just didn't see myself reflected in the faces of other attendees at GBBF.

The Great American Beer Festival is an enormous gathering where thousands of people just like me converge in Denver for one reason: beer. Everyone at GABF is crazy about beer and many people I encountered during the first session showed a level of beer fanaticism that far exceeded my own. I went to bed feeling like your average, everyday beer geek and it felt good.

After our media pass applications had been approved a few months earlier, a flurry of invites to lunches, talks, and even a walking tour of Denver's beer history came our way. As first-time attendees to GABF, and our biggest media pass event to date, we accepted everything we could fit into our schedule. Friday's media lunch presented by the Brewers Association, the group that organizes GABF, was our first media corps function of the festival. Information we received on the function warned attendees that it would be a "working lunch." What that meant, we eventually found out, was that along with lunch we were bombarded with facts and figures to presumably use in our articles on GABF. We were also treated to a keynote address by Greg Koch, founder and CEO of Stone Brewing Company, a brewery we'd be visiting in November.

Shortly after the lunch was over, a walking tour of Denver's brewing history started. Our tour group was comprised of other freshmen beer media like ourselves. I guessed that all the veterans had already experienced it and once was enough. During our walk, we learned that Denver, founded in 1858, had a brewery just one year after it became a city. The Rocky Mountain Brewery was subsequently overshadowed when Coors in nearby Golden started production in 1873. When we started off, Chris and I weren't exactly sure how long the tour would last. Two hours later, during a stop at Wynkoop Brewing Company, we saw our chance to quietly slink off into the sunset. Or at least down the street. When we felt far enough away to be safe, Chris and I heaved a sigh of relief. Two hours in Denver during GABF was just too long to go without a beer.

"To Falling Rock?" Chris asked.

"To Falling Rock," I answered.

We arrived at Falling Rock to a full house. There we saw Bruce Paton—aka the Beer Chef and our friend from Barclay's in Oakland—and joined him near the entrance at the top of the stairs to the basement. Always looking for the optimal see-and-be-seen spot, here we could catch those coming in, up from the downstairs, or to and from the bathroom. Like a high school reunion, we grouped with the people we knew and saw frequently, while doling out everything from polite "hellos" to "Oh my god! It's so good to see you" hugs to those who passed by.

Downstairs in the basement, *All About Beer Magazine* was hosting a tasting of Dogfish Head's less common beers with founder and president Sam Calagione in attendance to pour. Our friend Rick Sellers, who at the time was the beer editor for *Draft Magazine*, came up the stairs with his taster glass of Theobroma, a beer brewed with Aztec chocolate, cocoa nibs, honey, chilies, and annatto. Released only a few months before, it was the hot, highly discussed beer of the moment. The recipe was based on a chemical analysis of an ancient Honduran pottery fragment, which revealed the earliest known alcoholic chocolate drink. I readily accepted when Rick offered me a sip.

"Oh, wow!" I said. "That's an amazing beer!"

"And it was brewed by Sam," Chris added.

Rick laughed along with us before he moved on to mingle. A man approached us and introduced himself. One of Chris's Facebook friends recognized him from his profile picture and *thebeergeek.com*.[27] It gave us an ego boost and even a bit of a thrill to be recognized.

"Hey, that was kinda cool," Chris said. "Stay here, I gotta use the little boy's room."

Bruce snickered and said, "Okay. Thanks for sharing."

Gone for longer than I expected, Chris eventually returned bragging that he talked with Sam while waiting in line.

Shortly thereafter, Sam walked towards us on his way back downstairs, an effort that was riddled with slaps on the shoulders, greetings, and handshakes. Our group watched as he approached.

"Sam," Chris said.

Sam turned and Chris pointed to me as if to say, "Look, Sam. It's Merideth." Sam looked at me and I extended my hand. He gave me a hug instead. Shocked and taken aback, I managed to get out a "nice to see you."

I waited for Sam to disappear downstairs before whacking Chris on the arm.

"Why did you do that? It's not like he knows me," I said.

"Yeah, but he gave you a hug," Chris said smiling.

We stayed at Falling Rock a little longer, but, in the interest of pacing ourselves, it was time to take a break. A walk up to Great Divide Brewing provided just the break we needed.

Great Divide is long and narrow. Seating includes the bar, a few tables at the far end of the room, and places to stand

27 At the time, Facebook had not yet exploded in popularity and the beer community was not nearly as well connected through social media as it is now, making this encounter all the more unexpected.

along the wall. With GABF going on, every beer place in town was working on overdrive and Great Divide was no exception. With nowhere to sit, we stood to the right of the front door by the bathrooms. If I wanted to pick up a date for the night, it might have been a good spot. People waiting for the bathroom are a captive audience, at least until it's their turn.

Not thrilled with our drinking spot near the bathrooms to begin with, we became even less enthralled as traffic increased. Vastly different from Falling Rock, I felt just below Kathy Griffin on the D-list at Great Divide. We didn't know anyone, nobody recognized us, and we were stuck at the worst seat in the house. We did drink great beer, though.

"I guess we peaked at Falling Rock," Chris said.

Saturday morning Chris, who had worn shorts up to this point in the trip, broke down and put on pants.

"I curse you Denver," he said. "Two days ago it was 75°F; today it's in the 30s."

"That's why you should never promise," I told him.

Later, Chris filmed his mea culpa for breaking his April promise to not wear pants again until December.

With Chris in pants and me bundled up, we joined the *Beer Magazine* crew, including Brad and Rich, at the Sam Adams American Homebrew Contest breakfast at Marlowe's, a restaurant located in Denver's Central Business District. Also known as the Longshot Competition, it actually consists of two separate contests, one for Sam Adams employees and the other for homebrewers from around the country. The winning beers from each group are included in the Sam Adams Longshot six-pack that is distributed nationwide. The breakfast is the media forum at which the winners are announced.

We arrived to find representatives from each of the major beer publications in addition to a handful of internet-based beer media like ourselves. We tasted a variety of Sam Adams beers, as well as the final three employee homebrews. Later, over brunch from the Sam Adams beer-inspired buffet, we listened to Boston Beer Company founder Jim Koch announce the winners.

Television personalities often look much different in person, but not Jim Koch. His face and voice were so familiar that I had to remind myself that the event was live, not a TV commercial.

The ubiquitous face of a large corporation, Jim was used to public speaking. He impressed me with the way he flawlessly introduced the employee finalists by name and position without using notes. A national account manager, legal team contract manager, and a senior manager of operations finance, the finalists weren't exactly employees whose names would be expected to roll off the founder/CEO's tongue. I viewed Boston Beer Company's corporate image a little differently after that. Carissa Sweigart, a national account manager, won with her Cranberry Wit.

Full from the "beerunch," as beer brunches are often called, we walked to the Convention Center for the member's session of the festival. This session, open only to members of the Brewer's Association, was the one where the first, second, and third place winners in each category would be announced.

Before the PowerPoint presentation of winners, we had time to explore the vast array of festival entertainment. Off in the far corner, several beer pong tables were set up. The testosterone level was a little too high for me as we watched a pair of guys in their late-twenties become fiercely competitive during their match. I nudged Chris to keep walking.

Across from the games, we passed a woman who laughed hysterically as she took a picture of her male companion with his head sticking out of a wooden cutout. His face on top of a German fraulein's figure with melon-sized breasts falling out of her dress was almost too much for the photographer to bear. It appeared to be one male-centered entertainment activity after another.

As we ventured over to the other side of the convention hall, we encountered an activity the whole family could enjoy: a silent disco. A group of twenty people twisted their bodies, shook their hips, and flung their arms in the air. From our perspective, they grooved in silence. Not familiar with silent discos, we asked someone nearby to tell us how it worked.

"They're all listening to the same music in the headphones," a woman explained.

I looked over at the DJ as she continued. "And every once in a while, the DJ will tell them to do something, like 'strike a pose.' That tells him if everyone's headphones are working."

A middle-aged man in a green shirt danced with no one in particular as he threw his arms above his head and moved them from side to side. Next to him a younger couple got a little freaky. "Get a room," Chris said of their dancing style. One man was doing his own thing as he shuffled his feet around. Suddenly, everyone stopped briefly then started dancing again.

Chris noticed that the awards presentation had started, so we joined the overflow crowd standing behind the seated viewers. Enormous screens were positioned on either side of the podium on stage. A category was introduced, followed by the announcement of the bronze, silver, and gold medal winners. The crowd cheered wins by their favorite breweries and groaned when their least-favorite brewery placed.

"Category 61: Belgian- and French-Style Ale," the announcer said without emotion. "The bronze medal goes to Rare Vos, Brewery Ommegang. Cooperstown, New York."

A bullet point with the medal and name of the brewery popped up on the large screens on either side of the stage. Claps and cheers rang out.

"The silver medal goes to Pride, Midnight Sun Brewing Company. Anchorage, Alaska."

A slightly louder roar of cheers filled the air.

"And the gold medal in the Belgian- and French-Style Ale category goes to Redemption, Russian River Brewing Company. Santa Rosa, California."

The crowd exploded with excitement, as Russian River is a favorite among craft beer fans. In contrast, the American-Style Specialty Lager category, swept by Anheuser-Busch, elicited little more than polite claps.

I nudged Chris. "Look, that's Garrett Oliver."

"Oh, you're right," he whispered back.

Garrett Oliver, the Brewmaster at Brooklyn Brewery and author of *The Brewmaster's Table*, stood in front of us. As the author of one of the first comprehensive books ever written about beer, including the idea of pairing it with food, Garrett Oliver is truly a beer industry legend. At that moment I was about as star struck as I have ever been (no offense to Sam Calagione!). In his collarless sport coat and neatly groomed hair, he resembles nothing like a typical brewer. In all the pictures I had ever seen of Garrett, he wore posh, fashionable outfits. Seeing him now, I wondered if he even owned a pair of jeans or a t-shirt.

Watching the announcement of the medal winners, we learned that if no beers in the category met the standards for a silver or gold, those medals were not awarded. This happened in the English Style India Pale Ale category.

Soon after the awards presentation finished, the mad dash to taste the medal winners commenced. As if by magic, by the time we got to the tables with medal winners, stickers indicating the medal won appeared on the signs next to the beer, making them easy to find. However, everyone had the same idea as we did and several beers were already out.

Chris managed to get Arquebus, a summer barley wine, from our Boston favorite Cambridge Brewing. It won gold in the Experimental Beer category. Made with honey and white wine grapes, the brewery describes it as a "barleymalt-based interpretation of a dessert wine, meant to be sipped on sultry summer evenings." Chris tilted his head and raised his eyebrows after he sipped.

"Uh, yeah. This is experimental alright," he said. "It's syrupy and sweet like an ice wine."

With the one-ounce pours, there wasn't enough left in his glass for me to try it.

"I want to try that Kölsch that won," I said.

Consulting our floor plan, we walked over to the Mid-Atlantic region to find Stewart's Brewing Company and the Wind Blown Blonde. A volunteer happily poured my taste. As I walked away from the table and toward Chris, I examined my beer. Chris had the camera rolling to capture my expression.

"Check this out. I got shorted on my one-ounce pour," I remarked. "That really sucks."

We managed a few more medal winners, but mostly wandered the aisles. We eventually made out way back to the *Beer*

Magazine table to hang out with Rich and Brad. When we got there, the guys were in full Guitar Hero mode. Rich sang Duran Duran's Hungry Like the Wolf while Brad played guitar. After Rich failed singing several times, I decided that I could do better.

"Here, let me try it. I was a teen in the 80s. I loved Duran Duran," I said.

A bit out of character for me, it was amazing how just a little beer could reduce my inhibitions and any concern of making a fool out of myself.

I had never played Guitar Hero, but more or less understood how it worked. I grabbed the mic and Rich picked up the bass. Chris turned on the camera. Shy and stiff at first, I intently watched the screen for the lyrics. On my left, Brad shook the guitar up and down. He added a few whoops and hollers now and again while Rich stood quietly playing his part on my right. By about the tenth round of "Strut on a line, it's discord and rhyme, I'm on the hunt, I'm after you" I rocked like a pro. The lyrics whizzed by on the screen. I got a little lost at one point, but did my best to keep up. Brad bounced around sticking his tongue out occasionally. As a group, we got through the whole song and my singing earned an 87% score. I turned around to find a crowd had gathered. Mix beer and Guitar Hero and you've got the makings for embarrassing fun. Chris got it all on video.

Soon after my Guitar hero debut, the lights came up signaling the end of the session. We didn't plan to attend the Saturday night session, so our visit to GABF ended. Chris and I set up to record the closing scene of the episode.

"We came. We drank. I even sang Hungry Like the Wolf, but the lights are up and GABF is over. So, we're outta here. I hope you enjoyed this episode," I said into the camera.

We initially had reservations about attending the Great American Beer Festival because of its size. As it turned out, it was the enormity of it all that differentiated GABF from any other beer festival we'd attended. Magnitude isn't everything, though. Oktoberfest, for example, is also a huge gathering involving beer, but it's about participating in the biggest party most of us have ever seen. GABF, on the other hand, is an enormous party meant for beer lovers.

From the minute we arrived in Denver we felt right at home. We connected with beer friends from around the country, met new people and were recognized by fans of *thebeergeek.com*. I even got a hug from a beer celebrity. The Great American Beer Festival is the one time of year that just about every beer person in the U.S. converges on one location. Chris was right. If Trekkies, comic book geeks, and computer lovers could have their annual gatherings, so could beer people.

At the end of our trip I thought back to high school and pictured the kids we called "geeks." They differed from us by being into their own thing. There were the music prodigies, wannabe thespians, and during my time, the computer nerds. I imagined that each one of these types found others just like them when they moved on from high school. They were no longer geeks in the bad sense of the word, but part of a bigger group who all shared the same interests. It was only after I thought of these high school misfits that I realized every geek has her day.

At the Great American Beer Festival, I blended in with all the other beer geeks. I wasn't extreme or thought of as beer-obsessed because those labels served as a baseline for every person who attended. On this trip, I found my people.

NOVEMBER

LOOK BEYOND THE HYPE

Chris calls San Diego one of the hottest beer scenes around and when we planned the Year in Beer, we knew it had to be included. The greater San Diego area had experienced a craft beer explosion since our last visit over fifteen years ago and we hadn't yet visited some of the latest, most talked about breweries in the country. At GABF, beer geeks lined up and down the aisle for a taste of beer from places like Port Brewing, The Lost Abbey, Green Flash, and Stone. We had tasted beers from these breweries and knew they were worthy of the attention, but the hype about San Diego's beer scene felt over the top. Bandwagons come and go in the beer industry and beer geeks get on and off them just as quickly. We didn't want to believe the hype simply because it was the popular thing to do. We wanted to experience it for ourselves.

November's trip to San Diego was a good old-fashioned beer vacation. With the exception of a brewery bus tour, our itinerary consisted of discovering the area's beer community all on our own. Thus far, the Year in Beer had been extraordinary in that we had attended festivals, volunteered at events, and met with brewers almost every month. This trip, however, was different.

Chris picked me up after work on a rainy Monday night and we hit Highway 101 South for our final North American Year in Beer destination. To break up the seven-hour drive to the newest beer holy land, we planned to travel halfway down to Hollister Brewing Company in Goleta and stay the night in nearby Camarillo. We arrived at the brewpub just before 9:00 P.M. Hungry and cranky, I got out of the car and dashed to the door in the drizzling rain.

Hollister Brewing served over a dozen beers. We chose a six-beer sampler set, three for Chris and three for me. Chris went hoppy, of course, with The Pope IPA, Beer with Hops, and Hip Hop Double IPA—the 2008 GABF silver medal winner in the Imperial or Double IPA category. As soon as I realized we hadn't missed the dinner hour, my mood greatly improved. I happily chose Pumpkin ale, Orange Blossom Special, and Sands Session Ale to go along with my white bean puree and flat bread.

So-called "session beers" are low alcohol brews that allow for long periods of drinking with friends without getting completely snockered. Often these beers are mistaken for flavorless lagers, but that is far from the truth. Given the skewed sense of modern West Coast beers, 5.5% ABV was now considered a session ale.

"Enjoy it now," Chris told me. "We're headed into big beer country."

I sighed with resignation. Chris was right. Of the twelve breweries we aimed to visit on this trip, a third of them made their name with bold-flavored, high-alcohol content beers that made my taste buds cower. As I fell asleep that night, I vowed to suck it up and not grumble.

Tuesday morning, Election Day, we awoke full of hope. Hope for a new era in American history. Hope for a fruitful day of beer hunting. After driving four hours further south, we found the first brewery on the day's agenda, the newly opened Breakwater Brewing in Oceanside. New brewpubs often open for business before they're allowed to serve their house brews. Once the final permits are obtained, they replace other craft beers with their own. We crossed our fingers that Breakwater Brewing was all set to go.

From our front-row barstool, we scanned the tap handles. They had a great craft beer selection, none of which were their own.

Chris asked the bartender if they were serving their own beer. Just as we'd feared, he told us that they were adding the final touches to the brewing equipment in preparation for the city's last inspection. He expected the final approval within a week. Obviously that didn't help us.

We had planned to drink Breakwater beer and have some lunch. Instead, we drank someone else's craft brews with our pizza. Any other time it would have been a nice day out, but it was hard not to be disappointed. We had hoped to add Breakwater Brewing to The List.

We recovered quickly, though, because our next stop, Stone Brewing Company's World Bistro and Garden in Escondido, was a sure thing. As a speaker at our GABF media lunch the month before, Stone's CEO and co-founder Greg Koch informed his audience that the World Bistro was the third largest attraction in North San Diego County behind Legoland and the San Diego Zoo's Wild Animal Park. Praise for the place ran rampant through the beer geek community and we wanted to see it for ourselves.

Thirty minutes after leaving Breakwater, we ended up in a sparsely developed industrial park. I stared down at the map to make sure we hadn't missed a turn. When I looked up again, an enormous building appeared on the left. Although there was no sign, we knew that had to be it. We pulled into a parking lot fit for an amusement park. On a Tuesday afternoon, the lot had plenty of spaces.

Massive granite boulders guarded the long pathway to the Bistro's entrance. Tall craggy walls with veins of ivy rose up on either side, funneling my attention forward and preventing my thoughts from drifting to the outside world. When we stepped onto the path our aim was to get from there to the front door. However, now we slowed down to appreciate the effort it must have taken to create such an amazing work of natural art. Heavy vines created a canopy of filtered sunlight above our heads. Bushy greenery brushed against our legs as we continued toward the entrance.

Like wide-eyed kids, we looked up and around as we stepped inside, taking in our first impressions of the establishment we had heard so much about. The foyer, with its tall ceiling, fit my vision of a mansion entryway, except light-colored marble had been replaced with dark gothic décor. We continued to the right into the Bistro.

Now when I think "bistro," I think intimate French café. Obviously I wasn't expecting to enter a croissant-eating, espresso-sipping establishment, but I was hardly prepared for what I did find. The three-story high ceiling and open floor plan could have fit ten French cafés. Combine willowing trees, a koi pond, and boulders set into the floor with the beer and food and you get a self-contained biosphere. Once again, the sight temporarily derailed us from our mission to get beer. A complete view of the brewery could be seen through the glass wall on the left. Opposite, a wall windowed from floor to ceiling exposed the outside patio and gardens. In a case of Feng Shui gone wild, every natural element was represented. World beat music rounded out the sensory experience as we sat down.

I ordered a pint of Stone Pale Ale, which was the first beer they ever brewed, and Chris opted for the Cali-Belgique, a Belgian style IPA. We needed to drink at least one of the Stone beers to count it on The List, but if we chose to, we could have picked any one of the craft beers from their extensive guest tap selection. I soaked in the atmosphere and, for a second, thought I heard the sound of happy, chirping birds.

"What do you think?" Chris asked.

"I like it, but I bet this place gets loud when it's busy," I said.

"Did you see all the fixtures? They have the devil logo everywhere," he pointed out.

Chris nodded toward the lamps with shades made of welded metal. On each lamp, the light bulb's glow showed through the cut-out of Stone's devilish logo. I looked at it for a while—a winged creature with horns and a tail sporting a sinister grin. Was it a devil, a demon, or an escaped gargoyle, I wondered.

The bartender arrived with my deep-fried mashed potato balls (otherwise known as Spud Buds) and Chris's hummus plate. I dipped a golden brown ball in the side of BBQ sauce and stared up at the enormous devil/gargoyle/demon creature etched into the cement wall. His wings were spread wide. With one leg bent slightly and the other firmly extended, he hovered above us with a pint in his hand. I felt small under his gaze. The fact that we were two of only a handful of customers in the huge restaurant only added to the feeling.

We ordered another round of beers and took them out into the garden. The acre of lush garden was so full of life that it was hard to believe that not one blade of grass existed there when construction started in 2005. We followed the path that wound through the property, sipping our beers as we went. A grove of bamboo grew tall in the far corner. Fruit trees huddled together, forming a small orchard. Across the grass lawn was a row of avocado trees growing near a pond. I stopped to admire the waterfall.

We completed our loop of the gardens and returned to the large patio. As the only people out there, we had our pick of places to sit. Round stone tables that reminded me of the wheels on Fred Flintstone's car dotted the area. It was at one of these tables that I went on to lose to Chris in Scrabble. However, the quiet serenity of the garden gave me the inner peace to let the loss go. An entire day could be spent relaxing in the garden, but we had more places on the agenda. Out the door and back toward the car, we left what felt like paradise and re-entered the real world.

The evening's plans included a visit to San Marcos Brewery, which wasn't going to count on my list because I had visited the year prior during a work trip. For the second month in a row, Chris would be counting breweries that I already had. Now Chris's lead in The List count would be further extended.

We exited the highway and drove onto W. San Marcos Boulevard, an area known as "Old California Restaurant Row." The street looked familiar and I knew to look for an adobe-style building on the right. We found it with no problem.

Not many patrons sat inside and the place was quiet, save for the bartender chatting with a few people at the bar. A waitress loitered at the server's station trying to stay busy. We realized right away that it was not where we wanted to end our night, but Chris needed at least a taster set in order to count it on his list. We sat at the bar and watched the presidential election coverage on the TV. The political commentary from the man a few stools down confirmed that this wasn't our scene. With such an historic election, Chris and I sought a livelier, less conservative crowd. Chris counted San Marcos Brewery on his list and we left for Hensley's Flying Elephant Bar and Grill in Carlsbad, a fifteen-minute westward drive away.

At the time, the Flying Elephant was owned by Matt Hensley, a former pro skateboarder and the current accordion player for Flogging Molly. Visible from the San Diego Freeway, the pub looks like an old Denny's from the outside. On the inside, a coat of black paint with red accents, together with skater and music memorabilia, give it a punk makeover. It isn't a brewery, but our love of Flogging Molly made us want to support any side project of a band member. We stepped in the door to roars of applause. Looking at the election coverage playing on the big screen TV, it was clear that the cheers signaled approval of Barak Obama's increasing chances of becoming the first Black President of the United States.

This was most definitely our crowd. Twenty-something girls with Betty Page hairdos and colorful tattoos covering their arms accompanied by 1950s-style rockers in rolled up jeans and black t-shirts dominated the room. At the same time, middle-aged regular folk drinking pints of Guinness were also scattered about. At one table, a man who ran for local public office celebrated with his supporters. Eyes from vastly different walks of life all focused on the big screen TV showing the election projections.

We took the last two seats at the bar and caught the attention of the bartender. I ordered a Sierra Nevada for Chris and a pint of Guinness for myself. Our own eyes were now fixated on the TV. Another deafening round of applause, cheers, and whistles rang throughout the pub. Obama was projected to win yet another state. This was the kind of atmosphere we wanted to be part of on this very special election night. When the bartender came our way again, I ordered a trio of pulled pork sliders and Chris opted for tacos.

Before leaving, we bought two Hensley's t-shirts. One for me and one for our friend and fellow Flogging Molly fan Ute who we'd be seeing in December. Chris and I finished our night in our hotel room watching the broadcast of John McCain's concession speech and Oprah getting teary-eyed as Barack Obama and his family came out on stage for his acceptance speech. With optimism about our new president and a plan to visit at least ten more new breweries on this trip, the future looked bright.

Wednesday's beer tour started at Ballast Point Brewery in a northern San Diego business park. A half-hour drive from our hotel, Chris timed our departure so we'd arrive at opening time. He even included wiggle room to allow for any unforeseen navigational errors (read: me getting us lost).

Much to our delight, I successfully directed Chris to the brewery without any wrong turns. Fifteen minutes early, we sat across the street on a grassy knoll and enjoyed the warm sunshine. At the sight of the front door being propped open, we jumped up and crossed back to the other side of the street. We climbed a short set of concrete stairs and entered the nondescript business park office. On the way in we passed a woman with a large banner. "Oh, hi," she said. "You guys are right on time. I'll be right back in." She planted the colorful banner in the ground and promptly returned.

As the first customers of the day, we received the undivided attention of Amber, the aptly named tasting room hostess. We laughed when she told us her name. She smiled knowingly. "I know, I get that all the time," she said. Amber lined up nine beers along the bar, five from their year-round selection and four specialty brews. She chatted a little in between her set-up duties, but mostly left us to our tasting.

"Here, I've got something for you to try," she said as she walked toward the backroom.

Chris and I made eye contact with a look of "All right, we're getting the double special VIP treatment."

Amber returned with a bowl of pale-colored spread and placed it on the bar with a bowl of pretzels. “This is the last of it, but this is a cheese spread made with our porter,” she told us.

“Thank you. This is perfect,” I said. “I always like to snack while I’m tasting.”

We stood at the bar for close to an hour eating cheese spread-laden pretzels and tasting the Ballast Point beers. The barrel-aged Porter, one of the specialty offerings, proved too strong for me, causing me to cough. Instead, I enjoyed a real session beer. The Even Keel Session Beer was only 3.5% ABV and full of flavor. Chris took the opportunity to remind me again of what was to come. He suggested that I enjoy my session beer while I could because in a few days, there would be none in sight. I wished he didn’t keep reminding me of that.

We purchased several large bottles to take home, thanked Amber and hit the road. While planning for our San Diego trip, our friend Mike had told us about a craft beer bar called O’Brien’s. It was the next stop on our agenda.

The self-proclaimed “Hoppiest place on earth” didn’t exactly dress to impress, but its substance more than made up for the lack of flashy presentation. We stepped up to the bar to examine the beer menu, a whiteboard filled with beer names written in a variety of colors. The messiness of it grated at my orderly sensibilities, but I admired their commitment to content over form. “Sierra Nevada Harvest” was scrawled in blue just above “Russian River Blind Pig” in purple. “Alpine Brewing Pure Hoppiness” stood out in red. In the bottom left corner, in plain black, “Wine by the glass.”

When the bartender brought our beers to the table, she said, “The beer geek dot com. Is it a coincidence that you both have that shirt on?”

We laughed. Chris always insists that we sport our logo wear. "Flying the colors," he calls it.

"No. It's our website," Chris explained. He launched into a well-practiced spiel explaining the site. After eleven months, it now rolled off his tongue.

As we waited for our lunch, Chris flipped the bottled beer list over and over again. He pointed out different beers to me as he ran his finger down the tiny type of the single-spaced list.

"I know. It's impressive," I said. "Can I look?"

It was hard for Chris to give up the beer menu and he continued scanning it as he handed it over. Within a few minutes, he asked for it back. When we came in, Chris had failed to notice a pair of televisions, one on either end of the pub, each showing a different Champions League soccer match. Now at a table, however, Chris's attention was soon diverted to the TVs. I sat quietly drinking my Moonlight Boney Fingers Black Lager and watched Chris sip his beer while turning his attention from one game to the other and back to the bottle list during breaks in the action.

We tore ourselves away from O'Brien's and its remarkable beer list for the last new brewery of the day–Firehouse Brewing Company located near Qualcomm Stadium, the home of the San Diego Chargers. Within craft beer circles, there are many examples of giving back to the community, but I'd never seen one quite as inspirational as Firehouse.

Established by two brothers, Firehouse was a labor of love for the pair of third generation firefighters. Motivated by the tragedies of 9/11, these firefighting homebrewers decided to start a brewery where they could raise money to help firefighters and their families. Through their Firehouse Foundation, a portion of brewery proceeds went to a widow and orphan fund to assist the families of firefighters who had died or been seriously injured in the line of duty. An additional percentage helped local fire departments buy safety equipment they couldn't otherwise afford. Unfortunately, Firehouse Brewing declared bankruptcy in March 2011 and the brewery's assets were subsequently auctioned off.

At the time, Firehouse brewed two beers, a Hefeweizen and a Pale Ale. While we tasted, our host told us the story of the brewery and the firefighters pictured on the wall. He even offered us a taste of another beer that wasn't currently being served. I don't remember exactly what the beer was, but it was described as a "work in progress." He invited us to follow him on a quick brewery tour, something we'd done hundreds of times, but enthusiastically accepted anyway. We ended up on the other side of the building from the tasting room and out near the cold storage area. Chris bought a six-pack of the Hefeweizen and our host expressed an appreciation for our visit.

We concluded our evening at Pizza Port in Carlsbad. It didn't count on The List because we had visited before, but we still looked forward to spending time there. A family-friendly joint, Pizza Port is loud and crowded with plenty of pre-adolescent kids bouncing around the inside like pinballs. The atmosphere could easily be confused with the Straw Hat Pizzas of my childhood, but Pizza Port Carlsbad was no ordinary pizza place: it had just won six medals at GABF.

As we sat eating our grilled chicken pizza, washed down with a pitcher of Port Pale Ale, I thought about the personality differences from one brewery to the next. From the eco-friendly oasis and passionately philanthropic to the family friendly and non-descript business park setting, they were all so different. Some were well known, while others were new to us, but they all had one thing in common: great craft beer.

When people heard that San Diego was a Year in Beer destination, they offered recommendations of places we had to visit. Each person had their own take on the area's beer scene, but standard suggestions included Ballast Point, Green Flash, and Stone. However, those with the most passion didn't simply suggest that we visit Alpine Beer Company in eastern San Diego County; they told us we absolutely *had* to go there. Before hitting the brewery, we planned a hike in the Cleveland National Forest.

We stopped at the ranger's station to find out about the trails. The older woman dressed in an olive green uniform pulled out a map from below the counter and ran her finger along the thin squiggly lines as she described the terrain. After showing us a few routes, she pointed to one and said, "We don't recommend this one here because, being so close to the border, it's popular with smugglers, both drug and human."

Chris and I snickered. We had never been issued such a warning before. The woman stared back at us in all seriousness. We stopped smiling.

"Thanks. We'll keep that in mind," I said.

Back in the car, we went in search of the trailhead. "You know, I'm actually feeling a little nervous now," I said.

"Relax. It's not like we're going on that trail," Chris reassured.

I was just letting go of my worries when a man dressed in military fatigues and a rucksack on his back popped out of the bushes and onto the trail. He acknowledged Chris, who walked in front of me, with a head nod and a "sir" then sprinted down the trail and off to the right.

"They must be doing some map reading exercise," Chris explained.

Half an hour into our hike, we came upon a teacher presenting to a group of ten year olds. Scattered on either side of the trail, the students listened with varying degrees of attentiveness. I felt bad about passing through the middle of the class, but the teacher didn't miss a beat. When we got on the other side of them, Chris informed a teacher's assistant that we had come upon a camera and thought it might belong to one of the students.

On our return journey, we encountered the class again and again we had to cut through the middle of the teacher's lesson. As we passed, the teacher thanked us. "These are the people who found Zoe's camera," he announced. The class responded in unison, "Thank you people who found Zoe's camera."

We survived our two-hour hike and drove back into Alpine and parked in front of Alpine Beer Company, a small brewery situated on the main drag of the town. Chris was especially excited because Alpine brewed one of his favorite beers at GABF, Pure Hoppiness.

Inside we found an employee behind the counter eating a late lunch. With his mouth full, his cheeks bulged as he tried to smile and gave a wave to acknowledge us. We said hello and turned to the long side of the L-shaped counter. I scanned the small room as we waited for someone to assist us. Stacks of white malt sacks lay on the floor, almost going unnoticed against the whitewashed brick wall. Empty cardboard boxes were piled haphazardly in the corner. What personality-type does this place have? I wondered. A man wearing a baseball cap, t-shirt and jeans emerged from the backroom. His friendly, casual demeanor matched the décor and feel of the brewery: relaxed and not the least bit pretentious.

He set us up with ten beers to sample; everything from a vanilla version of their Willy Wheat to a spiced Dunkel Weizen. While Chris chatted with the brewer, I sipped from my row of small, plastic cups and continued my character assessment of the brewery. A half-dozen oak barrels rested on a rack at the end of the counter and several stainless steel tanks were little more than an arm's length from where we stood. What did those things tell me? Nothing came immediately to mind, so I took a sip from the next sample in line and joined in the conversation.

Looking up, an array of award plaques hung proudly on the wall above. Then it hit me. Alpine Brewing's character, including both the brewery and the brewer, was understated, humble even, in its public display of achievement. Not ones to use flash and show to get noticed, they let their award winning brews speak for themselves.

Satisfied with what seemed like a brilliant analysis, my focus returned to tasting the beers. The brewer presented Chris with two small, plastic cups of a dark brown brew.

"Here, I'll let you try these," he said. "You have to try this one first, though," pointing at the beer on our left.

Chris took a sip. "That's the stout."

The brewer smiled. Chris picked up the cup on the right and looked at it. "Hmm. The color is throwing me off a bit," he said before bringing the cup just under his nose. He inhaled. "Oh, this one is vanilla."

"That's right," the man said. "That's the Captain Stout mixed with the Willy Vanilly Wheat."

Chris took another sip of the mixed brew and said, "I still think the Pure Hoppiness is brilliant."

At the time, the town of Alpine not only supported a great brewery, it was also blessed with a world-class beer bar. After a quick lunch at the taqueria next door, we went a few short blocks up the road to the Liar's Club. Another place that people told us we *had* to visit, the original Liar's Club had lost its lease in San Diego and had recently relocated to Alpine.

If we hadn't noticed the Liar's Club on our way to the Cleveland National Forest, we might have missed it during the three-minute drive from Alpine Brewing. No colorful roadside signs to lure passing motorists inside. You either knew it was there or you didn't. Only a couple signs facing parallel to the road indicated you were there and that was only after you'd already found it. The attitude of this not-so-secret secret place ensured a clientele of people who knew exactly what they were there for. It was the same reason we were there: the beer.

Our friends described the old Liar's Club as somewhat seedy—dark-colored walls, wobbly stools, and booths with stained and ripped upholstery. What we walked into was obviously a newer, sanitized version of the original. A light, airy place with white paint and brick wall accents, it appeared the complete opposite of what we had heard about. The décor may have looked different, but to us the grungy spirit of the place was just as our friends had described it. Unfortunately, the change was just too drastic for the likes of the original Liar's Club's customers and the new Alpine location closed a few months after our visit.

Green Day played on the jukebox and a Flogging Molly flag hung above the threshold into the restaurant. The flag's green background with serpents intertwined in a white four-leafed clover shown prominently against the white wall. A tightly packed row of tap handles lined the wall behind the bar. We instantly liked Liar's Club.

I'm usually the one who has difficulty deciding what to drink, but on our first visit to the Liar's Club, it was Chris who didn't know where to start.

"Oh man," he said. "They have Blind Pig, Pliny the Elder, Bear Republic Hop Rod Rye…" He trailed off, too many favorites to name them all.

Panic developed on Chris's face.

"I'll have a Firestone Little Opal, please," I told the bartender.

Chris's mind worked furiously: What should I have first? How many can I have? Okay, I've got to order something. I need to order something. But what do I get?

He eventually settled on Russian River's Damnation, a Belgian-style Strong Pale Ale, as his first pint. The indecision crisis over, we parked ourselves at a table near the bar. I pulled the latest edition of *Draft Magazine* out of my backpack. On the cover, actor David Boreanaz casually leaned against a bar with a pint of beer in his hand.

"Let's see what beer Angel likes," I said while flipping through the magazine. As a huge fan of *Buffy the Vampire Slayer* and a moderate fan of *Angel* and *Bones*, I was especially keen to find out his thoughts on beer. You know, in case the opportunity to buy him one ever arose.

"Well, it says here that he likes Guinness on draft." I continued reading. "Oh no, and Stella. He drinks Stella." My shoulders dropped and I slumped in my chair.

Stella Artois, a mass-produced lager brewed in Belgium, was not high on our list of beers.

Chris shook his head and said, "Sorry."

"He's still cute, though," I responded.

"But we need to get on camera the real reason you bought that issue," Chris reminded.

I sat poised and ready for the signal that the camera was rolling. When Chris raised his eyebrows and shook his head up and down, I put on my jazz hands.

"Angel is on the cover of *Draft Magazine*, but I guess the more exciting thing is…" I fumbled through the pages to the back of the magazine. "…that Chris's 400th brewery picture made it to Backwash."

Backwash, a regular feature that appears toward the back of the magazine, is a collection of photos sent in by readers.

Chris zoomed in on the collage of pictures. In the left top corner, next to a picture of Zane Lamprey chugging a Beck's, was a picture of Chris giving two thumbs up and a wide grin. The caption read, "Chris Nelson at his 400th brewery at Hopworks Urban Brewery in Portland."

The time drew near for Chris to order another beer and I readied myself for a 'second beer choice overload' meltdown. Chris tilted his glass high to drain it empty. Up at the bar, the back of his head moved from side to side as he scanned the taps. He could have easily been watching a slow motion tennis match. I went back to reading my magazine, figuring it was going to be a while. In a surprising show of decisiveness, however, he approached the table before I even had a chance to find where I'd left off. I picked up the video camera to capture the candid moment of him starting a fresh beer.

"I found the Dissident on draft," he said practically stroking the side of the glass. He spoke with such emotion in his voice you'd have thought he was presenting a priceless object.

Chris had tried Deschutes Brewery's Dissident, a Flanders-style sour brown ale, at GABF and loved it. The special reserve brew would never make it to our craft beer backwater at home, so he didn't want to miss the chance to have it again.

The Liar's Club's owner, Louis Mello, came out of the kitchen to chat with us. He brought us bottle after bottle of beer to check out. He was very helpful and a good salesman, but we couldn't possibly buy or drink all of them. The barrage of beer only stopped when he was called back to the kitchen by a food order.

"Did you notice that it's been all punk music playing?"

"I know. I really like this place." Chris shook his head with satisfaction. "Do you want to play a game of Scrabble?"

If Chris had a vision of heaven, this afternoon might have been it—good music, good beer, and a good Scrabble performance.

We left Alpine early on Friday morning and returned to San Diego. We intended to take it easy because we had a big afternoon of beer touring to do. With the help of Brewery Tours of San Diego, we planned to visit five breweries.

Our idea of taking it easy was to start the day off at Toronado San Diego, the sister taphouse to the Toronado in San Francisco. We wondered how the dingy charm and the gruff bordering on verbally abusive staff of the original Toronado would be recreated at a second location.

Our customary early arrival meant that Toronado San Diego wasn't open yet. So, we explored the neighborhood on foot to kill some time. Along our looping route, we turned up a street one block over that exuded next to none of the hipster chic of the main street. Waist-high chain link fencing enclosed neglected front yards. The houses themselves looked in need of make-overs.

Kylie Minogue played on the overhead speaker in the Von's grocery store where we went for bottles of water. I wasn't sure if it was a grocery store with a dance club or a dance club that sold groceries. The middle-aged woman in front of us talked to the credit card machine as she checked out. Upon leaving we passed a burly woman with short, dyed black hair and a barbell through her nose. The tattoos that covered her arms brightened her otherwise dark ensemble of black jeans and a black t-shirt.

"Well, that's one similarity between the two Toronados," Chris said. "They're both located in colorful neighborhoods."

When Toronado San Diego's door opened, we were the first to walk in. Absent was the confined dive bar darkness of Toronado San Francisco. The room was bright, spacious, and having only been open for six months, the walls were bare of bumper stickers with pithy sayings.

"It's so clean," Chris repeated several times.

The appearance threw us off, but the beer selection, every bit as good as the original, didn't disappoint. My Victory Prima Pils started my day off right and Chris enjoyed one of Sierra Nevada's Beer Camp beers, a Saison, as we chatted with the bartender.

The three of us mulled over the differences between the original and its new little sister. The bartender explained San Diego's philosophy this way. "We didn't want to fake the atmosphere," he said. "With over twenty years head start on us, we can never be the same as the original. We'll develop our own spirit as the years go on."

I liked that answer. I also liked the idea of experiencing an establishment in its infancy. In twenty years, I could use a cranky old lady voice to say, "I remember when you could see bare walls and it was sparkling clean."

Back at our hotel later that afternoon, we waited out front for Jon McDermott from Brewery Tours of San Diego to pick us up. While researching for the trip, Chris had found them online. He loved the idea of someone else driving us to breweries, so he called and booked a special tour.

We watched the street and eventually a large white van pulled into the hotel driveway. "That must be him," Chris said.

We introduced ourselves and climbed into the back of the ten-passenger van. Jon gave us a quick rundown of the route. The tasting hours for Lightning Brewery in nearby Poway were just about to start, so Jon took us there first.

Along the way, we chatted about *thebeergeek.com*. Jon told us about how he started doing brewery tours and what services his business now offered. Unlike Jon's usual groups, Chris and I remained relatively quiet as we rattled around the van with plenty of room to spare. With only the pair of us, we didn't exactly constitute a brewery tour group, more like a brewery tour twosome.

We arrived at Lightning, a brewery we knew little about, before the official start of their tasting hours. It surprised us to see several people already there when we walked in. We joined a few middle-aged guys who appeared to be regulars. Chris and I moved toward the taps, as Jon hung to the side. Like a museum, a small rope prevented us from getting too close to the row of spigots. On the other side of the rope, a man with a thick head of hair and graying temples came over to help us.

He handed us each a taste of the Elemental Pilsner, our first sample.

"So what do you do here?" I asked him.

"I come in to help out," he said. "I'm the brewery cat."

"Brewery cat?" asked Chris.

"Yeah, a brewery cat, a brewery regular," he explained. "You know how bookstores have the shop cat that lounges around the bookshelves and in the window. They come and go minding their own business, but overall seem to be a permanent fixture. Think of someone like that hanging out in a brewery."

Before the man completed his story, Chris had finished his beer. The man, now identified as the brewery cat, handed Chris his next sample. It took me a few more minutes before I moved on to the Hefeweizen. I stepped away from the taps and over to the side near Chris. Jon stood nearby patiently drinking his bottle of water.

"Did you want to film something here?" I asked.

"Yeah, we probably can," Chris said.

"Our first stop this afternoon is Lightning," I started, "and I'm totally stoked because they do German lagers. We already had a Kölsch and now I'm on to the Hefeweizen."

Later, when the San Diego episode came out, our friend Matt Venzke demonstrated why he deserved the title "Beerdrinker of the Year." He was the only person to catch that neither beer I mentioned is a lager. They're both ales.

A few more samples and we turned to Jon and told him we were ready to go. Our quick style of tasting surprised him because he was used to bigger groups who lingered at each brewery. In and out of our first brewery within a half hour, we were now ahead of schedule.

"Wow! You guys are quick," Jon said.

"We're professionals," I told him.

We piled back into the van to drive to the next stop on our tour: Alesmith Brewing Company. My day was now more or less finished. All but one of the remaining breweries brewed the highly hopped, high alcohol content beers that I feared. I may not have been as excited about the rest of the afternoon as Chris, but a small taste at each new brewery added them to The List just the same.

Jon confidently led us through Alesmith's front office into the brewery. Chris and I stepped up to the bar, an area carved out on the left hand side. Jon, once again, drifted off to the side without making a peep. Behind the bar, a petite woman with a girlish face waved at Jon and smiled. I realized then that he must know everyone at the breweries because he visited them so often. I turned around to look at Jon, who was smiling back.

Initially the only ones there, we were soon joined by regulars who talked about their homebrews as they waited for their growlers to get filled. At GABF the month before, Alesmith had won two gold and two silver medals. They were named Small Brewing Company of the Year and their brewing team won Small Brewing Company Brewer of the Year.

Jessica Oliver, who dubs herself Alesmith's "Jess of All Trades," served us their usual beers: IPA, X, Imperial Stout, Horny Devil, and Wee Heavy, their Scottish Ale. You'd think being named 2008 *small* brewery of the year would give it away, but Chris was surprised at how small Alesmith was and told Jessica so.

"For being such a big name, you guys are really quite small," he said.

"Yeah, well, we just expanded," she said.

Although I admit to enjoying the Lil Devil, a Belgian-style ale, which came in at a low 5.5% ABV, I sipped just enough of the others to count Alesmith on The List. I even declined my own taster glass of Wee Heavy. Sweet and malty, I almost never like Scottish Ales, so there was no point in wasting it. Instead, I reached my hand into the basket of leftover Halloween candy on the bar and came up with a lime Starburst.

"Oh here," Chris said. "You should try this." He handed me his cup of Wee Heavy.

"But I just stuck a candy in my mouth." I took a sip anyway and paused. "Hey, yeah. I can actually drink this."

A few minutes later, when the tart lime flavor wore off, I took another sip.

"Oh, blech. No," I cried.

"That's a gold medal winner right there," Chris said.

"Yeah, well, if you like this style, I'm sure it's a fabulous beer."

We visited Alesmith on what many beer geeks would say was a most special day: the first day their Yule Smith Holiday Ale, an Imperial Red, was available. Chris excitedly purchased several bottles before we left.

We were well acquainted with Alesmith, but with our next stop, Oceanside Ale Works, we completely changed gears. Chris had only become aware of Oceanside during an internet search prior to the trip. When he booked the tour with Jon, Chris requested that we go there. We had no idea what to expect.

The outside was unassuming, being located in an industrial park, and quiet. However, we opened the solid door and the muffled sounds of a party could immediately be heard. It was not yet 4:00 P.M., but Chris and I stepped into a party mobbed with people drinking full pints. I squeezed passed a man in a City of Oceanside work shirt on my way to the bar. Chris was close behind me, but overwhelmed by the level of activity, we temporarily lost track of Jon.

A trio of middle-aged women in tight jeans and t-shirts darted back and forth between the bar and the taps behind them. The woman who helped us appeared shocked at our request for a taster set. Determining which order to serve the beer samples flustered her, so to ease the confusion, Chris and I purchased several tastes each and moved away from the bar to make our own sample set. We stood close together and raised our voices to be heard above the crowd noise.

The order in which we tried the beer was a little different than protocol would dictate, but without a place to set a line up of samples, we made the best of it. We observed the scene as the crowd, made up of mostly men, milled about. A hot dog cart with a red and yellow umbrella attached was parked outside the open warehouse door. A band was setting up its equipment.

Chris and I filmed a few short clips and then looked around for Jon. We'd seen and heard enough and we were ready to move on. Before we got back in the van, I gave Jon the opportunity to film a promo bit for us to include in the *beergeek.TV* episode. A little reticent at first, he eventually agreed. After I asked him, I had second thoughts. He hadn't really said much so far on our excursion and if the clip proved boring, Chris wouldn't use it. I feared that I might have gotten Jon's hopes up. However, as soon as the camera started rolling, Jon brightened up and, in his own reserved way, cheerfully plugged his business. He even showed good jazz hands.

Chris became increasingly more excited about the last two breweries of our tour: Green Flash Brewing Company and

Port Brewing/The Lost Abbey. "Hoppiness here we come," he said as we pulled up to Green Flash Brewing Company.

"Yippee," I replied sarcastically.

Jon laughed. He'd heard us all afternoon and by now was getting a sense of our personalities, including our likes and dislikes in beer. It was at this point that he finally admitted that it's sometimes hard to be driving people to these great breweries every week and not be able to drink. "Well, you can let me drive the van and you can drink because I'm pretty sober," I told him. He laughed again.

With the popularity of Green Flash West Coast IPA, we expected a big party for their public tasting hours and we were right. We walked into a brewery several times bigger than Alesmith. Happy young people chatted in small groups. Thousands of cases of West Coast IPA were stacked on pallets around the edges of the warehouse. Chris and I weaved through the loose crowd to the taps located in the corner.[28] It pleasantly surprised me to see a varied line up of beers. We started with the Saison, a beer I thoroughly enjoyed. I admitted to Chris that drinking the Saison, a Green Flash beer I actually liked, at the base of mountains of beer was awe-inspiring. The spirit and friendliness of the other brewery visitors made it hard not to get swept up in the Green Flash fanaticism.

Chris was in heaven as he went on to sample the Imperial IPA and the Palate Wrecker, a Double IPA. Le Freak, a fusion of an American Imperial IPA and a Belgian Trippel, was another favorite among beer geeks, including Chris. While the brewery describes Le Freak as "a zesty brew with…delicious malts and a complex layering of hop flavors [to] quench and refresh

---

28 In June 2011, Green Flash opened a new brewery that included a tasting room.

your pallet," our friend and fellow beer geek Renee Brincks described it more succinctly. "It's a hoppy, poppy party in my mouth."

With a small glass of Le Freak in my hand, I couldn't resist quoting Renee on camera. I also couldn't wait until the camera was off before I scrunched up my face and stuck out my tongue. Le Freak popped a tad too much hop for me.

Chris returned from the bar with a small glass of dark beer with a tan-colored head. A special brew, Chris had been told earlier that the serving size of the double stout on cask was smaller than the other beers, but his glass was almost full.

"I see that you got a huge pour. Were you supposed to get that much?" I asked.

"Well, it's like when we were serving cask at GBBF, it's hard to regulate the pull," he replied.

Chris took a sip of his beer. "You know, I knew this was going to be good, but this is really cool," Chris said as he looked around. "This visit is all I hoped it would be."

"So, Green Flash really lives up to the hype?" I said.

"Yep, it really does."

With that, we left for what Chris considered "the crowning glory:" Port Brewing Company and The Lost Abbey. It may have been the crowning glory of the trip, but it also posed a conundrum for us that we wouldn't resolve until we actually got there.

The Lost Abbey is a line of beers derived from the Port Brewing chain of pizza joints and Director of Brewery Operations Tomme Arthur oversees both brands. While each Pizza Port location brews their own beer, our next stop brewed Port beers for distribution, also known as a production brewery. In addition, it brewed all of the Lost Abbey beers. We had added

Port Brewing to The List years before with our visit to Pizza Port Carlsbad, so we knew we couldn't count this as a visit to Port. The big question was could we count this as a visit to The Lost Abbey and add it to The List?

In the weeks leading up to the trip, we polled our friends about what they thought. Most people argued both sides, but never settled on an answer as to whether The Lost Abbey was a separate brewery. For us, this question was not simply fodder for philosophical musings over pints of beer. We needed an answer.

On our way to the brewery, we took one last stab at it and asked Jon for his opinion on the matter. Like most of our friends, he was non-committal, but did lean toward it being one brewery with two brands, rather than two breweries under one roof. Clearly this issue was ours to sort out. The answer was obvious from the moment we stepped in and saw just one set of brewing equipment. We didn't let this outcome mar our visit to the brewery, however.

The bar teemed with customers and all the seats, kegs with malt sacks on top for padding, were occupied. Chris started with the Port Brewing beers. Flip flop-shaped tap handles in green, yellow, blue, and black were lined up in a row as if a group of kids had taken off their shoes before coming in the house. I waited to the side as Chris ordered his samples.

"Imperial IPA," Chris said as he held up a small glass of golden colored brew.

"Yum," I said.

Chris held up the glass in his other hand. "And a wet hop beer, High Tide, which you've had," he said.

"Double yum." My sarcasm was unmistakable and Chris took full advantage.

"Oh, Merideth needs a hug," he said tenderly into the camera.

Although I didn't have to drink the beers (it wasn't counting on The List anyway), I indulged in a few pursed-lip sips. Shark Bite Red, an American Amber/Red Ale, had a "prominent hop profile," as some might say. The hop flavor washed over my tongue and my lips immediately pressed together with dislike. Chris watched and laughed.

"Hey, I'm being a pretty good sport, you know," I said. "I don't really even have to drink these."

Chris quieted down as I tasted another beer. The Shark Attack Double Red, at 9.5% ABV, was a strong sweet tasting beer that produced much the same reaction as the Shark Bite had.

Leaving Port Brewing's surf-themed beers behind, it was time to move on to the more pious Lost Abbey, a line-up of beers honoring monastic brewing traditions. A large Celtic cross was painted on the wall above the threshold of a room to the right of the bar. Upon closer examination, the usual Celtic knot work was replaced with images of the four main ingredients used in making beer. Barley, water, yeast and hops were each integrated into the four arms of the cross. I relished the thought that two of my favorite things, ancient Celtic culture and beer, had been combined into one.

From high on the wall, the cross commanded reverence from its flock on the warehouse floor. It kept a protective eye over the scores of barrels stacked four and five high. Dozens more oak brandy, bourbon, and wine barrels overflowed beyond the confines of the barrel room. All were filled with beer aging patiently and motionlessly for eighteen months or more. Chris had entered the Promised Land and, although not a fan of barrel-aged beers, I did find the scene a majestic sight to behold and could appreciate Chris's admiration.

Spending a day drinking beers not fully to my liking, I found myself nearly sober at the end. The one time we were treated to a chauffeur and I could have easily been the designated driver. It didn't matter, though, because Chris thoroughly enjoyed himself and it made me happy to see him so relaxed.

It was only 7 P.M., but the early darkness of late fall made it feel like we'd been out all night. I'm sure the fact that we'd been out for almost six hours and visited five breweries had a little something to do with it.

Led by Jon, the three of us walked toward the wide warehouse door to leave. Chris, whose body practically hummed with excitement from the day's activities, made various comments to no one in particular. I, on the other hand, was quiet and quite simply tired. Near the exit, a black streak darted across my path and disappeared into the brewery. I smiled at having caught a glimpse of a real, live brewery cat.

We started out our last day in San Diego with the final brewery visit of the trip: Coronado Brewing Company. The blue, cloudless sky and a 75°F temperature made it perfect for a romantic ferry ride to Coronado. We sat in the back of the gently rocking boat and Chris put his arm around me. "This has been a great year," he said as he smiled and gave me a kiss.

"It really has. So, where are we going next year?" I teased.

The motor revved and the boat surged forward. We knew romantic time was over when a set of parents with two school-aged children joined us in the back. Chris got up and readied the camera for filming stock San Diego footage. I sat back, closed my eyes and felt the wind through my hair and the sun on my face. The father's voice filled my ears. His running commentary on everything from the scenery to debris floating in the water didn't end until the boat arrived at the Coronado Ferry Landing. We enjoyed a quiet walk over to Coronado Brewing Company.

A beautiful red brick building with dark green awnings, Chris and I opted to sit outside at one of a half-dozen tables that were tightly arranged on the small patio. When the waiter came around, we requested a taster set.

"Which beers would you like?" he asked.

"One of each, please," Chris said.

"There is a three taste limit," the waiter told us.

I looked at Chris. "Okay, you pick three and I'll pick three."

"It's a three taste maximum for the whole table," the waiter corrected.

The table next to us watched the interaction and chuckled to themselves. The waiter accepted our final order of three samples, the Pale Ale, IPA, and Nut Brown, before he retreated inside. Our patio mates shrugged and smiled when it was all over. In all our brewery travels, we had never encountered this policy before. Chris remarked that he wasn't sure if it was odd or admirable. On the one hand, it was somewhat moralistic and eliminated all sense of personal responsibility but, on the other, it was an easy way to combat excessive drinking. From our limited exposure to their beer offerings, we each ordered a pint to go with our lunch.

"How am I supposed to taste all of your beers?" I asked when our food arrived.

"Well," the waiter hemmed, "You can go inside and ask for a few at the bar."

We followed his suggestion on our way out and stopped at the bar to get a few more samples. We quickly tried several more of the brewery's offerings and we were out the door. As we left, I noticed a sign hanging in multiple places around the inside of the restaurant: "3 drink limit."

On the ferry ride back to San Diego I admired the city's skyline. Tall buildings in various shapes and sizes stood along the waterfront with mountains guarding them from behind. It was easy to focus on the towering edifices, but I also considered the smaller, less conspicuous places in between and around the larger buildings. In many ways, this view mirrored the greater San Diego area's beer scene—multiple, showy standout breweries with lesser-known gems hidden in the shadows. Through a willingness to explore and look beyond the hype surrounding the renowned big name breweries, Chris and I discovered modest hidden treasures. Humble award-winning breweries every bit deserving of notice that were happy to remain quiet in their greatness. The big names attracted us to the area, but we found that there was much more to San Diego than just the hype.

When we reached the shore, I became painfully aware that the Year in Beer was nearing its end. Finishing this trip, we only had one more to go. What was I going to do with myself when it was all over? Just go back to my normal life? I didn't want this dream year to end, but I also knew the truth was that things *would* go back to normal. They had to because it would be a long time before we could afford to do something like the Year in Beer again.

DECEMBER

NEVER SAY NEVER

Once back home, the moment of troublesome reality I had experienced on the ferry in the San Diego Bay became almost constant. Each day brought us closer to our last trip, Belgium and the Netherlands, and closer to the end of the Year in Beer. Thoughts of the end were bittersweet. On the one hand, I was relieved it was going to be over. My life had moved nonstop all year. It was high time I slowed down and enjoyed what I had at home.

On the other hand, we spent the whole year focused on beer, living our dream life. Our friends and followers of the website started asking what we planned for the following year. They had become accustomed to our frequent blogs and endless tales of beer travel, as well as a new *beergeek.TV* episode each month. Chris and I were the Year in Beer and the Year in Beer defined the two of us. Who was I going to be when it was over?

The answer to my existential dilemma came from the most unsuspecting of Messiahs—the four-legged face-licking kind. The night before we left for Belgium, Stout refused to play ball or snuggle with us on the couch. Instead, he hid in his "happy place" under the bed. Stout had had enough of the Year in Beer and he was letting us know it. His not-so-subtle message reminded me of all the things that had been brushed aside during our beer-centric year: our house, the yard, our families, the dogs. Suddenly, my post-Year in Beer purpose became clear. The following year would be about re-focusing on the domestic front. The thought of having a purpose beyond the Year in Beer comforted me. But first, we had one last trip to go.

The main part of our final Year in Beer adventure consisted of a Christmas beer festival in Belgium and perhaps our most ambitious travel goal ever: to visit all seven Trappist breweries. However, when Chris learned that Flogging Molly and the Street Dogs would be playing just a train ride away from where we planned to be, he added a couple of shows to the front of our trip. This was the last hurrah for the Year in Beer and we planned to go all out. There was nothing holding us back from making it a very special ending to a very special year.

The day before we left, I figured out the time difference and planned my sleeping schedule accordingly. Usually it was a voluntary effort to stay awake as long as possible when we arrived in Europe. This time, however, it wasn't optional. The difficulty was that we were scheduled to arrive in Brussels at 7:30 A.M. and had plans to attend a Flogging Molly show that first night. Our friend Ute was coming over from Germany to join us for a few days.

After landing in the predawn darkness at Brussels Airport, we joined morning commuters as we waited in the cold for a train bound for Antwerp. When we arrived an hour later, we were happy to discover that our hotel room was available for check-in. Chris, knowing that we would need to conserve our energy, had planned a leisurely first day that included lots of walking and only two beer stops. Propelled forward by the second wind generated from a shower and fresh underwear, Chris and I set out to find Antwerp's only brewpub, 'T Pakhuis.

We were a little nervous about our visit to 'T Pakhuis (The Pack House) and we expected it to be a challenge. This was the first trip in a long time we were visiting a non-English speaking country where we didn't know the language at all. We had previously traveled to the Ardennes, a French-speaking area of Belgium, but in Antwerp, the language is Flemish, a regional dialect of Dutch.

An old warehouse located on a quiet street south of the old city center, 'T Pakhuis was a half-hour leisurely walk from our hotel. We were the first customers of the day and the restaurant was idle, save for the creaking wooden floor and the cheesy pop Christmas music. We sat down at a bistro table with a front row view into the brewery. It was clearly visible to the bartender, a tall thin man with a 1980s David Bowie hairstyle. Travel weary and unfamiliar with both the language and pub culture, we patiently waited as the bartender polished glasses behind the bar. When he was good and ready, he came over to serve us our first beers of the trip: a *Bruin* (brown) for Chris and the Blonde for me.

Our somewhat inattentive bartender eventually returned for our next order. I stuck with the Blonde, but this time Chris went for the 9.5% Tripel. By the time our aloof server came back with our beers, I had mustered the courage to ask him how to pronounce the name of where we presently were.

"Pahk-oose," he repeated until I could pronounce it reasonably well.

He also taught us two helpful phrases, *Alstublieft* ("Please," pronounced all-stew-bleeft) and *Dank u* ("Thank you," pronounced dahnk-oo). Between the bartender and our Dutch dictionary, we pieced together, "Twee bier, alstublieft" ("Two beers, please"). It's an essential phrase that all traveling beer geek couples should know in any language.

After a couple of beers, a few new phrases, and a newfound confidence, we left Pakhuis ready to hit the town. "Dank u," we called out as we left.

Our second beer destination of the day was Kulminator, a world famous beer bar and a must-stop for any beer geek. Although they boast less than a dozen taps, Kulminator is famous for its extensive cellar of both vintage and current beers.

A forest of overgrown houseplants obscured the windows of the pub, so we had no idea what to expect inside. Once through the door, I thought we might have made a mistake and walked into an antique shop or possibly a pack rat's den. Stuff was everywhere. Magazines and newspapers were piled a foot high on benches. Lit candles were corked in large beer bottles. Wax had dripped down the sides sealing them onto the tables. Metal beer signs and ones that lit up covered the walls. Faded cardboard beer advertisements hanging from the ceiling twisted gently above our heads. There was barely room on the bar to put your beer and it looked like there was a week's worth of mail accumulated on a far table. Everything appeared covered in two decades worth of dust.

In spite of it all, a few locals managed to wedge themselves in at the end of the bar. I hung my heavy coat on the rack and followed Chris to a table. A woman who I had barely been able to see behind the cluttered bar came towards us. Pleasant enough without being overly friendly, she left us with a 50-page beer list to look through.

Chris turned the pages of the spiral bound "menu," which was really more like a phonebook for a small city. I flipped through a pile of magazines, waiting for my turn with the beer list. Interspersed with the magazines were laminated articles in various languages about Kulminator and its owners. The pictures showed a clean-cut man in his sixties with short gray hair. A woman, identified as his wife and co-owner, stood next to him, the top of her head barely reaching his shoulders. Her smiling face formed two bulging rosy cheeks. I looked up at the woman behind the bar. It had to be the same person, but time seemed to have changed her. She didn't look nearly as chipper and youthful.

The daunting menu didn't go well with our jetlag. Also, at the time, my familiarity with Belgian beers was limited, which compounded the difficulty to choose. You could find every style of Belgian beer in Kulminator—Trappist, Gueuze, and Kriek to name just a few. I was vaguely familiar with the styles, but many of the brewery names were unknown to me.

Chris pushed the menu away. "I don't know if I should order the '93 Westmalle or the '94. I am way too tired to choose and we don't have a whole lot of time."

The Street Dogs, who were opening later in the night for Flogging Molly, had a short acoustic set scheduled at a punk store called Fish and Chips, conveniently located just down the street. Stopping there was part of the day's agenda.

"Just get me this," I pointed to a Belgian Pilsner. "Alstublieft," I added as Chris walked away.

Several cats darted in and around the piles and tables. Quick little things, they were too fast for me to catch on video. Then, with timing only seen in the movies, a cuckoo clock chimed as a door behind the bar opened. Well-camouflaged behind beer posters and wooden crates, I didn't even know it was there. A hunched-over man with his head hung low stepped out. His mop of wild white shoulder-length hair concealed his face. I took it to be the clean cut man captured in the article photo.

He emerged like a hermit from his cave and avoided eye contact with those in the pub. A gray cat, sprung from containment when the door opened, shot out from behind the bar and dashed to the left. The man disappeared just as quickly.

Despite feeling subdued and slightly spacey from jetlag, the somewhat bizarre scene in Kulminator was not completely lost on me. It felt like I had been dropped in the middle of a Grimm's fairy tale. It was as if something strange and sinister lurked in the shadows waiting to catch us off guard. We drank our beers in silence and I even zoned out a few times. Chris drank the Kasteel Bier Rouse, a Kriek he had seen listed on a sandwich board outside. Even in all our tiredness, we were grateful for the good fortune of being in the midst such an amazing collection of beer.

Chris got up and announced that he needed to walk around to keep from falling asleep. I watched as he peered through windows in the wall on the left. It was a room filled with hundreds of beer bottles sitting on wooden shelves. Some bottles looked reasonably clean and were neatly lined up on the shelf. But others lay on their sides in a haphazard pile, covered with a dull blanket of dust. These weren't just any old bottles of beer, though. Underneath that dust was a stunning array of rare vintage beers.

Soon it was time to go. We knew that we hadn't given an ample amount of time to fully experience Kulminator, but we had other places to be and a whole night still ahead of us.

After listening to the brief set performed by the Street Dogs, we returned to our hotel to rest before hailing a cab to Hof Ter Lo, the venue for the concert. Ute planned to meet us there before the show. Unfortunately, she was going to be alone. Wolfie had not been able to get the time off work to join us. Chris told the cab driver where we wanted to go and off we went across town in the dark. However, purposeful navigation soon turned random and confused. The cab driver was lost.

After asking a pedestrian for assistance, we finally arrived at the venue. Groups of people huddled out front, puffs of cigarette smoke and cold air floating above their heads. We hurried past the crowd into the warmth of the venue.

We arrived early with the assumption that the venue would serve good Belgian beer. Chris had visions of watching Flogging Molly with a Chimay Blue or La Chouffe in his hand. Unfortunately, the only beer they served was Stella Artois. After twenty minutes and much grousing, Chris decided to go ahead and give Stella a try. "Maybe it'll taste better in its home country," he reasoned. I propped myself up against a wall trying to stay awake while Chris went for his beer.

He returned a few minutes later with a red plastic cup full of Stella. "Well, here I go," he said.

I looked at him expectantly as he took a sip. Pulling the cup away from his mouth, Chris stretched his lips flat and stuck out his tongue like a lizard.

"Yeah, no. It's still kind of bland," he said.

Ute, frazzled from an agonizing journey of late trains and a missed flight, arrived moments before the show started. All three of us sighed with relief. Everything was now as it should be.

After the show, Nate Maxwell, Flogging Molly's bass guitarist, jumped down onto the floor. Adoring fans immediately surrounded him. When Nate saw us, he gave each of us a grossly sweaty hug. He also invited us to the after-party at Bar Mondial.

Once Chris got a look at Bar Mondial's beer selection, he was happy he didn't drink a lot of beer at the show. Too many beers too early and he would have been asleep already. Fully alert, we were at a concert after-party with band members drinking world-class beer at 3 A.M. I had never stayed up until 3 in the morning in my life and the fact that I did it on my first night in Europe was quite a feat. We were having a great time, and it's always difficult to leave at the height of the fun, but Chris was watching out for us and suggested that it was time to call a cab. While I knew it was for my own good, I reluctantly left for our hotel room.

Chris, Ute and I caught an 8:30 A.M. train to Amsterdam, where we planned to meet a few of Ute's friends and attend another Flogging Molly/Street Dogs show. One afternoon in the city is not nearly enough, but it was all we had. So, Chris and I did what we do best: took a whirlwind beer tour of the city. Ute knew the pace with which she would be expected to keep up because she and Wolfie had traveled with us before.

The weather was bitterly cold and after a short walk across the canal, we were all eager to get in from the nose numbing air. Our first stop, a specialty beer café called In De Wildeman, was a welcome sight.

Inside, the varnish on the dark wood paneled walls had worn in spots, creating tan patches of exposed wood. We sat down and stared up at the choice of beers listed on a chalkboard. The place looked like an old antique shop with its walls and shelves cluttered with faded beer signs and dusty steins. It was quiet and we naturally started whispering as we considered what beer to order. The bartender looked up from sorting and boxing glassware to tell us that there was no need to whisper.

The three of us sipped from thick goblets and watched outside as the snow started to fall. From our indoor vantage point, we thought it was charming weather for an early-December day in the Netherlands.

A few rounds later, Chris looked at his watch and determined it was time to move on to the next place. Outside, the distinctive earthy smell of marijuana filled the air. Many tourists in Amsterdam stop at coffee shops to experience the novelty of taking a toke off a legal joint, but not us. As beer geeks with only one day in the city, our time was devoted to Amsterdam's beer scene. We did, however, need a spot of lunch before continuing on our beer tour.

We quickly ate at a nearby café under the watchful eye of a begging cat before heading to Brouwerij't Ij, a brewery housed in an old bathhouse next to a windmill. In better weather, the long walk would have been nice. But it wasn't nice out and Ute and I just wanted to be warm and dry.

The interior of the building had been altered only slightly when it was converted into an organic brewery. The white tile running halfway up the wall and the cement floor may have been nostalgic reminders of the bath house days, but they also made the inside feel like a walk-in refrigerator. Much to my disappointment and discomfort, Ij was almost as cold inside as it was outside.

I opted for their Pils while Chris and Ute chose Ijnde Jaars, a Belgian Strong Ale only available from November to January. We sat at a long wooden table next to some locals to drink our beer and shiver. I looked around at the funky interior. Paint peeled off the plastered walls and an impressive collection of empty beer bottles ringed the room.

In the brewery a man in rubber boots and no shirt cleaned the kettles. The three of us laughed and averted our eyes. With very few exceptions, you really don't want to see brewers with their shirts off.

In between sips of beer my teeth literally chattered. Chris told me to "knock it off," but I couldn't help it.

I turned to Ute, who had remained quiet. She agreed that it was cold and suggested that we finish our beers and go somewhere else. Chris finally gave in to our complaining and we went to the next brewery, De Bekeerde Suster ("The Converted Sister").

As we approached, we could see the brewery's name glowing in neon against the darkening late afternoon sun. De Bekeerde Suster is located on a canal at the edge of the red light district in a building that previously served as a *bethaniënconvent.* A place where ladies of the night who wanted to pay for their sins could stay and convert to a sister or nun.

A welcoming bartender greeted us as we plopped ourselves on a few barstools and peeled off our damp outerwear. We chatted with him as we drank our beer from a chaliced glass. At De Bekeerde Suster, Chris sipped on what turned out to be his favorite beer in Amsterdam: De Manke Monnik, a Tripel. After accepting an invitation to tour the brewery, which we could practically touch from where we sat, Chris followed the bartender to get a closer look at two beautifully polished copper kettles in the corner. Ute and I chose to watch from the comfort of our seats.

Over beers, the three of us unanimously decided to forgo a rest before the Flogging Molly/Street Dogs show in order to visit one more beer café-'t Arendsnest. "Rest is overrated," Chris remarked. We had one more hour before we were supposed to meet Ute's friends at a pub across town, so we had to move quickly.

Known as *the* bar for Dutch beer, many people have included 't Arendsnest on their world list of essential beer stops and there's a reason for it. Most beer cafés in Amsterdam specialize in European beers, but 't Arendsnest is proud to offer only beers from Dutch breweries.

Ute and I followed Chris up a few stairs to the stoop and in through the wide glossy black door. The pub burst with a sparkling brilliance. A shiny copper tap system and cleanly polished glasses ran the length of the bar. Bottles of distilled spirits on glass shelves glimmered under the lights. It was all majestically presided over by a brass eagle atop the center beer tower, his wings spread strong and proud.

The owner, Peter van der Arend assisted us in navigating the extensive list of beers, many of which we were unfamiliar with and had no idea how to pronounce. While his depth of knowledge was not surprising, he also demonstrated a high degree of patience in educating us about Dutch beer. Then Chris had to go and ask the question, "What is your favorite beer?"

"What is a favorite to me may not be a favorite to you," Peter said.

Somewhat uncharacteristically, but also fueled by an afternoon of beer drinking, Chris doggedly pursued an answer. "Well, what is the best Dutch beer you serve here?"

This went on for a few minutes and I even tried to quiet Chris down with a few pats on the leg, but there was no stopping his persistence. Ute shook her head and laughed.

"I'm not going to answer that question," Peter finally said in a polite, yet clearly annoyed tone.

He went on to explain that Michael Jackson (the famed "Beer Hunter," not the gloved one) had attended the opening of 't Arendsnest in July 2000. Michael apparently told Peter that if he were to find the best beer in the world, he would no longer be the beer *hunter*. Chris had no response to that. After all, who was he to question the wisdom of the beer God himself.

After Arendsnest, we met up with a few of Ute's friends at an Irish pub near the venue. Here Ute was in her element. Holding court at a table of a half-dozen Flogging Molly fans, she was the most animated I'd seen her all day. I drank a Guinness along with everyone else at the table, except Chris, who explained that he only drinks Guinness in Ireland. We gave him a hard time about his pretentious comment, so he rephrased his stance to something about the importance of enjoying local beer.

We stayed out until 2 A.M., at which point I was convinced that I could actually feel my immune system deteriorating. Time to get to bed and start drinking beer again the next day.

Friday, Chris and I left Amsterdam on a mid-morning train to Roosendaal on the Netherlands/Belgium border, while Ute flew home to Germany. Along the way, we readied ourselves for the main event of our trip.

Chris and I hailed a taxi at the train station in Roosendaal and shortly thereafter arrived at the rental car office. Once in the car, Chris handed me CAMRA's *Good Beer Guide Belgium* by Tim Webb. Serving as our most essential guidebook of the trip, we would refer to it often throughout our travels in Belgium. I slipped it into the pocket on the passenger side door and turned my attention to the map, which Chris had already started to unfold. It was my job to remember what Chris showed me and to get us there. If all else failed, the car had GPS.

His game plan entailed traveling along the border, hanging a right at Eindhoven and arriving at Brouwerij der Sint-Benedictusabdij de Achelse Kluis, known more simply as Achel. It marked the first stop on our Holy Grail quest of all beer travel adventures: to visit all of the Trappist breweries. A very special type of brewery, there are only seven of them in the world, six in Belgium and one in the Netherlands.

The Trappist order, started in 1664 by the Abbot of La Trappe in France, was a modification of the Cistercian order.

One of the primary tenets of his new more conservative order required the monasteries to be self-sufficient. Monastery breweries originated as a way to sustain their own community and today have evolved into a funding source for charitable works.

In 1997, eight of the approximately 170 Trappist abbeys worldwide formed the International Trappist Association as a way to limit the commercial misuse of the name Trappist.[29] Today, the "Authentic Trappist Product" logo of the association indicates the use of specific production guidelines for items such as cheese, beer, and wine. For beer, the criteria include the following:

- The beer must be brewed within the walls of a monastery or its vicinity
- The beer must be brewed under the direct supervision of Trappist monks in accordance to a proper monastic way of life
- The proceeds must be used to sustain the monastery and/or fund charitable causes

Brewing some of the best and, in certain cases, the rarest beers in the world, our goal was to visit all seven Trappist breweries during our trip. Given the unpredictability of beer travel, it would be a major feat if all went well.

Chris double-checked that I understood the route he wanted to take. It looked easy enough and I told him so. And it might have been just that easy if it weren't for the city of

29 The German abbey Mariawald, which also produced other food products, no longer brewed beer but joined with those who did to create the association.

Eindhoven temporarily transforming itself into one big construction zone.

After some trial and a few errors we reached the abbey in the drizzling rain. To offer a little perspective on what we were up against, the abbey's own website describes its location as "somewhere in an out-of-the-way place of the Flemish Country, hidden between fields and forests on the boundary with the Netherlands, situated near the water of the Tongelreep." Yep, that pretty much describes it.

Through a set of archways, we entered a large courtyard. I imagined that in the summer it was filled with tables, but in the cold December rain, it was a barren field of shiny terra cotta tiles. Surrounded by the building on three sides, the courtyard was lined with a series of doors and windows. So far our day had been one big guessing game—navigating Eindhoven, locating the abbey, and now figuring out the building entrance. But, if we could make it to this "out of the way" abbey, we could surely locate the front door.

We picked the right door and correctly guessed the main seating area inside was around the corner on the right. We would have never guessed, however, that it would look like a school cafeteria. Several 70-plus-year-olds drank coffee with their pie to the sound of Madonna's "Like a Virgin" echoing throughout the linoleum-floored dining room. Beer travel in December can be a quiet affair, especially places that get cold and rainy. In general we enjoy it, but admittedly off-season travel makes it difficult to blend in with the locals. The half-dozen pensioners watched us as we claimed one of the many vacant tables.

Chris slid a green lunch tray down the counter, reaching into the different cases for pie and a small bowl of cubed cheese as he went. My contribution to the tray was something that looked like a custard tart topped with a cinnamon roll. We ordered beers at the register from a young woman and paid.

We drank the two available beers, a Blonde and a Bruin, as we used toothpicks to pop artisanal cheese into our mouths and forks to defend our respective pastries. Even with the elementary school service style and distinctly older crowd, the beer was amazing and the experience memorable. It was and always will be our first experience at a Trappist brewery. Our beer and snacks gave us just enough energy to get to our bed and breakfast a few kilometers away.

Villa Christina in nearby Hamont was housed in an old mansion that dated back to 1758. From the pictures we saw on the internet, we knew that it was ornately furnished with antiques. Not our usual type of accommodation, the winter rate made it impossible to pass up.

We knocked on the door and a neatly dressed man in his forties welcomed us into an entryway tiled in a dramatic gray and black pattern. The classic furnishings added to the provenance of the hotel, as did the ridiculously steep, narrow original staircase.

At the top of our radical climb to the first floor, we were happy to find ourselves at the threshold of our room. The elegantly decorated accommodation was fancier and more delicate than we were used to, but after several late nights of partying, it had what we needed most: quiet comfort.

Our host offered us a dinner suggestion located nearby, but it wasn't exactly our style. We could handle a fancy room, but dining at a chichi restaurant would have put us completely out of our comfort zone. Further down the street in the town square, we found the Hotel de Klok. It looked more like our speed.

The dimly lit pub was filled with regulars. Quiet and cozy, it bordered on romantic. A gracious host with a warm smile met us at the door and led us to a small table. He recognized us as visitors from out of town and made it his mission to introduce us to his best beer offerings.

A young woman came out of the kitchen with a tray of complimentary nibbles. I enjoyed a warm croquette, but passed on the sliders when she came around a second time. Apprehensive outsiders when we walked in, it didn't take long to feel part of the local scene.

Our waiter suggested a regional specialty *Stoverij met Frietjes*, a traditional beef stew with fries, to Chris. We don't generally eat red meat, but this meat was marinated in Belgian beer. Chris couldn't pass on that. He wanted an authentic cultural experience and didn't want to offend our new friend, so he ordered one.

When our dinner arrived, Chris's eyes grew big. He was served a hearty crock of potatoes and beef chunks. Chris took one bite and knew he'd made a good choice in accepting the recommendation. He insisted that I try a bite. It melted in my mouth and seemed the perfect comfort food for the season. As silly as it may sound, Chris's stew summed up our short stay in this historic town: a welcome and comforting embrace that warmed the soul.

Saturday's journey took us out of Flemish-speaking Belgium and south into the French-speaking region of the country. No beer travel adventure would be complete if it went off without a hitch and we hit our snag at our very first stop of the day, Brasserie Fantôme in a small village called Soy.

We arrived around noon to find the front door closed. A man intercepted Chris in the yard as he looked around to investigate. There were a lot of hand gestures, then the nodding of heads. I heard Chris say, "Okay, merci," and he turned back toward the car.

The brewery wasn't open for another two hours, so Chris rearranged the day's agenda. We'd first go to the town of Rochefort, home of the Trappist brewery of the same name, and return to Fatôme later. The downside of this new plan was that we would miss the tasting hours for another nearby brewery.

It didn't take long for us to recover from our disappointment at losing an opportunity to add to The List, however, and after a half hour drive we arrived in Rochefort. After entering the town from the opposite end and taking several wrong turns, we finally found the abbey.

Rochefort is unique among the Trappist breweries in that it is the only one that doesn't have its own brewery tap. We parked the car and went to film in front of the abbey gates. I let my verbal knife loose on the French language.

"Behind me is the Abbaye de Notre-Dame de Saint-Remy. It's the home to the Trappist Brewery rohk-fur. Rohk-for? Rohsh-for," I stumbled. "Unfortunately it's not open to the public so it doesn't count on The List, but it does count as having visited our second Trappist brewery."

This demonstrated our first crack at butchering the French language, something that would be shamefully documented on video throughout the duration of the trip.

We had read in the *Good Beer Guide Belgium* that a nearby restaurant served the Rochefort beer. A sign down the road conveniently pointed the way to Le Relais St. Remy.

There was just one other car in the parking lot when we arrived, which made us think that the restaurant might be closed. In winter, the slow season for many establishments, business hours can be scant and unpredictable. Fortunately, through the window we noticed an older couple eating a meal.

Chris and I whispered as we attempted to decipher the menu. Finally, Chris consulted our pocket dictionary and decided that the item we contemplated was a ham and leek quiche served with a *salade*, which we correctly identified as a salad. Our quiches went well with our gold-rimmed chalices of Rochefort 6, the lowest ABV (7.5%) of their three Strong Dark Ales.

When our hostess came to clear the table, I held the dictionary up to her and pointed to a few phrases. The hope was that she would understand I was asking where we could purchase bottles of the Rochefort beer. Fortunately, she did understand and proceeded to offer me directions, in French of course. The first sentence I roughly understood, but then she continued on for another few minutes. I nodded and said, "Okay" even though she had lost me a few dozen words back. I did catch "*Chinois*" and "*marché*."

"Did you get that?" Chris asked outside.

"Uh, not really, but I saw a Chinese restaurant back there. I think she said something about the market being close to a Chinese restaurant."

We found the market, but no Rochefort, so we hit the road empty handed for the 26-kilometer drive back to the tiny village of Soy and Brasserie Fantôme.

Fantôme has a reputation for brewing unique beers using unusual ingredients, not all of which have resulted in successful brews. The quality of the beer is known to vary and its availability is unpredictable. For all his efforts, the brewer, Danny Prignon, has been described as a "lively character" who is alternatively creative, mysterious, and eccentric.

The best way to describe Fantôme's ramshackle tasting room is unconventional. We sat at a table near the front bay window where ceramic figurines of happy ghosts were arranged in the windowsill. Odd knick-knacks, such as a laminated picture of dried ham, were scattered about. Everything had been brought inside for the winter, including a stack of folded up patio chairs and an outdoor heat lamp, which was on.

After first ordering a pair of Saisons, we chose the Fantôme Brune for our second round. Much to our delight, we discovered in the *Good Beer Guide Belgium* that the Brune was a rare occurrence. It was an amazing stroke of luck that helped us enjoy the visit even more. Everything about the place was quirky and we loved every minute of it.

Now the early evening, we traveled further south, almost to the French border, to the town of Bouillon, our home base for the next few days

Our biggest goal for Sunday was to visit Orval, our third Trappist brewery. Chris was a little unsure of the hours and wondered if they would even be open. With crossed fingers and a little apprehension we set off on the 33-kilometer drive to find l'Abbaye Notre Dame d'Orval.

A half-hour later, the car approached the sought-after road and I instructed Chris to turn right. Bam! We were faced with one of the most striking visions I've ever seen.

The abbey loomed in the green valley and seemed to reach the heavens themselves. We passed a few small buildings on the left, including the official brewery tap, and continued down the road toward the abbey. As we got closer, I realized that the front façade was a 60-foot high relief of the Virgin Mary. The look on her simply-carved face as she gazed tenderly upon the baby Jesus in her arms enveloped me in an overwhelming sense of spirituality. I was simply speechless.

We parked the car near the entrance and stepped out into the bright sunlight. It was the first time we'd seen the sun on the whole trip. We walked back a hundred yards to A l'Ange Gardien, the official brewery tap, and added Orval to The List.

In a high chair next to his parents, a child with round rosy cheeks and a head full of curly hair giggled. With the look of a cherub, the child seemed right at home in the shadows of the abbey. A Christmas tree with brightly colored bulbs stood in one corner. Despite the short brisk walk in the sun, the winter air still packed a chill, so Chris agreed to sit at a table by the fire.

We started off with Petit Orval. A 3.2% diluted version of the regular Orval, it's found only at the abbey and is created especially for the monks. In an unusual method of identification, the beer comes in the same bottle as regular Orval but it has no label. One beer to secure Orval on The List and we were ready to visit the abbey.

Orval Abbey, founded in 1070, became a Cistercian monastery in 1132. The monastery was built and rebuilt several times over, but was completely razed during the French Revolution. In 1926, a group of Cistercian-Trappist monks returned to the site and the brewery was established in 1931 to fund the building of the new monastery.

As a working monastery, the main grounds were closed to the public. We could, however, wander around the remains of the original abbey. Along the boundary on the left side, I came across a round pool of water that looked like a small hot tub. The sound of rushing water could be heard through a grate in the ground nearby. As I stood over the pool staring into the clear water, Chris came up alongside me.

"This is Mathilda's Fountain," I told him. "The water comes from the same source that's used in both the beer and cheese."

As legend has it, around the year 1076, Countess Mathilda of Tuscany accidentally dropped her wedding ring into a clear gushing spring. Given to her by Godfrey the Hunchback, her deceased husband, the Countess was deeply saddened at the loss. She reportedly prayed in earnest to the Virgin Mary for its return. Within days, a trout appeared at the surface with her ring in its mouth. In good royal fashion, she declared the site a blessed valley and became a benefactor of the abbey. From this romantic story of love and devotion, Orval's logo of a fish with a ring in its mouth, was born.

We passed through a few more stone archways and the medicinal herb garden before returning to the tavern for more beer and food. Our visit to Orval was all we had hoped it would be—a truly amazing experience.

Tuesday was my birthday and we were ready for whatever adventures the day might bring. Chris and I plotted our northern route to our fourth Trappist brewery, Chimay, before hitting the road. Confusingly there is a town called Chimay, but that's not where the brewery is located. The easiest way to get to Chimay (the brewery, not the town) was to head east into

France before going north back into Belgium. Thus far, the GPS on the dash had served as a backup to ensure that I steered us in the right direction. However, there was one small problem with this backup system. Upon entering France, the screen went black, except for a wobbling yellowish dot. The only thing our computerized navigator could show us was that we were still moving.

Despite the apparent nonexistence of roads in France, l'Abbaye Notre-Dame de Scourmount was easy to find and we arrived without any wrong turns. The challenging part of the day so far had not been the navigating, but the weather, which had turned from a cold rain into sleet. Once at the abbey, I had to go out to film.

"Another cold day here in Belgium," I started. "We made it to the Abbey Notre Dame de Score-mont. Scower-mont?" I laughed at myself for mangling the name then continued. "Which is the home to Chimay. It's not a day we can take a tour, though. So we're headed down the street to their official tavern. It's freezing out here so I want to get going."

The second largest of the Trappist breweries, Chimay started brewing in 1862 and, up until 1970, sold its beer and cheese out of the abbey's gatehouse. While the church, garden, and cemetery are available for visitors, the brewery is closed to the public. For us, the cold weather quashed any desire to visit the grounds and we just wanted in from the cold. At that point, any place would have sufficed, but we knew that Auberge de Poteaupré, Chimay's official tavern, was just down the street.

A small bistro table provided the perfect view of the taps at the bar. I could see only a few other people in the restaurant, but the crowd must have been somewhere because the bartender filled one ceramic pitcher after another with beer. A sign on the wall at our table advertised a special beer.

"Spéciale Po-to-pre. Po-to-pray?" I said. "How do you pronounce that?"

"I don't know, but that's what I'm starting with," Chris said.

Spéciale Poteaupré (pronounced paw-toe-pray) is a 4.5% golden colored beer that is drawn from a cask and is only available at the Auberge de Poteaupré. The glossy brochure-like menu suggested pairing it with the Poteaupré cheese. "The cream of the Trappist cheeses," it explained. The menu also listed a variety of what they called cheese "planks," a fancy way of saying cheese board. We opted for one with a selection of four cheeses served with homemade bread.

Both the camera and video camera were in frequent use as we ate our snack. It was like a photo shoot at our table. I had my birthday portrait taken with a goblet of Chimay Rouge. Chris had his picture taken with the cheese board before he offered me a birthday toast on camera.

"Today we are not only visiting our fourth Trappist," Chris said, "We're also celebrating Merideth's 21st birthday."

He clinked his glass against the camera. "Happy birthday to my beautiful wife."

One by one, each of the cheeses disappeared. The bread soon followed, leaving an empty cutting board sprinkled with crumbs. With the last sip of our beers gone, we stopped to purchase an armload of beer before stepping out into the now falling snow.

In the warmth of the car, we continued on to Brugge, making two more stops along the way. First was the farm brewery of Dupont, located down a narrow country lane.

Brasserie Dupont set the industry standard for the Saison style of beer. Summer and harvest are the traditional times of year for Saisons, as they were originally brewed to nourish agricultural workers. Judging by the farmlands surrounding Dupont, there were probably plenty of laborers around to taste the beer and help the brewery perfect their recipe.

After a few minutes of checking out the farmhouse across the lane, we crossed back over to "Les Caves Dupont." Inside, a woman behind the bar and a few farmers drinking beer turned to look at us with surprised faces. We used our best hand signals and French pronunciation to order a pair of Saisons. It may not have sounded pretty, but the woman understood what we wanted and that's all that mattered.

We sat drinking our beers and listening as the bartender and the farmers chatted in French. A pet bird repeatedly squawked from another room. The unfinished framing above our head amplified the sounds as they echoed throughout the room. Through it all, we absorbed the atmosphere of what felt like the brewery's staff cantina.

When the pair of farmers finished their beers, they set their empty glasses on the bar and said good-bye to the bartender. They said a few words in our direction that I assumed to be friendly salutations and left. The door closed and for a brief moment, the room was quiet. We finished our beers and made our own exit as the bird resumed its squawking.

A short fifteen minutes down the road, we shifted from workingman's casual at Dupont to the sleek and modern décor of Trolls and Bush, Brasserie Dubuisson's tavern and visitor's center in Pipaix. "Another One Bites the Dust" blared as we entered the brightly lit room. We sat down and ordered beer from a slight young man dressed all in black.

A mural of a troll with curly-toed elf shoes and a hop cone hat grabbed my attention. Kind of creepy, yet verging on cute, he wore a happy grin as he leap-frogged over the word "Trolls."

After a look at the menu I realized I was in for a special treat. There was a highlighted section that I surmised meant you get a free taster set on your birthday.

When our waiter returned, I pointed at the menu and showed him my passport. Thoroughly unimpressed, he nodded his head to acknowledge that I was correct. We ordered shrimp croquettes and a Croque Monsieur (a grilled ham and cheese sandwich) before he walked away to pour my free gift.

"So how's the birthday going so far?" Chris asked.

"Terrible, just terrible. It's awful to be in Belgium for my birthday."

"Yeah, it must be a bummer to spend your 21st birthday here."

"You have to stop saying that because I look really old for 21. You're supposed to say I'm 50. That way I look really good for 50," I said.

"Well, I think you look pretty good for 39," Chris complimented.

I smiled and gave Chris a kiss. "You always say the right thing."

When our lunch was finished and our beers were dry, we left for our final and much anticipated destination of the day: Brugge. Chris expected the drive to be a little over an hour, but a missed exit prolonged our arrival and brought the unwelcome challenge of navigating the city in the dark.

Once we parked the car in an underground garage and picked up a map from the tourist information center, we set out on foot to find our hotel. We did a quick check-in and set out in search of one of the most famous beer cafés in the world: 't Brugs Beertje, The Little Brugge Bear.

We walked the streets of Brugge's city center, passing a Christmas market in full swing along the way. Each winter many cities throughout Europe set up festive street fairs with dozens of stalls selling crafts, Christmas gifts and specialty foods. Christmas was over two weeks away, but spirits were already high. The markets are a sure-fire cure for the bah humbugs and one of the reasons we thoroughly enjoy Europe at Christmastime.

Excited chatter filled the air as business people in full-length wool coats mingled with tourists in short parkas and knit hats. The sweet smell of Belgian waffles and the savory aroma of grilling sausages drifted through the merchandise stalls. The cheerful feeling was contagious.

We walked a few more blocks before turning down a dark side street. The front windows of 't Brugs Beertje were fogged like a car parked on Inspiration Point. Laughter and lively banter carried out into the alleyway. The small front area was standing room only, so we continued past the bar through to a second, even smaller room where we found an empty table in the corner. Some might call Beertje cramped, but we thought the close quarters were cozy.

Daisy Claeys and her husband Jan De Bruyne had previous restaurant experience, but their dream really came true when they opened 't Brugs Beertje in 1983, a time when an interest in Belgian beers was just starting to grow. Located in a brick building that dates back to 1632, Beertje has developed into a Brugge tourist destination for beer geeks and non-beer geeks alike. Daisy, a native of Brugge, is an icon in the specialty beer industry. She possesses an incredible amount of beer knowledge, yet none of the pretense that could easily go with such expertise. No passing fad, Beertje has earned its place as one of the best beer cafés in the world.

Chris looked wide-eyed as he leafed through the beer menu. He decided to start with Christmas beers and ordered a vintage flight of De Dolle Brouwers Stille Nacht. I chose the Dupont Saison as a way to buy myself some time. I could sip away at a beer I knew while perusing a whole list of ones I didn't.

We ordered a portion of cubed cheese with celery salt. Chris stuck a toothpick in a piece of cheese and popped it in his mouth.

"My strategy is going to be to drink lower alcohol beers, so I can try a lot without being crazy drunk," I announced.

Chris, on the other hand, decided to enlist the assistance of our waiter for his second round choice. He described to the waiter, who luckily spoke impeccable English, what he was in the mood for and ended up with Oude Kriek from Brouwerij Drie Fonteinen.

A few hours later when we were ready to leave, I finally got up the courage to ask Daisy for a picture. She had been behind the bar all night and Chris had repeatedly badgered me to take a picture with her. All it took was a little liquid courage. Despite my good intention, low alcohol content beers can still add up to tipsy.

Daisy was hesitant and tried to politely decline, but she eventually agreed.

"Okay," she said, "but only because it's your birthday."

I moved closer to Daisy as she came to the end of the bar. Chris snapped one picture before a man seated nearby offered to take the picture so Chris could be in it. The spot we had chosen wouldn't do for our photographer, however, and he pushed Chris and me behind the bar with Daisy.

We thanked our new friend and I gathered my coat. Before we squeezed our way through the crowd to the door, Daisy handed me a brand new stuffed brown bear that fit in the palm of my hand.

"Happy Birthday," she said.

Wednesday was the day Chris was most excited about. Unfortunately, his health didn't completely cooperate. He'd been sniffling for the past few days, but this was the first time he finally admitted he didn't feel good. He even ignored the alarm clock in the morning, causing us to be an hour behind our self-imposed schedule—very unusual for Chris.

Our first stop of the day was the St. Sixtus Abbey, home to the most sought-after beer in the world, Westvleteren. St. Sixtus monastery has the smallest production of all the Trappist breweries and the beer is rarely available outside Belgium. This scarcity has created a mystique unrivaled by any other brew, Trappist or otherwise, and it has spurred many a beer geek to make a pilgrimage to the brewery. A visit here meant we could tick off our fifth Trappist brewery.

It was a longer drive from Brugge than Chris planned and the last few kilometers took us down one-lane country roads. We barely saw any houses and certainly nothing that looked like a monastery, which added to both the frustration and concern that we had ended up in the middle of nowhere. Fortunately, we came around a curve and found a large complex on the right and the official café, In de Vrede, across the street.

It was another moment of truth in our quest to visit all seven Trappists as we stepped up to the front door of the café.

I pulled the front door open and we both let out a big breath. Westvleteren was checked off the Trappist list. Large inside, we easily found a table near a 12-foot tall Christmas tree. Chris was so anxious to get his hands on the beer that he didn't wait for a waitress. He went to the counter to order.

With a beer in each hand, he returned looking much more relaxed.

In the far corner there was a small store where, among other things, the beer could be purchased to go. Afraid they might sell out, which occasionally happens, I immediately sent Chris over to buy some. He came back with just one six-pack.

"I'm such a dork," he said. "I tried to buy a six-pack of their Blonde and two of Westvleteren 8. Those are the only two beers available for purchase today."

To discourage re-sale and price gouging, the brewery imposes a purchase limit with a highly organized system of sale. The system includes calling for a reservation and providing the license plate of the car in which you will be picking up the beer. Only one case per month can be purchased per vehicle and the system will interrupt your reservation if it detects that a second order in the same month is being placed using the same phone number. Lucky for us, they also sold six-packs at the café, but there were purchase restrictions there, too.

"I had read that you're allowed only one six-pack. So I don't know why I tried to buy more. I got a six-pack of the Blonde, so now it's your turn. Go buy a six-pack of the 8."

With that I went to make my purchase. I had never had the beer (not even a sip from the one right in front of me) and had no idea what it even tasted like, but I was excited nonetheless. That's the power of short supply.

"So how does it feel to be drinking the most sought after beer in the world?" Chris asked as I finally took a sip.

"I'm speechless actually. I think it's way too cool," I answered.

Chris took a sip of his Westvleteren 12, a 10.2% ABV Belgian Quad, and summarized his experience. "My life is complete. I have been here."

Our second stop of the day was a brewery equally revered as Westvleteren in beer geek circles: Rodenbach. Fortunately there was an English language tour already scheduled by another group that we could join. We learned later that English tours were a rare occurrence, so we appreciated their willingness to allow us to tag along.

Rodenbach brews a unique beer that the late Michael Jackson called a Red Ale. Some call it a Sour Ale, while the Belgians categorize it by a whole other name: Brown Sour Ale. Whatever you call it, though, this beer is as tart as unsweetened lemonade. The unique sour flavor is the result of organisms such as Lactobacillus (a bacteria) and Brettanomyces (a yeast) that are allowed to propagate in the oak vats where the beer is aged. Consistency is maintained by blending young and mature brews. It was the magical oak vats that we came to see.

Our guide first led us through the old malting facility. The historic round brick building was from the time when Rodenbach malted its own barley. During our visit to the malt house, we learned that we had joined the tour of a NATO work group. Consisting of people from several different countries, English was the common language.

After much anticipation and patience, the moment that Chris had been waiting for finally arrived. Our hostess guided us through huge rooms filled with almost 300 wood aging vessels. The vats, held together by reddish-orange metal hoops, sat atop short brick walls. To stand near them was like being in an old growth redwood forest. The age, some vats are as old as 150 years, and enormity of the vats was awe-inspiring.

The tour ended in an expansive banquet room. Chris ordered a Grand Cru (an unblended maturely-aged brew) for each of us and we sat down at one of the large round tables. Chris looked on top of the world. He was so happy it was hard to remember that he felt lousy. While the visit wasn't really much of a sacrifice, Chris had been a real trooper. It had been a full and exciting day and it was time to get him back to the hotel to rest. No time for serious illness, we still had four days, two Trappist breweries, and a beer festival to go.

A good night's sleep helped Chris to feel a little better and Thursday we were ready to explore Brugge. First, we went on a tour of the only brewery left in the city.

Chris guided us along city streets to De Halve Maan, home of the beer Brugse Zot. Beer geeks easily identify Brugse Zot by the logo: a joker with a Cheshire Cat grin dressed in a red and green hat with jingle bells. A stone marker with a gold half moon marked the entrance to a cobblestone courtyard. We were early for their regularly scheduled brewery tour, so we bought our tickets and drank a quick beer in the brewery tavern. It was here that Chris broke the bad news to me.

We had had a goal of visiting our 450th breweries (respectively) by the end of the year. Chris, being a few ahead of me, was still on target, but because of forgoing a visit to Brasserie Caracole a few days before and stopping at another brewery that failed to list updated business hours on their website, I would end the year two breweries shy of meeting that goal. It was a disappointing discovery, but I didn't have much time to dwell on it. The tour was starting.

We explored the different parts of the multi-level brewery before entering their brewery museum, located in the attic. There, our guide outlined the use of hops in the brewing process. She explained that the hop plant is related to marijuana and that's why it gives us the "kick" in beer. Holding her thumbs and index fingers together near her head, each time she said "kick," she split her fingers apart to indicate brightened eyes. Her delivery was as dry as Melba toast and her expression just as stiff, which made it even funnier. Chris and I couldn't understand why no one else was laughing because we thought the whole thing was absolutely hilarious.

After concluding the tour on the rooftop with a beautiful panoramic view of the city, we returned to the tavern for the glass of Brugse Zot that was included in the tour ticket price.

We spent the rest of the afternoon browsing through the Christmas market in Market Square and taking in the sites. As we climbed the Bell Tower, Chris and I recited lines from the movie *In Bruges*. While not everything depicted in the movie was exactly accurate, the top of the stairs of the Bell Tower most certainly got narrow.

Our final evening in Brugge was spent at Brugs Beertje. It was Daisy's day off and the pub didn't emit the same vibrancy as it had a few nights before. It was also much less crowded. We enjoyed ourselves in the mellow atmosphere as we explored the beer menu for a second time. We felt more confident on this return visit and alternated between asking for recommendations from our friendly waiter and taking wild guesses. It made for hours of fun.

On our walk back to the hotel, we stopped at a Belgian waffle stand. Chocolate sauce dripped down my chin when I took a bite. Chris's mustache caught a dab of sticky caramel sauce as he bit from his waffle. We tripped along the cobblestoned street wiping each other's faces. Puffs of breath floated around us as we laughed in the cold air.

We left Brugge Friday mid-morning and drove east across foggy Belgium to our sixth Trappist brewery. Westmalle, the largest of the Trappist breweries, is famous for having developed the Dubbel and Tripel styles of beer. Like the other Trappists we had visited, the brewery itself was not open to the public because it was located within the walls of the active monastery. There was, however, a brand new brewery tap conveniently located across the street.

After accidentally parking on a back service road, we tromped across an unfinished brick patio to the front door of Café Trappisten. A nicely dressed waiter in a long black apron and silver tie served us a pair of Dubbels. He added to the sleek and modern dining room, which was a world away from Achel's elementary school cafeteria style.

Chris held up his chalice and announced into the camera, "Congratulations to me. Westmalle is my 450th brewery."

For as excited as Chris was to reach this milestone, he was also anxious to arrive at our seventh and final Trappist, La Trappe. We had only a small window of time to make it there. If we missed the limited tasting room hours, our quest to visit all seven Trappists would fail. At the time, their winter tasting hours were a scant three hours in the afternoon. Saying goodbye to Trappist brewery number six, we drove 60 kilometers across the Dutch border to the outskirts of Tilburg.

La Trappe—known as Konigshoeven in the United States until 2010— is the most commercialized and the only Trappist brewery outside of Belgium. The brewery was established in 1884. However, nearly a century later, an aging monk population made it difficult to continue as a Trappist brewery and by 1999 the monks no longer managed the day-to-day operations. This violated the criteria for using the Authentic Trappist Product label and in December of that year, the brewery labeled their beer as *Trappistenbier*[30] instead. In 2005, the monks returned to take control of the daily business of the brewery and La Trappe was able to use the Authentic Trappist Product logo once again.

We located the Onze Lieve Vrouw van Koningshoeven Abbey and easily found a spot in the large car park. To reach the monastery grounds, we crossed a footbridge. Wild greenery filled in the shallow gulch below. Trees, the tops of which were visible over the red brick wall, came into full view once we passed under the archway and onto the grounds. Leafless branches exposed the trees in all their winter nakedness.

"We did it, hon," Chris said stopping to hug me. "We visited all seven Trappists."

"We haven't added this one to The List yet. But yes, we've been to all seven." I replied.

The tasting room itself was situated in front of the monastery entrance. The patio nearby was empty, except for a couple of men who suffered in the cold as they smoked their cigarettes. It was quiet and peaceful.

Inside was a different story and we encountered two different large tasting groups. We chose one of the long birch tables

30 Literally translated as "Trappist beer," this label still identified the beer as a product of a Trappist monastery.

far away from the crowd and close to a modern cube-shaped fireplace. Our waitress served us a taster set and we ordered an assortment of their cheese to go with it. The sampler came with six beers: Witte, Blonde, Dubbel, Tripel, Bock, and Quadrupel.

Chris picked up the cute 25 cl saucer of the Tripel sample and held it towards me in a toast. I met his glass with the sample of the Blonde.

"Here's to us," Chris said. "We did it."

"Yep," I replied. "Here's to the joy of beer travel."

We clinked glasses and both let out a sigh. Having achieved our major goal of the trip, the pressure was off. Now all we needed to do was return the car in Roosendaal and attend the Kerstbierfestival over the weekend.

Friday night, Chris and I stayed in Roosendaal, the last train stop in The Netherlands and a quick 10-minute train ride to Essen, Belgium,[31] the small town where the Kerstbierfestival is held. The festival didn't start until 2 P.M. the next day, so we had time to enjoy a restful morning. On the go for the last ten days and with advancing colds (I was now sniffling, too), we were grateful for the slowing pace. Our plan for Saturday included exploring Essen and having lunch there before the festival opened.

Shortly before noon on Saturday, we caught our train and, upon arriving in Essen, braved the extraordinary cold on the 2-kilometer walk into town. The weather greatly diminished our interest in exploring the town, so we strayed little from the route between the train station and the Heuvelhal, the town's

31 Not to be confused with the bigger, more industrial city in Germany with whom it shares a namesake.

sports hall and site of the festival. We found a small restaurant along the way and sat down at the bar for a bite to eat.

A half hour before the festival started we made our way down the road to the Heuvelhal to wait in line. Standing out in the crispy air wasn't really appealing, but we had no idea what to expect in the way of a crowd. Most of our reference points for beer festivals had been grossly over-sized rowdy affairs and we thought maybe we needed to arrive early to secure ourselves a seat.

We joined the line behind 25 fellow beer drinkers who were even more anxious than us to get a good place to sit. The line was in constant motion as each person shuffled around to keep the blood flowing.

Eventually the line started to move forward and we filed through the small door and into a high school gym, complete with basketball nets on either end. Strings of large banners advertising beers like Delirium, Duvel, and Maredsous criss-crossed the room.

While Chris waited in line to purchase tokens and tasting glasses, I secured two seats from the dozens of long tables draped in white cloths. Miniature poinsettias served as centerpieces.

Admission to the Kerstbierfestival is free, but tokens are used to pay for everything from tastes and snack items to full bottles of beer to go. The program told us all we needed to know about attending the festival. The "House Rules" included things like: there is no table service, order beers by number to avoid any confusion due to language differences, and the bar is conveniently organized into three parts: draught, bottled, and exclusives. It also requested that attendees keep the tables "neat and tidy and don't make a mess by fiddling with the candles or decorations."

As far as beer festivals go, it was an oddly civil scene. No whooping. No hollering. The frenzied hurriedness to get that first beer was entirely absent, as people calmly made their way to empty seats. The sound level in the Heuvelhal was that of a distinguished gathering rather than the pen full of hyenas we usually encountered. Different from what we had ever experienced before, the scene took us by pleasant surprise.

I opened the program to pick my first beer. "It's back! A Belgian exclusive on draught," the program said of the Van Honsebrouck Brigand Christmas. I decided that anything "exclusive" was a good place to start. Chris started with a copper-colored beer that the program described as "dry hopped."

Most beers were one token but rare or special ones could cost as many as three. Despite being "exclusive," my first beer cost me just one token. The beer was served on draught, so I found it with the other draught beers on one end of the long counter near the glass washer.

I held my glass upside down by the stem and pressed it down onto the jets. Water shot up into the glass with a ping and slid down the insides. My clean glass was now ready to be filled with beer.

I moved to my right in front of a volunteer server who was behind the counter. Placing my glass on the counter, I extended my thumb and index finger. "Number two, alstublieft."

He nodded his head slightly as he took my glass. He turned his back to me for just a moment and when he turned to face me again, my small snifter was foaming with a light amber colored brew.

"Dank u," I said.

"You're welcome," he replied in an American accent.

I chuckled. Who knows if he was actually American, but at a small beer festival in a small Belgian town, it was the last type of accent I expected to hear.

Chris and I sat comparing notes on our beers. We looked around and noticed that others in the mostly male crowd were doing the same. Glasses were held up in the light to get a better look at the color. Copious tasting notes were scribbled down for future reference. Frequent flashes went off as people photographed their beers, a sure sign that you're dealing with beer geeks.

In all its subdued nature, the Kerstbierfestival may sound boring, but it isn't. It's just more adult than many beer fests. Even as the Heuvelhal filled up and all of the few hundred seats became occupied, the noise level stayed about the same. That is until the sound of an accordion rang through the air, rising above the conversation noise. A group of middle-aged men gathered around a man playing a blue accordion. I didn't recognize the song and the men didn't seem to either as they sang along in sounds other than real lyrics. They were neither in tune nor in sync, but it was still festive and more importantly, it wasn't annoying.

It took three beers before Chris discovered one he truly liked—#102, Slaghmuylder's Kerstbier, a Czech style pilsner. In the ensuing hours, we developed a strategy of focusing on beers that were described as "Exclusive!" and "Rare!" The Bush des Nuits from Dubuisson, a three token beer, was listed as a "Festival debut and rare!" in addition to the automatic status enhancer, "When it's gone, it's gone!" Chris gave it three stars.

While the drunken camaraderie of Oktoberfest was missing, we did manage a short chat with our tablemates, exchanging beer suggestions. We determined that the table next to us was a Belgian beer tour group from the United States. A man in a long sleeved denim shirt stood over the table, dispensing various tidbits of information about Belgium, Belgian beer, and proper beer tasting techniques to his 10 charges.

A group of people dressed in cheap Santa suits and fake beards weaved passed us through the crowd like a snake. One of the women carried an oversized stuffed fish like the ones we seen used to tease tourists at Pike's Market in Seattle. How exactly the fish fit in with the outfits or the festival was a mystery, but the group was clearly enjoying themselves. Other festival goers got a kick out of them as they exchanged toasts, shared smiles, and took pictures.

Chris and I had had our fill of extraordinary beer for the day and it was time to get back to the hotel. As we left the Heuvelhal, I stopped at the 6-foot laminated world map on the wall and pressed a red pushpin below San Jose, the closest I could get to our hometown.

"There," I said. "Now they'll know we were here."

We returned to the festival at opening time on Sunday, the last day of our final Year in Beer adventure. No line formed outside and the crowd inside was a fraction of what it had been the day before. Saturday's mood may have been subdued, but there was an undercurrent of enthusiasm that kept the room abuzz. Sunday, however, the mood went beyond subdued and into the solemn range. For us, our trip was winding down. We were tired, missing the dogs, and our colds had forged ahead. As for other people, we assumed that an overindulgent Saturday night was to blame for their dulled sense of enthusiasm.

I purchased a portion of cheese and one of salami, each of which came on a small paper plate, and dropped them off at the table with Chris before going in search of a beer. With only three beer tickets left, I was down to choosing my last few beers of the trip. In fact, I was down to my last few beers of the Year in Beer.

"What'd you get?" Chris asked when I returned.

"It's called Christmas Beer," I laughed. "from Strubbe."

"Aptly named, I guess," Chris said.

For the next 15 minutes, we spoke little as we sipped our beers and ate our snacks. In the absence of the usual chaotic beer festival chatter, thoughts of the Year in Beer ending intruded upon my otherwise peaceful frame of mind.

"Do you realize that we're only one day away from the end?" I asked Chris.

"Yeah, I've been trying not to think about it." He stood up. "Okay, here I go to get my last beer of the Kerstbierfest."

It saddened me to think about our life without the Year in Beer. For the whole year, our lives were organized by and scheduled around the Year in Beer. For all its crazy making, the Year in Beer would be missed. Without it, my life was going to feel empty and ordinary.

But how many times over the year had I looked into Porter's sad little face before walking out the door? How could I forget the smell of the carpet when I lied on the floor trying to coax Stout out from his "happy place" under the bed just before we left. Even without the Year in Beer, there was no way my life could be empty when I had my dogs, my family, and my friends to re-connect with. For the second time in as many weeks, I experienced that "Aha!" moment; one that relieved me of the heavy heart created by the impending close of the Year in Beer.

Chris approached the table with a light golden beer in his hand and picked up our conversation where we left off.

"It seems like not all that long ago that we left for Anchorage," he said.

"Yep," I nodded my head in agreement.

"What am I going to do? For the first time in a year I don't have any travel arrangements to make."

For a few moments, we looked at each other without speaking. I could see in Chris's face that he was trying to pull his thoughts together, perhaps to make some profound concluding statement about our trip to Belgium or even bigger, the Year in Beer.

"So what'd you think?" Chris asked. "Was it a good trip?"

"It was. I guess I can never say that I don't like Belgian-style beers because I actually like them now."

And just like that, in a most poetic turn of events, my newfound fondness for Belgian beers provided a convenient conclusion for not only December's adventure, but for the Year in Beer as a whole. From my simple answer to a simple question, I realized that I had just learned the most important life lesson of the entire year. I learned to never let reality stand in the way of my dreams and to never view seeming impossibility as a reason for not even trying. I learned to never doubt my ability to accomplish something great. I learned to never say never again.

EPILOGUE

Several years have passed since the Year in Beer ended, but it feels like a lifetime ago. Dozens of new beer adventures have been logged since then and The List now boasts over 700 breweries. We traveled to Australia twice and returned to both the Kerstbierfestival and to Alaska. My beer geek identity has moved along the evolutionary continuum, but one characteristic has remained constant: Chris and I are, and always will be, beer travelers.

That's not to say that we didn't need to recover from our yearlong travel binge. When it was all over, we were tired, out of money, and somewhat disconnected from our family and friends. We planned on lots of rest, but what we didn't anticipate was the emotional let down. The satisfaction of sitting at home on the weekends felt rejuvenating for a while, but it soon turned into restlessness and an overwhelming desire to hit the road again.

Two months after it was all over, Chris and I talked for the first time about our post-Year in Beer feelings. Without a trip to organize, Chris didn't know what to do with his time. The wheels in his head furiously turned as he yearned for a trip to plan, but they didn't get him very far. It drove him crazy.

Chris proclaimed his readiness to go back to Europe. Although we had been to Europe five times during the Year in Beer, I shared his sentiment. We decided that our next trip would be to Wales and Ireland.

When I approached my supervisor at work with my time off request, she acted surprised. As she approved my request, she stated," I thought you were done with all of this."

Her comment confused me. "It's just the Year in Beer that's over," I told her. We never once considered the Year in Beer to be the end of our beer travel and I couldn't understand why she would think that it was.

Later, when I told my mother of our plans, she responded with almost the exact same words.

"Why did you guys think we wouldn't be traveling anymore?" I asked.

"I don't know. I just thought you'd be home for a while," my mother replied.

"Well, by the time we leave, we will have been home for four months," I said.

Four whole months, I thought. By the time our next trip came around, we'd have stayed home for four months. Given that the previous year we'd gone on six different beer adventures in the first four months of the year, I thought we demonstrated remarkable restraint. The truth is, the level of Year in Beer travel could not be replicated for a long time. Lack of money and vacation time guaranteed that. A period of readjustment back to normal life was necessary, but beer travel was not going to be abandoned altogether.

I looked into my mother's eyes. "Don't worry," I assured her. "I'll always come back."

"I know. I just like to know that you're home safe," she said.

I hugged her. "You'll always be more important than beer," I said softly into her ear.

"Well, I hope so," she laughed.

An unexpected transformation had occurred during the Year in Beer, one that can never be undone. My worldview changed as I lost my naiveté, gained a more realistic sense of my place in the beer community, and accepted my nomadic tendencies. The Year in Beer was the experience of a lifetime, just as we expected it to be. The scale of it is something one only does once, though. Any subsequent attempts are bound to pale in emotional comparison.

Beer travel has taken us to distant places, but the road is long and winding. While some adventures may be out of my line of sight now, I know they're out there. The final life lesson to be learned from the Year in Beer? Life is an open road, so don't forget your map.

GLOSSARY

ABV – Alcohol By Volume. Standard measurement for alcohol content.

Ale – A beer produced with a top-fermenting yeast and brewed at a temperature of

60-75°F.

Barley wine – A strong ale (8-12% ABV) most often associated with the winter season. The color can range from a deep gold to a ruby dark and its malty flavors are rich and sweet. American versions tend to be hoppier than their English cousins.

Belgian (-style) Dark strong ale – A category of high ABV Trappist/Abbey beers. The taste is rich and smooth, with a lot of malt sweetness. The addition of '-style' means the beer was brewed outside of Belgian/Netherlands.

Black lager – A dark variation of a lager. Also known as Schwarzbier.

Bock – A seasonal German beer noted for its higher ABV and rich body. There are two traditional variations: a spring release called a Maibock and a winter release called Doppelbock. *Bock* means "goat" in German.

Cask – A term for a beer barrel. Also refers to a specific method of dispensing beer without gas.

Double/Imperial/Triple India Pale Ale – A hoppier, bigger-bodied, higher ABV version of an American IPA. First developed in the United States in the 1990s.

Festbier – A German pale-colored lager associated with German beer festivals. Most commonly used in reference to the special brews made by the Munich breweries for Oktoberfest.

Hefeweizen – A top-fermenting German wheat beer, with the most common types coming from Bavaria. A special yeast, housed at the Weihenstephan Brewery in Freising, Germany, gives the beer its unique banana/clove taste and character.

Helles – A standard Bavarian beer. It is a light-bodied, somewhat hoppy lager. *Helles* means "light (in color)" in German.

Growler – Half gallon glass jugs popular at brewpubs for buying beer to go.

Gueuze – A beer native to the area around Brussels made from a blend of old and young lambic beers. A Gueuze is golden in color and has a musty, sour flavor.

Imperial Pilsner – A higher ABV version of a Pilsner beer. An American invention, it was developed in the 1990s.

Imperial Stout – A high ABV stout developed in England during the 19th century for the Russian czars. A strong alcohol flavor dominates the roast/coffee/chocolate notes of a regular stout.

India Pale Ale (IPA) – A pale ale made with higher alcohol and more hops. Developed in England in the 1800s, the name is derived from the brew's popularity in India, a British colony at that time. American brewers resurrected the style but made it uniquely American by using more assertive native hops. This gave the brew a more pronounced bitter flavor.

Kölsch – A pale, straw-colored, top-fermenting beer native to Cologne, Germany. It is light-bodied and fruity in taste. Kölsch is a protected designation of origin in the European Union.

Lager – A beer produced with a bottom-fermenting yeast and brewed at a temperature of 48-55°F.

Pilsner – A pale, straw-colored lager. Introduced in 1842 in the Czech town of Plzen, most beer consumed in the world is a Pilsner or Pilsner derivative. This beer style has a spicy hoppiness that differentiates it from other pale lagers.

Porter – A dark ale. First appearing in London in the early 1700s, the beer got its name from its popularity with the dockworkers. The flavor profile includes coffee, toffee, caramel and nutty. Like most ales, American versions tend to be hoppier than English versions.

Quadruple – A dark ale with a sweet, rich flavor. The strongest of the Trappist/Abbey beers, the ABV can be as high as 12-13%.

Radler – A mixture of lager and lemon-lime soda or lemonade (also known as a Shandy).

Rauchbier – A smoked beer. The flavor is obtained by the use of smoked malts, which gives the brew a ham/bacon flavor. The most famous smoked beers originate from Bamberg, Germany. *Rauch* means "smoke" in German

Stout – A dark ale. Derivative of the Porter style beer, Stout was made world famous by Guinness. There are three main variations: Dry, Sweet/Oatmeal and Imperial. The dominant flavors of a stout include roasted malt, coffee and chocolate.

Trappist/Abbey ale – A beer meeting the standards established by the International Trappist Association. Criteria for the use of the *Authentic Trappist Product* label are: The beer must be brewed within the walls of a monastery or its vicinity;, the beer must be brewed under the direct supervision of Trappist monks in accordance to a proper monastic way of life; and the proceeds must be used sustain the monastery and/or fund charitable causes. There are only seven breweries in the world that can use the term Trappist, all others are called Abbey Ales.

Tripel – A pale, strong Belgian Ale known for its spicy character. It was first developed at the Trappist brewery Westmalle in Belgium. Sugar is used to increase the alcohol content, which ranges from 7.5-9.5% ABV.

ABOUT THE AUTHOR

Merideth Canham-Nelson is one of the most experienced female beer travelers in the country. For over two decades, Merideth and her husband Chris have traveled the world together looking for the next great beer experience. She has visited over 700 different breweries throughout the United States, Canada, Western Europe, and Australia.

Merideth lives in Carmel Valley, California with her husband and their two dachshunds, Porter and Stout.

Made in the USA
Lexington, KY
15 August 2012